KNOWLEDGE
MANAGEMENT

To Sylvia, Luke and Anabelle
Paul

To Samantha for her patience
John

KNOWLEDGE MANAGEMENT

A STATE OF THE ART GUIDE

models & tools

strategy

intellectual capital

planning

learning

culture

processes

PAUL R GAMBLE & JOHN BLACKWELL

KOGAN
PAGE

First published in 2001
Reprinted in 2002

Kogan Page Limited
120 Pentonville Road
London N1 9JN
UK

Kogan Page US
22 Broad Street
Milford CT 06460
USA

British Library Cataloguing in Publication Data

A CIP record for this book is available from the British Library.

ISBN 0 7494 3649 2

Typeset by Saxon Graphics Ltd, Derby
Printed and bound in Great Britain by Biddles Ltd
www.biddles.co.uk

Contents

Acknowledgements

This book is based on many years' experience working in the field of knowledge management with managers from companies all over Europe and the United States. All of these managers have taught us a great deal. In particular, we should like to thank the managers from the following companies, who spent time giving us their perspective of issues in knowledge management. The research for the book was carried out in 1999 and 2000 by a project run from SEMS, the graduate business school of the University of Surrey. Paul Gamble is the Director of the school, and led the research project with the able assistance of Melanie Chalder and guidance from John Blackwell. The views and opinions quoted are those of individual managers interviewed in the research. Sometimes, more than one manager was interviewed from each company. The insets represent individual views, not corporate positions. The remarks are reflective and thoughtful in character. As such, they share wisdom, not analysis, and are all the more valuable for that. They are personal insights, not statements of corporate position, and this is why we have not attributed them to individuals.

ABN Amro, Andersen Consulting, Anglian Water, AT&T, Barclays, BG plc, BOC, BP Amoco, British Telecom , Buckman Labs, Cable & Wireless, Cap Gemini, CGU, Ericsson, Ernst & Young, Glaxo Wellcome, Hewlett-Packard,

KPMG Consulting, McKinsey and Co, NatWest Markets, Nokia, NStar, Orange (Hutchison Telecom), PowerGen, PricewaterhouseCoopers, Procter & Gamble, Reckitt & Colman, Rolls-Royce, Royal & Sun Alliance, SEEBOARD, Siemens, SmithKlineBeecham, Swiss Re, Unilever, Zeneca. (Note that Zeneca are now called AstraZeneca and that Arthur Andersen's consulting arm is now called Accenture.)

1

What do we know? The state of the art

All wish to possess knowledge but few, comparatively speaking, are willing to pay the price.

Juvenal

Hewlett-Packard

When we designed this building, you saw that there was this big coffee area downstairs. The idea was that we created spaces where people can actually meet and talk.

It was probably Groucho Marx who first observed that the race may not always go to the swift, or the battle to the strong but the smart money was probably better placed on the fastest and the strongest. Running any kind of organization is very much a question of playing the odds. Perhaps it is for this reason that Napoleon always claimed to prefer lucky generals to clever generals. In today's rather complex world you cannot always depend on luck, there is therefore quite a lot to be gained by stacking the odds in your favour. The days when the saying 'What you don't know won't hurt you' was true have long gone. In a commercial environment where, during the summer of 2000, a 'Love Bug' virus written in the Philippines can bring half the world's trading systems to a crashing halt within 24 hours, being aware of what is going on can make the difference between survival and profitability, or failure and loss. Knowledge management is simply about rearranging the odds so that they favour the survival and growth of the organization a little more. Effective knowledge management policies do not guarantee success or survival, they simply improve the odds. As an approach, knowledge management is difficult to define and implement. It may also be expensive in terms of time and human resources, not to mention technology backup but it is an essential basis of effective competition in a modern knowledge economy.

The immediate reaction of most managers to the idea of knowledge management is that they are managing knowledge already.

Andersen

A client in Taiwan said to me, 'Knowledge management is just old wine in a new box'. All he meant was that many of the ideas within knowledge management, in terms of knowledge sharing and packaging knowledge and research, have all been predetermined by centuries. Previously, communities of people have got together and developed new ideas and things that we now take for granted. In that sense, many of the components of knowledge management are not new.

It seems that this is what most organizations are all about. They either recruit expert people who are qualified to do a job, or they train inexpert people to do their jobs better. They then set up procedures and processes to capture and record their knowledge in the form of memos and reports. The problem is that this is only half the story. As far back as the 1950s Peter Drucker, one of the earliest contributors to the theory of knowledge management, remarked that the memos and reports gathering dust on company shelves probably contained more knowledge than all the libraries in the world. In essence, all organizations are awash with 'knowledge' but much of that knowledge cannot be accessed or used. Indeed, in some cases much of that knowledge is not even visible since other members of the organization, or customers of the company, are not even aware of its existence.

Turning knowledge into action first requires commitment to change based on the kind of learning and innovation that contributes to competitive advantage. It then depends on:

- recognizing that knowledge exists both socially and contextually (in other words, it is quite different from data, or information);

- understanding who holds the knowledge and in what form;
- somehow making the knowledge available at the right point in time;
- making it available to the relevant people.

Defining knowledge is not easy.

Swiss Re

We had a project within the group two years ago now, where we decided to try to come up with a knowledge management strategy for the Swiss Re group. It said that, 'knowledge management is identifying, organizing, transferring and using the information and knowledge both personal and institutional within the organization to support strategic objectives'.

Like many terms, the word 'knowledge' carries a depth of meaning that goes beyond simple dictionary definitions. For example the word justice might be defined as 'the state that exists when all the laws are enforced'. However, it is easy to think of examples when the enforcement of law falls a long way outside socially accepted concepts of justice. The victim who turns on the hooligan after weeks, or perhaps even years, of abuse to wreak a savage revenge may well end up in prison despite huge popular sympathy. Although the law has clearly been enforced few politicians, journalists, or even ordinary people are likely to recognize that state of affairs as justice. Nevertheless, it is very useful to have a working definition of terms. We would offer one modelled closely on that given by Davenport and Prusak (1998: 5):

> Knowledge is a fluid mix of framed experience, values, contextual information, expert insight and grounded intuition that provides an environment and framework for evaluating and incorporating new experiences and information. It originates and is applied in the minds of knowers. In organizations it often becomes embedded not only in documents or repositories but also in organizational routines, processes, practices and norms.

This is a pretty comprehensive definition. Let us simplify it a little. Basically what we are after is the management of organizational knowledge for creating business value and generating a competitive advantage. In itself, it is not a particularly new idea so at least we are spared the embarrassment of using the term 'paradigm shift' yet again. In fact the ideas behind knowledge management go back some 50 years and many management theorists have written about them. For example Drucker (1999) stressed the growing importance of information and explicit knowledge as an organizational resource.

Senge (1994) has focused on the learning organization that is a cultural dimension of managing knowledge. Work at MIT in the 1970s and in places like Carnegie Mellon emphasized the growing importance of organizational knowledge through augmentation of machine processes with work on artificial intelligence. This was followed by technologies such as hypertext or groupware applications. By the early 1990s, a number of management consulting firms had begun in-house knowledge management programmes, not least because they were galvanized into action through the realization that their businesses depended on selling expertise and that some of this expertise was simply being lost. Perhaps one of the most widely read works around the middle of this decade was Nonaka and Takeuchi's book (1995) on how Japanese companies were creating knowledge and innovation.

Barclays Bank

I can give you text book answers if you like but having worked in the business, to me knowledge management is obviously making sure that everybody within the organization has access to the right expertise that they require. But also it's making sure the people within your company feel that they are contributing to the bottom line by their involvement in business processes and procedures. I think, having seen it develop, actually mushrooming within Barclays it is very, very much a 'people thing'. For me, if you can get buy-in from people and your colleagues you can make anything work.

Most large organizations around the globe in a wide variety of industrial sectors have now introduced knowledge management initiatives. This can be a little dangerous if knowledge management is treated simply as the latest management panacea following on from total quality management (TQM) and business process re-engineering (BPR). What we must do is recognize that the nature of business itself has changed. Technologies like the Internet, the mobile phone and digital television are the most visible external signs of this change but the change goes much deeper than that. Knowledge work is fundamentally different in character from physical labour. Whilst knowledge workers may use these technologies, accessing and leveraging knowledge goes far beyond clicking onto the Internet or turning on the digital television. It is perfectly apparent that you cannot solve most problems or gain competitive advantage simply by providing people with more access to information. This realization has emerged as a result of a number of new management approaches over the last five decades, as a quick review will show.

Cap Gemini

What was knowledge management before?

Knowledge management was a combination of things. It was business process re-engineering in the light or hard sense. It was also embedded in e-mail systems. The thing that is quite interesting is that knowledge management as a concept has been going on forever... I heard this chap once say... 'I was in the room when knowledge management was invented'. I thought that was very interesting, as I hadn't met a two and a half thousand-year-old man before! The early concept of knowledge management probably originated with Greek philosophy and probably has elements of Zen and whatever. It evolved through education. I think education was probably the primary mass-market example of knowledge management, where people were taught how to read and write. The second most important mass-market example of knowledge management was apprenticeships, where people taught other people how to do certain tasks, eg how to weave or how to work a farm or whatever. Then we had things like newspapers, which again were another example of knowledge management in communication. Books were a perfect example of it. All of these evolved and then suddenly we had this thing called the IT revolution. I guess it is very important to see this as a communications and technology revolution and not just a technological one. The invention of the telephone was also incredibly important. Television too has also become an important knowledge management medium, especially as both those media tend to focus on the elements of tacit knowledge transfer.

THE DEVELOPMENT OF KNOWLEDGE MANAGEMENT

The 1950s was the decade of electronic data processing. This decade was associated with quantitative management techniques such as PERT and highly structured management approaches such as management by objectives (MBO). The 1960s saw something of a reaction to this with a focus on different forms of organizational structure and an interest in the effects of centralization or decentralization. This was the 'touchy feely' decade of theory Y managers and sensitivity training by T-groups. It led to an interest in the effects of interpersonal dynamics, an early attempt to harness the power of people working as a community. In the 1970s therefore, it seemed useful to try and get all the members of the team rowing in the same direction. This was the decade of portfolio management, the experience curve and strategic planning as advocated by people like Henry Minzberg. By the 1980s, the competitive effect of all this coordination came to the fore, best captured by the work of people like Michael Porter, whose writing had a profound impact on the way we looked at the basis of competition. Management now took more interest in corporate culture, downsizing, management by walking around (MBWA) and TQM. The caring 1990s focused even more strongly on releasing the competitive potential of human resources. Management was now much more concerned with learning, unlearning and taking into account experience. On the human side of enterprise, the focus was on core competences and the learning organization. On the technology side strategic information systems planning came to the fore and the Internet began its spectacular rise. It became increasingly apparent that traditional organizations based on the strategy–structure–systems approach were no longer likely to be as successful as they had been previously. BPR, therefore, led to a shift towards the three 'P's – purpose, people, process – of Ghoshal and Bartlett (1998). It was accepted that communicating a shared sense of values across an enterprise was more likely to engage people in organizational forms that were less rigid and even less identifiable than they had been throughout the previous century. When the technology allowed a group of people scattered around the globe, who have never met, to create a product and service which is to be sold to customers that they can never see, it seems obvious that the control structure of a traditional organization no longer does the job. So at the beginning of the 2000s, knowledge management has emerged as a unifying corporate goal. Today the intention is to create enterprise integration through a knowledge sharing culture, to recognize the value of something that is called intellectual capital and to understand that competition depends not on the differential possession of physical assets, or even of information, but on the ability to deploy and exploit knowledge.

BG

We're quite an interesting organization in terms of how many customers we have. We don't actually sell gas in the United Kingdom but we do ship it. So we have about 35–45 shippers who are customers of one of our business units. Internationally, yes, we do sell gas to members of the public in fact through their households. So, how many customers do we have in the UK? Is it around 45 because they are the shippers? Or is it 19 million because we supply gas to 19 million gas meters? Ultimately, it doesn't matter because all customers are important. And again, picking up the knowledge, the expertise and in particular getting it around inside the organization is vital because if you've learnt a lesson somewhere, you don't now go and re-invent the wheel. It's a famous saying but it's true.

Knowledge management has come to the fore over the last 8–10 years, progressively brought into centre stage, driven by the networked economy, through increased competition, mergers and acquisitions and the all invasive Internet presence. The net result of all this has been a far greater dynamism in the economy as a whole. People have greater access to information than they have ever had before. There is a huge potential for learning at an accelerated pace, for change at an accelerated pace. What this had led to is a need to have a far more responsive organization.

Traditional economists cast the basic resources of production in terms of land, labour and capital. Most first-year business students have read about the way the Industrial Revolution changed the leverage that could be applied to different combinations of resource. What we have today is a far more intensive need, to respond on a shorter time-scale to a fourth basic unit of resource. Some writers call that entrepreneurship but we would call it knowledge because entrepreneurship uses personal creativity and innovation to put knowledge to work in new, highly competitive ways. To take a small example, over the last 10 years we have seen massive changes in the way that customer queries or complaints are handled. A decade ago the complaint would have arrived nicely on a piece of paper with an order number on it. Today, products can comprise a bunch of intellectual transactions connected together in the ether. So, what happened to the nice pieces of paper? Who cares? We can now treat the 'complaint' as a form of unsolicited feedback, link to other knowledge about customer behaviours in our customer base and use it for improving the basis of our value added. So, we are looking at running a business in a completely different way to that used a decade ago. Then the expected response time was typically a couple of weeks, now customers expect a response at Internet speeds. It was also expected that no one person could fulfil an order or request. Rather, the collective power of the organization was applied to solving a customer issue. This collected set of procedures and data from various sources were then synthesized and a response was made to the complaint. It all took time. On the other hand, the opportunities to develop strategy and for reflective thinking were far more accessible 10 years ago than they are today. The world moves much faster and thinking time is shortened. The knowledge available to the organization has to be tapped and synthesized much faster.

Siemens

Well, we have about 100 knowledge management projects in motion at the moment. With our global knowledge-sharing network, Sharenet, we have chosen to focus on one of our key business processes, ie sales value creation, which is very close to our customers, rather than say our logistics or our research and development. But it is also about our competitors and our products and finding solutions. So you can see that in a way it cuts across all areas. The next step will now be to get the customer involved in determining these sales processes. We will do this at first with a human interface because this is what our customers are most used to at present. However, it will be carried out by some form of intelligent agent or filter in a true e-business world.

All of this has come together at a time of increased competition and global-ization and at a time when information is exploding. The statistics from the NEC Research Institute show that the amount of information (note that this refers only to information, not knowledge) available across the network economy is equivalent to some 3 billion pages. It is estimated that this is growing exponentially, doubling every 18 months, as shown in Figure 1.1.

Keeping up with this rate of expansion requires a process like the proverbial duck swimming on a pond. Everything on the surface looks fine but just to stay still the duck's feet are working like crazy below the surface. All the research that IBM has undertaken in the area of knowledge management underlines this picture. Figure 1.2 gives a vivid demonstration of how this becomes a problem. Taking the term 'Bond' as an example, a search using Yahoo! or Excite would currently get in excess of 200,000 responses.

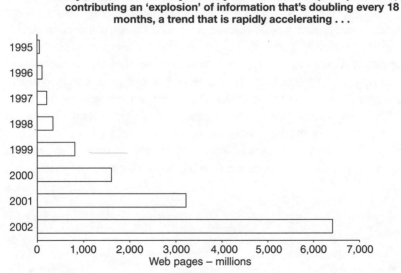

Today's network economy will only exacerbate enterprise problems, by contributing an 'explosion' of information that's doubling every 18 months, a trend that is rapidly accelerating . . .

Web pages – millions

Source: Nature, *Accessibility of information on the Web* (July 1999)
Steve Lawrence and C Lee Giles of NEC Research Institute

Figure 1.1 *Impact of the network economy: information available.*

Worse still, no matter how well those search engines have captured and filtered the information from the Internet, it is currently estimated that they will have indexed no more than 1.6 per cent of the data available. Yet the user will undoubtedly be overwhelmed even with what 'little' information he or she has got. Further, the information provided has no context and nothing to determine its relevance to the user's problem. In effect users are overwhelmed with insufficient data. This simple exercise indicates one of today's basic, fundamental drivers for the emergence of knowledge management. It has its origins in TQM when organizations were looking at the Japanese models of quality management that posed the question 'How do we learn from previous mistakes?' TQM then evolved into the idea of the learning organization. As with quality circles, people were seeking a collective understanding or solution to a problem. Progressively, that in turn led to an understanding that just working with documents or information was not enough.

Companies are becoming knowledge intensive, not capital intensive. Knowledge is rapidly displacing capital, natural resources and even location as the primary key to survival. This does not mean to say that all the other ideas that have been developed in the last 50 years should be thrown out of the window. All of those ideas are important and have something to offer. They

Merely using technology such as Search and Retrieval is now regarded as wholly insufficient . . .

- Searching today's 3 billion Web pages can demonstrate that the 'best' Internet portal sites will index approximately 12.8 million images:
  - representing 'only' 1.6% of the available information
  - this still offers access to a staggering 15 terabytes of information, but is it useful?
- For example, search for 'Bond' in your favourite search engine . . .

e**X**cite 210,029 hits

YAHOO! 281,858 hits

Were you looking for . . .
- *Financial Bonds?*
- *US Treasury Bonds?*
- *Euro Bonds?*
- *Bond Rates?*
- *Corporate Bonds?*
- *James Bond?*
- *Bail Bonds?*
- *Bonding agents?*

In which language . . .
- *English?*
- *French?*
- *Spanish?*
- *Dutch?*
- *German?*
- *Italian?*
- *etc, etc*

Figure 1.2 *Example search – for the term 'Bond'*

have led us to the place we are today. That place is much more unstable and dynamic than it ever was in the past. If your competitor in Argentina or China is six-tenths of a second, or one mouse click away, you have to be able to respond in the way and at the time that the customer prefers. Fixed positions and prescriptive marketing can leave you exposed as never before, however quick and slick your production system. It is no good being the hottest manufacturer of blue jeans on the planet when everyone is switching to khaki. The specific business factors that have to be taken into account include the following:

- Market places are increasingly competitive and the rate of innovation is rising. Downsized organizations need to replace informal knowledge with formal methods if most work is knowledge based.
- Organizations compete on basis of knowledge and the amount of time available to experience and acquire that knowledge has diminished.
- Competitive pressures have reduced the size of the workforce that holds valuable business knowledge. This is a problem when products and services are increasingly complex in a way that endows them with a significant information component. Early retirements and an ageing population in the West, coupled with an increased mobility of the workforce in general, has led to a loss of some important sources of knowledge.
- There is a need to manage increasing complexity as even small companies work in international environments.
- Changes in strategic direction may result in a critical loss of knowledge in specific areas.
- A need for lifelong learning is an inescapable reality.

AstraZeneca

I think the thing that's made some form of knowledge management possible is the development of groupware technologies, like Lotus Notes and the Internet. People will tell you that knowledge management has been around for a long time in things like apprenticeships and that is true. But I think you've got to be acting at a very local level, to sit down and eyeball the person to make that work. In our business, we have such a huge site that it's a 10-minute bus ride to the other side. So you've got to set aside half a day basically to share information and knowledge. You try and set up meeting for say June or July. But in July the Swedes are on holiday, in August the Brits are on holiday and the French are always on holiday. So you can't exchange knowledge easily. So, if we didn't have those Notes and Intranet technologies we couldn't even begin to do it on the required scale because any one of our projects spans the globe, time differences and functionality. It has been a global problem and the technology is now enabling you to do the sharing.

THE MODERN ENTERPRISE IS ABOUT KNOWLEDGE

Let's take the example of how to teach a young child to ride a bicycle. No matter how much we might try, it is impossible to write a one page, easily understood document that would delight a young child and help him or her understand how to ride a bicycle. There is no way that we could transcribe into a document feelings such as confidence and balance. How would we document the importance and benefits of overcoming disappointment? ('I've just fallen off this thing for the sixth time, and I am not getting on it again'). Of course, some people do persist and, indeed, some go on to win the Tour de France.

All of this is about tacit knowledge, it is about experience, about wisdom and about empathy. The very energy that creates great cooks, artists, musicians, poets and the same energy that differentiates an outstanding business person from a good one.

Reckitt & Colman

I think there will have to be an obvious trend or shift in the way that we now do business. The fact that most organizations are now not dealing with traditional manufacture but are selling services and people. The only way you can deliver a good service is to have the right people, the right knowledge and the right systems. If all you are doing is manufacturing widgets, then it's relatively easy to write down the processes involved in doing that, as it will be same each time. Whereas, when you are delivering a service or a solution, then it is different in every case and you need to have a learning organization structure behind you. If you look at the most successful knowledge management organizations, then it's those who have the best ones in knowledge terms, that have such good information management systems that they can hire new people. Being confident that they will pick up the requisite knowledge and skills very quickly through explicit means.

This brings us to the often quoted distinction first proposed by Michael Polanyi between represented knowledge (sometimes referred to as formal or explicit knowledge) and embodied knowledge (sometimes referred to as informal or tacit knowledge) The key distinction is that represented knowledge can be stored in an artefact, such as a piece of paper, a drawing, or a computer. Embodied knowledge is personal; it involves personal beliefs, perspectives and values. The storage medium for embodied knowledge is therefore generally people.

'FATHER KNOWS BEST'

Despite being banned by Congress for use in US defence industries as long ago as 1914, Frederik Winslow Taylor's idea of the 'scientific management' model heavily influenced the business world for much of the last century. Taylor himself never advocated such widespread use, suggesting the method as suitable for managing people with the 'intelligence of an ox' but unfortunately, the apparent attraction of organizing labour as if it were a cog in a production machine proved too alluring for many managers. Along with Adam Smith's famous recognition of the power of production lines in the 18th century, it helped lay the grounds for things like Henry Ford's famous assembly line. But this top–down approach, a sort of 'father knows best' management approach, as Stewart (1997) calls it, has proved inadequate to cope with modern technology, increasing mobility and the globalization of markets.

If an important management idea is misinterpreted or over sold to managers looking for quick fixes or instant solutions it can become discredited for all the wrong reasons. Another example was provided by TQM in the 1970s. TQM, a concept devised by W E Deming at the end of World War II to help revivify Japanese industry, set out to demonstrate that the cost of poor quality exceeded the cost of excellence. Quality, we learned, was free. It took a while before the power of these ideas, implemented very effectively in Japan, became more widely accepted. At this point, it was so avidly seized upon that some companies lost sight of the customer in their search for total quality. A formal procedure for getting something fixed quickly somehow took precedence over the more fundamental point that customers actually were not interested in fast repairs. They were interested in products that did not break down in the first place.

The 1980s therefore saw the emergence of BPR – the resurgence of Taylorism really. BPR set out to view everything in a very explicit process model with a focus on cost reduction. It shook up many of the major companies who then undertook substantial reorganizations. They became lean again and productivity climbed to new heights. However, most of the ongoing BPR projects struggled, many even failed. The reason has become increasingly apparent. The 'human factor' was underestimated in BPR. Treating your organization like a machine, disassembling it and reassembling it in a new and better way does not work. A more organic, humanistic approach is needed. The sort of factor that sometimes allows companies to become successful again just by exchanging the CEO.

THE COMMERCIAL SCANDAL OF THE 20TH CENTURY

The growing view amongst today's historians of commerce is that the simplistic focus on process efficiencies will come to be regarded as the greatest commercial scandal of the 20th century. As we organized ourselves into larger organizations and complex corporations, the neglect of knowledge based on people and ideas has undoubtedly reduced the corporate market place's capability for true innovation and sustainable competitiveness. It is therefore undisputedly true that if you are not managing your 'people and ideas' assets, you are negligent in managing the core of your business.

Cap Gemini

Quite often when I'm interviewed or doing conferences, I'm asked, 'What happens next?' It kind of frightens me a little bit as it really does make you think knowledge management is a phase. I'd like to think that if we accept the philosophy that knowledge management is a concept that has been evolving over two and a half thousand years, rather than three years, people would be less likely to suggest that it's a phase and about to come to an end. I think this mentality that people have, that it's a buzz word, that it's the hype of the year and it's going to go away, is something we have really got to address significantly. Otherwise we will get trapped in the hype ourselves. The number of organizations jumping on the bandwagon at the moment is just a distraction, causing problems in terms of proper understanding of the capability.

✓ ENTER KNOWLEDGE MANAGEMENT

This is where knowledge management comes in. It is not about managing knowledge as such in a mechanical sense. It is about extending the view of a process looking at the components of *embodied* knowledge, that which the knower intrinsically knows. It refers to the undocumented information, the intuition, empathy and experience that enables us to make the right decisions – at least most of the time.

This does not mean that decisions can or should be made without a framework. *Represented knowledge*, knowledge that is mostly contained in data, documented information and artefacts should still be the basis for decision-making. Knowledge in this form also has the advantage that it can be shared much more easily in an organization, eg by e-mail systems or electronic repositories. *Embedded knowledge*, the knowledge that exists in processes, products, rules and procedures, must also be considered as an intrinsic part of knowledge management.

As a broad generalization, commercial success in the 18th century and earlier was closely tied to the possession of land and what could be either grown or extracted from it. People were worked in a strictly hierarchical environment. With the Industrial Revolution in the 19th century this changed substantially, as the accumulation of capital became the driving factor. The structure of how people worked together was broadly the same though production line approaches and defined roles and responsibilities in a 'bureaucracy' became more prominent. The ownership of industrial resources became the basis for measuring success. Currently, such a measure is still predominant in the early part of the 21st century. It is still used as the basis for calculating the annual balance sheet.

Cap Gemini

It's hard to say which factor is the most significant, although the development of knowledge management awareness has been a very significant contributor. But I'd say that the most significant thing overall was the real growth and evolution of Internet and Intranet technologies. Recently, the most significant change has been the way in which organizations are now prepared to invest in knowledge management. About 5 per cent of the major businesses in the UK are now integrating knowledge as part of their strategy and policy, and they are the ones that are going to make the biggest and most significant benefit from it.

However, now business has to face a new kind of working together, networks of people working in different locations, some even working from home, within a very flat hierarchy. We also have to face a situation where shareholders no longer get much useful information about their companies out of the annual balance sheets. Examples of this can be seen in the current crop of Internet companies whose market capitalization can place them perhaps briefly in the Fortune Top 100 but whose actual assets are modest.

SKANDIA'S VIEW OF INTELLECTUAL CAPITAL

What makes the difference between asset value and market value? Early visionaries such as Leif Edvinsson, who works for Skandia financial services company, think this difference is mainly attributable to 'intellectual capital' (Edvinsson and Malone, 1997). In 1995, Skandia began publishing a supplement to its annual report to shareholders based on the intellectual capital that benefited the company even though the company can make less of a claim to own intellectual capital in the same way that it owns physical assets. This intellectual capital is usually not as visible as fixed assets, like buildings and machines. It is hidden in the patents, brands, customer relationships, expertise, intuition and skills in a company. The aspiration of knowledge management is to grow the hidden value that is often disregarded or even destroyed by older business management approaches rather than enhanced.

THE RISK OF KILLING KNOWLEDGE

A BPR example based on losing sight of real knowledge might illustrate the point. At the height of the BPR fashion, in the early 1990s, a major copier corporation took a close look at the activities of its field service engineers. It noticed that they spent a lot of time back at the depot, picking up works orders and parts or chatting in the coffee lounge. They decided to re-engineer the process. The coffee lounge was closed and a more efficient system for communicating orders and supplying parts was devised. A small department was set up to produce operating manuals for all the latest machines and every service van was fitted with a PC with a CD containing schematic graphics of the working parts of different machines. Engineers would be out on the road, customer facing more of the time and their information support would be up to the minute. However, repair efficiency went down, servicing costs went up. Then one observant manager noticed that in many of the vans the latest manuals had not been removed from their plastic shrink-wrapping. It was apparent that the CDs had never seen the light of a laser. Further investigation revealed that the engineers were very uncomfortable with the new system. It did not tell them the tricks of the trade. They felt foolish in front of customers having to consult a manual and the CDs were hard to use. Previously, when the engineers got together for a coffee, they were actually swapping ideas and tips about how best to tackle certain jobs. This information had high credibility because it came from another engineer who had actually done the job. So, back to square one. The coffee room was re-opened, a depot based supply system was introduced, the engineers were supplied with radio headsets that allowed them to talk to each other easily in the field and on the job: 'Hey Joe, how do you get the drum out of one of these ABC790s?' 'No problem, I did one last week, you just…'. Efficiency and repair costs rapidly climbed back on track.

In this case, the BPR exercise had killed knowledge exchange, at a time when the business need for knowledge was very strong. With a knowledge-based view instead of an ostensible cost reduction focus, the initial management decision would have been different. This is where knowledge management has something in common with TQM. Too much focus on process re-engineering, or on cost reduction, can extinguish valuable intellectual capital and reduce profit rates disproportionately. Reducing cost to a minimum can be more expensive than an investment in a knowledge management programme even though it might ostensibly increase short-run costs. Worse, a narrow focus on procedure or process might change the whole basis of customer value.

Most people have come across the joke about the time and motion study of a symphony orchestra. Instead of using 80 to 100 musicians, it was recognized that you could reduce personnel costs by converting to a chamber orchestra of approximately 40 players. Better still, you can cut personnel overheads even more by reducing to an octet. Of course, a string quartet or a trio is even cheaper. Indeed, why not have the piece played by a one-man band? A one-man band provides for very cost effective competitive position. Obviously, an enterprise using this approach could deliver very cheap music. Also, many instruments in the full orchestra were duplicating passages in a piece and some sections of music were being played more than once. A silly example? In late 1997, the Boeing Aircraft Corporation implemented a major 'downsizing programme'. Cost containment was dramatically improved but its distinctive competences were changed. Important knowledge was lost. The reduced corporation was no longer able to deliver customer value in the same way and in 1998, it posted its first corporate loss for 50 years. Boeing is not the only major corporation to have recognized a little late that downsizing can easily throw out the baby with the bath water. However, it did act quickly to recover its position.

WHY MANAGE KNOWLEDGE?

The example serves to illustrate the importance of managing knowledge. Managing knowledge requires a different perspective to managing land or capital. It is concerned with managing how people reason and how they make their expertise accessible. Let us look at the use of embodied versus represented knowledge, though the example of cooks. We might apply the title chef (as in chef de cuisine or boss of a professional kitchen) indiscriminately all the way from Escoffier (father of modern haute cuisine) to the person who hides behind a bit of stainless steel in Macdonald's. We could see them both as chefs. Both of them using the same basic food ingredients can produce a dish that delights and both dishes would have a value. However, these dishes would not be sold for the same amounts. The output from one chef would sell for tens of times more than the output from the other. The difference lies in the fact that the chef in Macdonald's is working within a defined process using very little personal knowledge. The knowledge is represented in the process, open a packet of burgers, grill it so long using automated equipment, present it in this form based on the picture you have been given as a model. The chef in a professional kitchen also uses (mental) models but combines them with intuition, artistry and flair (embodied knowledge), with things that we all recognize as the property of an individual expert.

Everyone can recognize such an expert, someone who is knowledgeable. We do it every day whenever we meet someone who does a job particularly well, with an apparent thoughtless skill. We find it possible to make decisions as individuals about someone who is knowledgeable, yet it is much more difficult to make that decision about an organization. The organization seems like an amorphous mass, its performance is more variable, it is harder to assess. What is needed is to be able make exactly comparable judgments. All the people in the organization are knowledgeable. They all know some things that may be more or less valuable if they were used on behalf of the enterprise. When we say someone is knowledgeable we mean they have artistry, intuition, or experience. Unfortunately, these are all things that tend not to get documented. They do not get transcribed into information and so do not easily offer themselves as a basis for judgment.

What has emerged over the last 10 to 12 years is an understanding that an information fire hose has been turned on us, we are in a digital, network economy that moves fast. The speed, access and globalization offered within this economy offers a special advantage to no one – since everyone has access to it. Anyone without access to it is playing a different game. There is an ever increasing need to respond to customers faster in order to be competitive. There is also a progressive understanding that the experience and wisdom, the collective brain as it were, of the organization is a hugely valuable asset. It is the valuable asset that turns explicit and tacit knowledge into something that can be leveraged competitively.

Imagine that you were allowed to walk into the computer centre of, say, a major international airline and someone were to say to you 'Here you can access every one of the computer systems, you can sit down where you like, browse the files, do whatever you want, take whatever you want'. Most people would have no idea where to start. They would have no context as to what is valuable or what actually makes a difference to the operation of an airline. The information held in the computer systems cannot be deployed or exploited without the insight and intuition that an expert uses to run the business. You would, in effect, be information rich and knowledge poor.

Over the last 10 years or so there has been growing awareness that beyond the knowledge represented by documents, or the embodied knowledge held by individuals in the form of wisdom and experience, there is a another important form of knowledge. This can be referred to as embedded knowledge. Those who provide products and services embed knowledge in the very products and services. Understanding this process emerged from the activities surrounding TQM and BPR. BPR in particular looked at process efficiency with the aim of making big, radical jumps in improving efficiency as distinct from the small, continuous improvements sought with TQM. The two approaches were not mutually exclusive and in many ways complement each other but BPR encouraged managers to examine the elements, sequence or location of a process and consider how they might be re-engineered to achieve massive improvements in performance. The idea was that instead of measuring how long it took someone to go from A to B to C and attempting to improve the process in a linear form, we could achieve massive improvements by radically restructuring so that we went from A to C or even D. The cost of the infra-structure and the logistics in the two alternative methods could be valued and the saving or improvement being sought could be measured.

There is a great example of this that goes back a couple of hundred years to the time of the emergence of the armed forces in the United State. As the United States established itself as an independent nation a lot of the observa-tions on how to form an army, how to train the armed forces and how to operate as an armed organization were based on how the British army worked. The transfer and communication of these ideas was not efficient in these early days. An old soldier might say, 'Well I've had experience in the British Army. Their procedure for firing a gun is, you stand up, aim very carefully, count for four seconds, steady yourself, aim low and then fire.' However, classic muzzle loading rifles took a long time to reload. Soldiers had to spend 15 or 20 seconds putting the powder in, carefully tamping it down, loading the musket ball and adding the wadding. A slow, very meticulous operation. Consequently, soldiers were careful about firing their shot. They knew they should take their time because a wasted shot allowed the enemy to approach more closely. In the mid-1860s there were several notable battles which resulted in considerable massacre for these new armies. It took three or four battles before it was realized that men were getting massacred by following the procedure of standing up, pausing to steady the rifle and counting to four before firing. They had not come to terms with the emergence of the repeating rifle – the competition fired at a much faster rate and did not even have to stand up to reload. The attacker no longer had 20 seconds to advance in relative safety between volleys. The process hadn't kept pace with the knowledge that drove it.

The BPR movement came about because of an analogous transformation in the corporate information environment. All of a sudden, whilst one company was processing customer needs in a traditional way, another realized that not only did the technology allow them to totally restructure their capabilities but that from within the digital representation of customer behaviour they could actually create new products and services. So what emerged was an under-standing that with an increasingly demanding market, more aggressive compe-tition and an ever increasing payload of information, it was necessary to harness the driving forces behind what was being done. In turn, these should be re-examined in terms of where value was being provided for the customer. That is when a recognition of embedded knowledge emerged, out of the learning cycle. We have seen some excellent examples of how this evolved and how companies looked at it in terms of the way they could use the emerging science of knowledge management. It is not just about getting more and more stuff into (and out of) databases, it is about exploiting knowledge in behavioural terms.

KNOWLEDGE MANAGEMENT INITIATIVES

What factors affect a company's ability to exploit its knowledge resources and what sort of initiatives have been taken already that we can look at?

BP Amoco

I think there are several [important factors]. Obviously, leadership from the top, which is what we have, is very important. But so is the overall culture of an organization, which must be empowering, encouraging and challenging. Tools and processes are also helpful particularly in the management of capital projects. We tend to have some key processes in place which we would call 'capital value processes' which amount really to a series of prompts for use by people when conducting a project, to make sure that they address the vital stages of shared learning where it could bring them advantage.

External structure initiatives

Gain knowledge from customers
Benetton, in Italy, mass-customizes its clothing to fit the latest colours in trends and designs by modifying its production lines continuously using sales data from key shops. In other words it uses examples of actual customer behaviour linked directly to CAD and CIM systems to maximize sales.

Since 1982, General Electric has collected all customer complaints in a huge database. This now contains the answers to 1.5 million potential problems and their solutions that allow telephone operators in its call centres to offer better service.

The National Bicycle Industrial Company in Japan uses CAD/CIM manufacturing possesses to customize its bicycles to fit customers' exact height, weight and colour preferences within 24 hours.

Offer customers additional knowledge
Agro Corporation of the USA sells fertilizers and seed. Data on soil types is combined with weather forecasts and information about crops to provide a better service to farmers when they are choosing the best combination of crops for their land.

Frito Lay, USA uses a similar system and a similar approach by collecting information about shelf space utilization for different brands. It allows its sales people to give retailers information about the best use of shelf space.

Internal structure initiatives

AstraZeneca

The technology usually isn't a barrier. Technology is everywhere in a business like ours. Everyone has a Web browser on their PC and we know there are about 40,000 of those around the company. So 80 per cent of our people are reachable by the technology.

Create new revenues from existing knowledge
Outokumppu, Finland, is a company that smelts copper and other metals. It has created a knowledge base on how to produce smelting plants which is used for the construction of new sites and for training. This business is now more profitable than the original smelting business!

Dow Chemical, USA, has put all of its 30,000 patents into a database that is used to explore how existing patents can produce more revenues. The technology behind this application has now been transferred into other intellectual assets, such as brands.

Build a knowledge sharing culture
3M, USA, is famous for the balance it achieves between creativity and conservatism. Having accidentally invented a glue which does not set, it had the insight to use the glue for the now ubiquitous 'Post-it' notes. With 60,000 products from its innovation processes, 3M actively encourages learning and risk taking but requires managers to link continuous learning to revenues.

Cap Gemini

I guess the most important thing is that the senior management of this company realizes that knowledge management is vitally important to our success. It's therefore part of the way we work. It's made it easier for us to integrate that into the way that our company is organized and structured. It's made it easy for us to embed and develop knowledge enabling processes within our business. It's made it easier for us to invest in enabling technologies that will help us to continue to communicate, develop and evolve effective knowledge and has enabled us to capture and manipulate the content that we need in order to conduct our business.

Oticon in Denmark has created a 'Spaghetti Organization', a chaotic tangle of interrelationships and interactions. Knowledge workers have no fixed job descriptions and work entirely on a project basis.

Capture and store tacit knowledge

Skandia AFS, Sweden, is probably the most famous international company in the knowledge management field and was probably the first company in the world to value intellectual assets on its balance sheets. Skandia created a formalized procedure to capture knowledge and as a result has reduced the cycle time that it takes to develop new financial services products to achieve profitability from two years to six months.

British Petroleum, another well-known company in the knowledge management field, emphasizes the transfer of tacit knowledge rather than the accumulation and transmission of raw data. Thus its technology emphasis is on its communications network that includes such things as video-conferencing and e-mail in order to facilitate the transfer of such knowledge.

Measure knowledge

Telia, Sweden, is Sweden's telecom company. Like Skandia since 1990 it has produced an annual statement of human resources including a profit and loss account which visualizes human resource costs and a balance sheet showing investments in human resources.

PLC-Consort of Denmark categorizes customers according to the value of their knowledge contribution to the firm and follows this up in its management information system.

Competence initiatives

Create careers based on knowledge management

Buckman Labs of the USA provides both financial rewards and accelerated promotion to management positions for employees who show themselves to be best at knowledge sharing.

IBM encourages its employees to switch between professional and managerial jobs in order to gain a more complete knowledge about the company.

Create microenvironments for tacit knowledge transfer

Honda in Japan routinely builds redundancy into some of its processes and procedures. People are given information that goes beyond their immediate operational requirements. Not only does this help to facilitate the sharing of responsibility but also produces creative solutions from unexpected sources.

Xerox in the USA provides convenient places where people can get together routinely in what it calls a distributed coffee-pot environment. These environments encourage cross-functional links.

Support education with communications technology

The Open University in the UK sells formal training via satellite to a number of international companies to encourage continuous learning and professional development. Members can interact via the Internet with each other and with professors electronically.

The University of Surrey in the UK has developed a Virtual Business School that allows students around the world to follow courses, interact with tutors and each other electronically, interrogate a knowledge base and even download snippets of information onto a mobile device such as a cell phone.

Learn from simulations and pilot installations

Matsushita of Japan launched a company-wide policy early in the 1990s to reduce its yearly working time to 1,800 hours. The objective was not to reduce costs but to change the mindset of managers. Matsushita created a promotions office with the task of facilitating experiments with the policy for one month by working 150 hours. The idea was to emphasize the use of quality time rather than quantity time. (Sveiby, 1995)

RECOGNIZING KNOWLEDGE-BASED PROCESSES

Andersen

I think a highly competitive external landscape is quite important because it generates a critical need for organizations to share knowledge and to maximize the speed of their innovation pipeline.

In BPR, a process was defined as a sequence that started and ended with a customer so that the process improvement achieved produced added customer value. A good example of this sequence can be seen in financial services, where some insurance companies cut out part of the process by selling directly to the customer instead of selling through brokers. Elsewhere, other companies cut layers of management, especially middle management. In some cases however, this produced an effect opposite to that intended. Gradually it was realized that some processes contained embedded knowledge. There was sometimes a good rationale as to why the original process was carried out in a particular way. Certainly, with the right infrastructure, cutting out some intermediate processes led to quantum improvements in performance and did indeed add customer value – usually where the 'hidden' embedded knowledge was captured in another form. This might not have been called a knowledge base at the time but that is what it really was.

This insight came from examining current policies and procedures and asking why they existed. Inside most corporations it is usually possible to find examples of policies that no longer make sense but which no one seems to question. If we go back to our culinary examples, we might ask ourselves why the service staff in up-market restaurants and hotels usually wear black, formal clothing? The reason dates back to the death of Prince Albert at the end of the 19th century. At the time, Queen Victoria put all her servants into black as a sign of mourning and 'good society' followed suit as a mark of respect. The practice was never changed though the relevance of this style of dress in the 21st century might not seem appropriate. When the rule was created, it was created by intelligent people for good reason. This sort of thing happens inside companies too (in a different form!). Corporate practices set up with good reason become outmoded. They are no longer relevant. Indeed, they actually start to slow things down, reduce internal efficiency, increase friction, and increase transaction costs: all of the issues that come about through losing sight of the knowledge as to why the process was created. Curiously, the importance of embedded knowledge often came to the fore in organizations that failed to capture it. Some companies shed middle management layers and then found that levels of customer service and even process efficiency fell to startling new lows. Some middle managers 'knew' how to provide service for some customers in ways that were not documented or formalized within the company. In these cases, the companies were forced to try and hire back people whom they had made redundant only a few months before. Knowledge initiatives tend to be most successful if they have a clearly defined objective in terms of how the knowledge embedded within a process can be used for competitive advantage.

SUMMARY

Management writers are always claiming that they have discovered the new, one best way of developing a sustainable competitive advantage. In many ways, knowledge management has been around in different forms for a long time. Formal ways of recording knowledge have evolved and there are long-established ways of passing knowledge from generation to generation, through mentoring and apprenticeships. As in so many things, the problem today is scale. We can trace the effect of management ideas such as MBO, JIT, competitive advantage through IT, TQM and BPR and the way this has led us to a recognition that human factors, in the form of knowledge, are what really counts. To a greater or lesser extent, all organizations are knowledge based and their success or failure will depend on the extent to which they can create, nurture, store, share and exchange knowledge.

2

Drivers of the new economy

Siemens

Internally, one of our major drivers was our CEO who understood the influence of all the external factors. He has seen the changing culture and the need to manage people differently and nurture their human capital. For him, if you talked about people, you talked about intellectual capital.

The drivers of knowledge became more prominent through increased competition and increased merger and acquisition activity. Figures 2.1 and 2.2 illustrate the changes from the old economy to the new economy. In the old economy people were able to have nice discrete packaging for what happened in their work, learning or social environment. People would tend to develop their career, much as the Japanese do even today, with one employer over their whole working life. Learning would take place in a classroom environment with a 'sage on the stage' – a teacher who explained a topic he or she thought you should learn about. Social lives were geographically bounded in the main, as was consumption. People remained loyal to their local store and shopped for the brands that store offered. Investments had to balance risk very carefully since there were high costs associated with disinvesting.

The new network economy blurs these edges and that is starting to change the dynamics of the marketplace. Knowledge is increasing at such a rate that no one can learn all there is to know about a particular area. People attune themselves to lifelong learning in an entrepreneurial sense, updating their skills continuously as and when they need to. Their portfolio of skills allows them to switch employers to take advantage of opportunities. They want to control what they learn and how. The 'sage on the stage' has given way to 'the guide on the side', knowledge nuggets downloaded over the Internet. Often people's social circle has global scope and they keep in touch with a wide, geographically dispersed circle of friends electronically (most probably using the short message service on their mobile phone). They are loyal to the best buy and can switch suppliers at the click of a mouse. They can also switch investments fast and if one market is too slow to meet their needs they will trade in another, unfettered by distance. These are the various forces in global markets that then accelerate knowledge drivers (see Figures 2.1 and 2.2).

Figure 2.3, based on research by Gartner Consulting, comes from a survey that looked at cross-global drivers of knowledge management to determine why managers might be interested in focusing their activities upon knowledge management. It demonstrates a range of pressures that affect variously all sectors of business. Notice that the figure divides broadly into two sections, knowledge push (the three issues at the top) and knowledge pull (the five issues at the bottom). Knowledge push is all about identifying and responding to customer needs more rapidly and these issues tend to be the most important reasons for developing a knowledge management programme. Knowledge

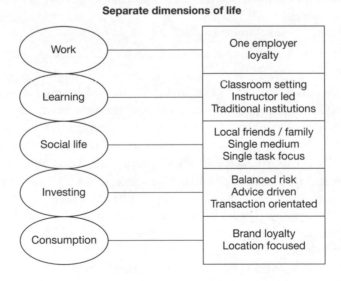

Figure 2.1 *Separate dimensions of life*

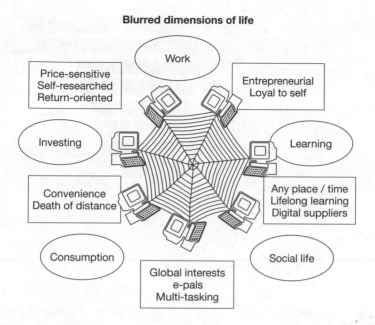

Figure 2.2 *Blurred dimensions of life*

pull is about responding to the competition, including getting into the game because to be left on the sidelines means that you do not get to play at all. It is clear from this research that the two most important influences are a recognition of the need for knowledge sharing across units and the importance of knowledge to improving competitiveness.

Research conducted by Ovum illustrates what is happening internationally. The international marketplace is being transformed and the global knowledge management landscape is growing apace. Figures 2.4 and 2.5 show quite a significant growth in the marketplace for knowledge management. Figure 2.4 illustrates the growth rate of the total marketplace which is expected to double in value to US $8.8 billion from 2001 to 2004. Figure 2.5 shows that nearly all of this growth is coming from the United States and Europe. The rest of the world market for knowledge management is growing significantly.

What Figure 2.5 does not clearly show is that this is knowledge management measured by services comprising both hard and soft technologies, which in turn hides a further differentiation. The difference between the US and the European knowledge management scene is that the Americans have moved very quickly through the early stages of knowledge management. This was characterized by adopting hard technologies which might be something of a

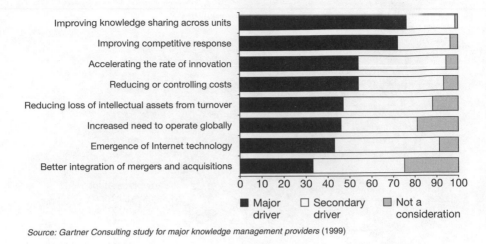

Source: Gartner Consulting study for major knowledge management providers (1999)

Figure 2.3   *Eight key business drivers for knowledge management*

cultural phenomenon in that the United States in particular is in a position to deploy high technology very rapidly. However, it is also characteristic of a general management behaviour which tends to prefer 'hard' solutions to 'soft' – in other words, to assume first and foremost there is something out there that will fix the problem. The assumption is that investing in these assets, establishing these databases, will make the enterprise smarter. Such thinking might have been coloured by the success of database management tools in the area of customer relationship marketing.

In general, understanding in the United States that knowledge management is really about people and that technology was mainly the enabler trailed behind the European view. In Europe the emphasis on soft solutions was greater, perhaps because the tendency was not to throw technology at problems quite so quickly, perhaps because Europe could learn from early experiences in the United States. The competitive landscape also played a part.

DIFFERENT DRIVERS OF KNOWLEDGE MANAGEMENT

The United States and Canada represent a market of about 350 million people. The United States has an especially dynamic economy notwithstanding a slowdown in early 2001. There are a number of factors that contribute to the dynamic nature of the US economy; some of them are to do with the structure of capital markets and some to do with the legislative framework. Above all however, it is probably influenced by different attitudes to business failure

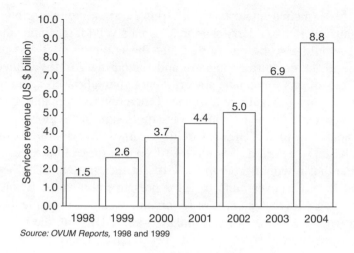

Source: OVUM Reports, 1998 and 1999

Figure 2.4 *Growth in the market for knowledge management services*

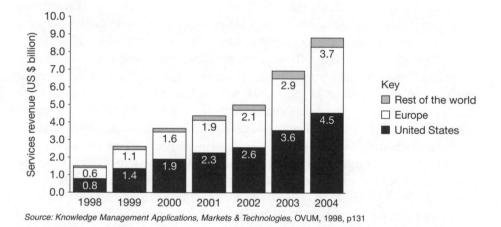

Source: Knowledge Management Applications, Markets & Technologies, OVUM, 1998, p131

Figure 2.5 *Knowledge management market – the United States and Europe*

than those that exist in Europe. There is a smaller social, legal and financial stigma to going bust in the United States than in most other countries. As long as you actually did not do anything illegal or dishonest and gave the business your best shot, should it fail you just pick yourself up, dust yourself off and try again. This encourages entrepreneurship and risk taking. Coupled with access to a huge domestic market, now even bigger thanks to NAFTA, a situation emerges where, for example, a couple of laid-back characters, one of whom professes his principal interests as ping-pong and eating, can grow a US $5 billion company, Ben and Jerry's, as an ice cream vendor in a niche market. Of course, it should also be mentioned that the company also has an expert knowledge of ice cream manufacture and flavourings. In the United States, niche markets of this sort can be powerful enough to allow companies to build sufficient size and gain sufficient financial momentum to enable them to step out of their national boundary and become quite significant global players.

By comparison, in the UK, it would be almost impossible to imagine a company based in a region of South East London, for example, Wandsworth, and assume that it would grow in scale to get recognition much beyond the immediate locality, never mind to get a presence across the whole of UK. Indeed, staying with the example of ice cream, expansion outside the UK to a European scale that compares in population and GDP with the United States would be even more difficult. British ice cream is famous in Europe as it contains little or no cream and therefore runs up against European food labelling laws!

The UK is only one-seventh the size of the United States but it is much more geographically constrained than that comparison suggests. The competitive issues of trying to scale up products and services to grow companies across a European marketplace present significant challenges in terms even of developing a common language. This refers to a common language, not from a linguistic sense but just from a business sense. Although English is the most widely spoken language in the world, within Europe its importance is as a leading *second* language. In a multi-cultural, multi-lingual context, simple ideas are sometimes hard to communicate. This creates greater difficulties in the communication of knowledge. When one manager says we go out into the market, do we all agree our understanding of what the market is? If we are referring to, say, a utilities market, are we all agreed on a common social or linguistic framework for the utilities sector? So there is a greater challenge for European companies although we have seen far more rapid deregulation and privatization across Europe than has been occurring in other parts of the world.

These factors, taken together, have meant that the pressures on the European marketplace have been to adopt a much broader understanding of the end-to-end principles of knowledge management and ramp up their activities far more quickly. Knowledge management is probably 80–85 per cent about people and their ideas. Technology is just an enabler. So whilst Figure 2.5 shows roughly that knowledge management activity in the United States and Europe are not dissimilar in terms of scale, the composition and substance of that activity are markedly different. This can be illustrated by comparing the proportion of knowledge management spending on technology in the United States as against services. In the United States 50–60 per cent of the total market figure is based on technology. Technology carries a bigger ticket in that it is a capital spend identified separately in most corporate accounts. Technology is a recurring business expense, so there is a much higher investment in technology in the United States than here. By contrast, in Europe the spend is much lower, maybe down at 15 or 20 per cent of the total.

Organizational transformation does not show up in the balance sheet in the same way. After all, the payroll might be similar before and after a knowledge management initiative. It is the people who will have changed and that is harder to value.

Organizations can learn to understand the soft issues around knowledge management and can be taught how to change. They can learn quite quickly, and can adapt and apply these ideas for themselves. Again, this 'internal snowball effect' is hard to value objectively. So what we have seen in Europe is a response to the need to embrace an overall end-to-end concept of knowledge management. The technology is just the tip of the iceberg and to some extent gives an illusion of progress that may not be real. After all, what is important about the technology is how it used, what it is used for and why is it used. Satisfying senior management by pointing to the installation of a range of information services can actually reduce the pressure to adopt an overall perspective of knowledge management.

BASIC KNOWLEDGE MANAGEMENT DISCIPLINES

Knowledge management draws from a wide range of disciplines and technologies:

- Cognitive science. This provides insights into how we learn and know which are used for improving the tools and techniques employed for gathering and transferring knowledge.
- Expert systems and artificial intelligence. These technologies are widely used to support automated learning.
- Computer supported collaborative work (groupware). In Europe knowledge management is almost synonymous with groupware. The leading product in this field is Lotus Notes that facilitates the communication and sharing of ideas.
- Library and information science. This is enormously important in knowledge management since clearly the way in which the content of knowledge bases are managed is fundamental to their usefulness.

- Technical writing. This is perhaps more usefully described as technical communication. It provides a body of theory and practice that is relevant to the effective representation and transfer of knowledge.
- Document management. These systems are primarily concerned with managing the accessibility of images and with making the content of documents accessible and reusable at the component level.
- Decision support systems. Broadly, this encompasses the quantitative aspects of information management in fields such as operations research and management science. Knowledge management uses a great deal of qualitative and unstructured data but it does not discard structured quantitative data.
- Semantic networks. These are formed from ideas and relationships. Basically, they involve a sort of hypertext without the content but with far more systematic structure according to meaning. They are often used in fields such as text analysis.
- Relational and object databases. These are the relational databases well established in fields like customer relationship marketing. Object-orientated databases are considered more appropriate for unstructured content and they may be more useful in representing and managing knowledge resources.
- Simulation. Computer and manual simulations as well as role-plays provide micro-arenas for testing out skills.
- Organizational science. Knowledge management expert Karl-Erik Sveiby has identified two tracks for knowledge management. The first concerns the management of the information. The second crucially concerns the management of people. Over these two broad areas three distinct themes can be identified:
  - mechanistic approaches
  - cultural and behavioural approaches
  - systems approaches to the management of knowledge.
- Network technology. The Internet and Intranets provide a communications background through which communities are formed and reformed.

Cap Gemini

Competition, ie a move towards the deregulation of markets, is also bringing up a new commercial challenge. For example, one of the things I find most fascinating in the utility sector is the emergence of call centres. They are probably one of the most knowledge-destructive facilities around because they do not allow people to learn anything other than scripts, thus destroying any knowledge, and it is making organizations detached from their client base. So there are no opportunities to learn from customers anymore.

EMERGING TRENDS

Figure 2.6 illustrates the rapidly accelerating knowledge management market. The market is definitely accelerating because the overall understanding of the benefits that can be achieved from knowledge management is becoming far more broadly accepted across organizations. Today, most enterprises are in the early knowledge management life cycle and are focused on tactical issues. In the future, priorities will evolve to intra- and inter-enterprise integration solutions.

There is in fact rapidly growing understanding of where the longer term strategic direction might lead an enterprise. An interesting comparison can be made here with the transformational effects of digital change, recognized under BPR. Early adopters tend to exploit innovation locally – perhaps using some Word documents linked by an Access database or some mind-mapping software. These initiatives then spread to surrounding departments or units but the underlying business processes are not integrated. Integration between departments or units represents Stage 3. Here the knowledge base is made accessible to a range of areas and functions which enables dispersed decision-making units to form their opinions from a shared perspective. This is then extended again to draw in parts of the supply chain, hence inter-enterprise collaboration. Legislation permitting, the customer database might be shared, or collaboration over solving technical problems of production scheduling might take place. Eventually, at the highest level,

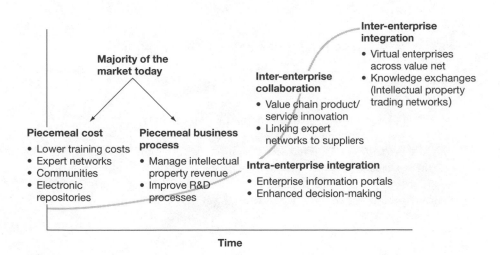

Figure 2.6 *Rapidly accelerating curve of knowledge management*

33

Stage 5, we might see inter-enterprise integration such that the customer does not notice a seamless division or boundary between one enterprise and another. If we were to extend the time line in Figure 2.6 to the right, say the equivalent of 2–3 years, it might also enable the distinction between the US and the European market to begin to blur. Both markets are likely to adopt a similar perspective on technologies. The buying behaviours for knowledge management systems and the customer segments to which they might apply is illustrated in Table 2.1.

In the conservative adopter stage, the enterprise is still at the point where knowledge management is a barely understood discipline. Quite possibly, most board members today have an understanding of the term but if they were to be asked what the organization would actually do tomorrow to make a difference to the business, they commonly struggle. Many companies are still very much in the evangelical, early adopter cycle. At the other end of the spectrum, self-sufficient integrators and business design innovators probably include about 5 per cent of the Fortune 2000. Examples might include, BP, MediaOne and Schlumberger – most already have knowledge management initiatives well underway. Solution buyers and fast followers constitute a further 55 per cent of the Fortune 2000. While some have embarked on knowledge management programmes, the majority are the next target for vendors. They are characterized by the disparate nature of their operations. They tend to view knowledge as an asset in the same way that say, patents are seen in the pharmaceuticals industry. Their activities are people intensive and they view human resources as their primary asset.

BEST AND WORST PRACTICE

KPMG

Everybody knows it is a good and noble thing to do but the trick is to make it really easy to amass content and then get it out again when you need it. If the systems, processes and the format make it really difficult to get the information out then people won't put it in. This place is brilliant at finding enthusiastic, ambitious people with solutions and that means that KPMG needs to maximize their innovation by making it accessible.

Table 2.1 _Five distinct knowledge management (KM) buying behaviours and customer segments which apply_

Percent of Total**	35–45 % **Conservative Adopters**	25–35 % **Fast Follower**	10–15 % **Solution Buyer**	1–2 % **Self-sufficient Integrators**	1–4 % **Business Design Innovators**
Segment Needs	• Basic KM functionality • Cost savings, process efficiencies, and service improvements	• Deep KM functionality in a few critical business processes • Less sophisticated companies use mitigated risk strategies • High IT needs but low capabilities	• Broad range and deep functionality across KM components • Cost savings, process efficiencies, and service improvements	• Innovative source of competitive advantage within their industries • Leading edge status in their industries	• Innovative source of competitive advantage within their industries • Derive competitive edge based on adopting new technologies quickly and sufficiently early to reap benefits first
Segment Profile	• Rely on groupware systems to provide KM functionality • Limited systems budgets • Willing to trade functionality for seamless integration	• Initiate projects for limited set of KM components • Expect large savings from solving their most significant KM problem • Adopt technology on a project by project basis preferring all-in-one solutions	• Typically larger companies with deep needs across a range of functions • Aggressively adopt technology on a project by project basis • Prefer all-in-one solutions from trusted advisors	• Market leaders • Led by risk takers who believe their competitive edge is based on adopting new technologies quickly, buying product and services on a best-of-breed basis.	• Market leaders, preferring 1–2 IT service providers • Often driven by visionary leaders who view advanced KM capabilities (eg inter-enterprise collaboration) as key to achieving leading edge status
Customer Case Example	'Our need for KM is not so great. We only have 30 products. Our small organization learns informally. It is helpful for dealing with customers and suppliers as well as sales proposals.' _Metal Component Manufacturer_	'We used KM to help make a wafer fabrication plant capacity decision which provided an alternative to having to invest US$500m in a new plant' _Electronics Manufacturer_	'We generated over US$100m savings and revenues by using KM to deepen our understanding of our world-class patent inventory. This allowed us to identify obsolete patents and generate royalties and tax credits from third parties to our business and our KM services vendor' _Global Pharmaceutical Manufacturer_	'The new world order is going to be swapping information for new revenues. We are taking what we've learnt internally and selling it to clients. Our vision is to create an electronic market place for intellectual property and intermediate between buyers and sellers' _Professional Services Partnership_	'We are extending our global KM Product Development 2000 project, which significantly improved efficiency by eliminating variation and improving performance. We are now using a "trading network" to leverage our entire supply chain and share best practices while driving down costs' _Automotive Manufacturer_

**Note: Data are directional only. Adapted from Lazard Freres (11/98)   _Source:_ McKinsey IGS 2003 analysis and Mercer SCM

WORST PRACTICE

Andersen

There are some companies that are practically off the map because they're hardly doing any of these things. Still worse, if they do, they're unconnected. Many people just blow money on training because everybody thinks that training is a good thing, that everybody should do training. Therefore, almost all organizations have a budget for some sort for training. But, if there's no link between the training that they do and the corporate strategy or business outcome – they've wasted money. We've spent huge amounts of money on training and whilst a lot of it is very good, there's sometimes a gap in the relevance of the training. I think that many other organizations also have that problem. A lack of coordination between training and business intelligence and between research and development.

A typically exhibited corporate approach to knowledge management that articulates the need for corporate coordination and strategy can be likened to the 'free-fall parachuting syndrome'. Consider the manager responsible for knowledge management across the corporation as a novice parachutist on his or her first jump. The flying school instructors pass the novice a rucksack and a book, saying, 'Trust me that there's a working parachute in the rucksack and the book will provide all the necessary instruction!' When the plane gets to 6,000 metres, the door is opened, the instructor wishes the novice success and pushes him or her out of the plane.

There are three clear phases that the novice experiences; the initial panic reading of the book (quickly!), the euphoric phase as it transpires that the book has very simple instructions (leave the plane, pull rip-cord at 1,500 metres, bend legs when landing), then the final stage where any previous euphoria is annihilated by the effect of the ground rushing up, the uncertainty of what is actually in the rucksack and the sheer panic concerning the outcome of hitting the ground. This technique clearly inspires confidence in the novice and obviously provides all the instructional support needed to ensure a successful experience. Even were the novice to survive the trauma of the descent, it's unlikely he or she would enjoy the landing – though, should it go wrong, nor would he or she have much opportunity to learn from the experience.

This might be compared to a corporate experience of knowledge management based on the 'just do it' approach with no clear strategy, negligible support, a blind trust in the technology (even if it's inappropriate for the task) and no learning from the experience. Clearly, not the way to build best practice in knowledge management.

AstraZeneca

We've done a number of pieces of work to try and figure it out. In terms of the quality of the stuff itself, I'm sure you can find good stuff. The difficulty is, that there is a lot locked away in different sorts of systems and repositories. We aren't instinctively knowledge management people. So a lot of it doesn't even have a title or an author on it. Anyway, our search engines try to go and find things but quite often they can't even find a title for a lot of the stuff, or a date!

In enterprise terms, the second thing that happens is the tendency is to implement something – (Don't just stand there, do something). For example, one large oil company started a video-conferencing initiative to encourage its remote managers to talk to each other. There was no strategy behind whether that was exactly what was needed for the organization.

Buckman Labs

That's a weakness we have. We don't learn from failures. I have never seen any discussion about why we failed in an open way and I know very, very few companies who do that, to be honest. We tend to highlight those places where we succeed and the reasons for our success. Informally, there may be communications which are not shared and that could be the reason why we failed.

In other cases, the organization might put in some groupware, on the basis that they have to have an Intranet (everybody else seems to have one) and they have to have something that is about knowledge management.

Certainly the quickest thing for organizations to do is put in some technology. So someone rushes to the nearest PC store and buys a nice shrink-wrapped box on the assumption perhaps that if it is sited in the middle of the office it will make everyone knowledgeable. Perhaps if the lights are turned down at 7 o'clock it will glow and we'll all be smarter in the morning. Obviously, that is not going to work and while the example is exaggerated, the general pattern can probably be recognized. It is a serious mistake.

N✳Star

Over the last few years we've found ourselves trying to do more with less people and documentation is probably the first thing that goes by the wayside. This is particularly true as we've moved into some of the newer technologies, since there is more pressure to get things done faster. Although we haven't felt the pain of not having it yet, I think we will soon.

BEST PRACTICE

Andersen

If you examine every organization at micro level, you can typically find at least something of all those activities going on. However, different organizations place their emphasis in different places and also there are drastically different levels of coordination and integration. In some organizations, especially relatively old fashioned ones, the level of integration is about zero. There's just no way that the left hand knows what the right hand is doing. In more modern organizations, in an organization like Microsoft for example, you find that there's an extremely high level of corporate awareness and that it is extremely well connected.

Technology of itself, implementing something, doing something without a strategy for knowledge management, self-evidently will not work. To be successful, knowledge management has to be related to the business. It has to have context and it has to have business drivers. There has got to be value to it. As Figure 2.7 illustrates, there are real costs to ignorance. Knowledge management is all about people and ideas. So you have to decide how to improve the productivity of people and ideas. If that is the objective, the main thing is to reach out to people's desks, to where they are working on Monday morning.

You have to convince them that you are going to introduce them to something that will make a difference to how they work, who they talk to, tell them who knows who and tell them who knows what. It will show them what is important that they were not doing on Friday afternoon. Invariably it is about people, changing the way they work, the way they behave and feel and the way they relate to other members of the enterprise. It does not really matter if you want to call it knowledge management. If the cap fits, great.

Is it worth doing? Well, there is some empirical evidence as to the price of being stupid. As Figure 2.7 shows, substantial costs can be attached to re-inventing the wheel, making the same mistakes at least twice, and simply not being able to find what the company might already know quickly enough to be useful for problem solving. It is estimated that in the United States alone, re-invention costs for the Fortune 500 companies alone will amount to a staggering US $31 billion.

SUMMARY

Knowledge management is a general term applied to almost any project that an organization undertakes which is designed to preserve, transfer or exploit knowledge from one part of the organization to another.

BP Amoco

We tend to have some key processes in place which we would call 'capital value processes' which amount really to a series of prompts for use by people when conducting a project, to make sure that they address the vital stages of shared learning where it could bring them advantage.

All companies are already involved in knowledge management but often it is done implicitly and informally. The job of a formal knowledge management programme is simply to make knowledge marketplaces operate more efficiently. The motive for undertaking formal knowledge management projects is very clear. Organizations are recognizing that ownership of knowledge is a key competitive differentiator. Quite simply the lack of a knowledge management programme means that they are losing money, or opportunities. Either because they are unable to find the knowledge that they need, or because they are re-inventing the wheel, or because they are making decisions based on inadequate information. Quantifying these losses is difficult and this makes it hard to design and justify knowledge management projects.

The easiest kind of knowledge management project to justify is a so-called knowledge base. A knowledge base is something that attempts to make the knowledge marketplace more efficient by making explicit knowledge easier to

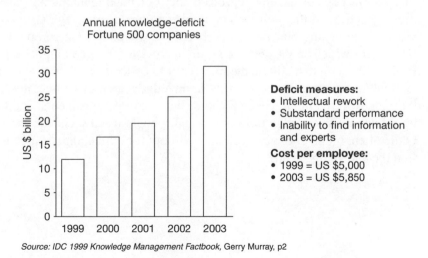

Source: IDC 1999 Knowledge Management Factbook, Gerry Murray, p2

Figure 2.7 *Knowledge-deficit due to lack of investment in knowledge management*

access. Unfortunately, making a repository of information available is not the same as transferring knowledge. It is only one (albeit important) step in a far more complex process.

Hewlett-Packard.

You know how people talk about HP's cultural practices? HP has got a reputation for having this particular type of culture. Interestingly one of the reasons that HP has done very well over the years, and actually what I think has happened historically, is that HP managed to incorporate in its normal management practices some of the things that have become much more fashionable in recent years. Because they have become embedded in the organization so deeply, they become invisible.

Knowledge is both and social and contextual. The person who holds the knowledge also knows what it means, what its limits are and how it can be used. This surrounding context of tacit knowledge is sometimes lost when the information is saved somewhere else. Even transmitting the information to someone else is not the same as knowledge transfer. The receiver must actually pick up the information and learn how to use it in appropriate ways.

Knowledge is most effectively transferred through interaction – preferably face-to-face interaction. The further one moves from learning through interaction the less likely it is that knowledge will transfer effectively. As a result many knowledge management projects focus on making interaction easier and more effective. At the high-tech end, this can be done through groupware, or video-conferencing but, far more cheaply and simply, one company set up talk-rooms which employees are required to visit for some minutes each day. Projects that aim to facilitate the transfer of knowledge work best when organizations recognize how the existing knowledge marketplace operates, so that they can work within it. Given a choice between asking someone and looking up a fact in a knowledge base or manual, people usually choose the former. Quite often, if that does not work they will opt for third choice, which is not to find the knowledge at all!

3

Practice orientation

N✱Star

It was all new to us. The concept of even doing something with knowledge management was only introduced last fall as part of the re-organization. So far, we've identified a position for a knowledge management architect within my group, although we haven't yet filled that position. So, we're very much in the infancy stages and at this point we haven't defined completely what knowledge management means to us. We recognize that it's going to have a place and that it's a concept that we want to introduce and build on. However, I don't think we'll be able to get too far until we can bring somebody in to help us get started.

Case example

As we have already made clear, knowledge management is largely about social processes and communities. From a commercial, not to say a profit-orientated view-point, those communities must involve customers. Sharing knowledge with customers can make a big difference to the bottom line. A good example is provided by United Parcel Services (UPS), a company that has always assumed that on-time delivery was the primary concern of its customers. As a result the cornerstone of its quality policy was guaranteed next-day delivery for all packages. In the mid 1990s everything that this company did was geared around a service quality which aimed to deliver every package by 10.30 on the morning following collection. The times taken to call a lift, the delay in answering doorbells were all taken into account in producing precise schedules. The company even shaved corners off its delivery drivers' seats in order to speed their entry and exit from their delivery vans. Having assumed that delivery time was critical, the company then set up a series of internal measures to monitor the reliability of its delivery performance. It simply assumed that if it met these targets customers would perceive it as offering high quality. Of course customers were very happy with this reliability and service standard but when UPS management broadened the questions on its customer surveys, managers received a big surprise. They found that customers valued an opportunity to chat with delivery drivers in order to get practical tips and advice on how to package and ship parcels. A driver that shot in and out of a delivery like lightning, in order to meet a tight performance target, didn't have time to share any knowledge. As a response, the company created a 13-minute space in each driver's day to allow the driver to chat with customers. When it was introduced this time allowance cost UPS US $4 million in drivers' time each year but the company reckons that the additional sales achieved are many times higher.

The UPS case illustrates what Pfeffer and Sutton (1999) describe as the 'smart talk trap'. This trap occurs when an organization falls into the gap between knowing and doing. It also illustrates an issue of critical importance in knowledge management, namely, the ability to ask the right questions. Market researchers have long known the dangers of asking a question that presumes its answer, or of developing a measure that is not relevant to the way a customer thinks. There is a strong inclination in all organizations to set up quantitative measures which examine rates and volumes, just as in the UPS example where the company was measuring speed of performance. In a call centre, measures of productivity are often established around the volume of calls handled by agents. In both cases the information obtained can be very misleading. For example, if quality declines, a call centre will have to process a higher volume of calls in order to deal with the rising number of complaints!

AstraZeneca

I think it depends exactly how you define knowledge management. I know we have some work groups where they have quality circles which are basically a type of knowledge management aren't they? I mean they exchange views on 'What happens if you try and do this with the tablets?' Similarly, if you're running a project, almost by definition the people working on it must be doing something in the form of knowledge management.

The smart talk trap refers to compiling information and knowledge which is not precisely relevant to customers, or finding relevant information which the company makes excuses not to put into action. The purpose of knowledge management is to provide a guide to productive and sound decision making which then forms the basis of action.

Advice about acquiring knowledge and wisdom is rooted in antiquity; the very word 'philosophy' actually means love of knowledge. This will help us to see knowledge as a step on the road to wisdom and to develop some useful definitions.

- Data – refers to chunks of facts about the state of the world. Data may be either quantitative or qualitative in nature. When thinking of data most people seem to emphasize the quantitative form that is easily stored and manipulated in computer systems.
- Information. Classically, information is defined as data that are endowed with meaning and purpose. A collection of books acquires meaning if it is conceived as a library. A slight difficulty here is that people may not agree on the meaning. One driver may regard 80 kph as a pleasant speed with which to cruise through the countryside but by the driver behind, seeking to make his or her next appointment, as altogether too slow. In both cases the drivers are obtaining data from their speedometer and structuring it in relation to another purpose.
- Knowledge. Information connected in relationships may be described as knowledge. At the individual level a person can relate information to his or her external environment or groups of people can agree how to interpret new information.
- Wisdom. When knowledge has been put into action repeatedly on the basis of interpretation and relationships and when it produces reliable and consistent results, it becomes second nature. Wisdom is the ability to make sound judgements and decisions apparently without thought. In the artificial intelligence community it is sometimes suggested that experts don't think – they know. Watching an expert at work is often an amazing experience for the lay person as the expert uses his or her wisdom (embodied knowledge) to achieve results seemingly without effort.

In a commercial environment knowledge must be put into work in three primary areas. The first of these concerns meeting customer needs. Every member of the organization or enterprise must understand how his or her work contributes to fulfilling customer needs and how the products and services of the enterprise provide customer value. People with direct customer contact need to understand the kinds of knowledge in which customers are interested and how they want it organized and presented. This may vary by individuals or by groups.

The second area concerns processes. Each person in the enterprise must understand how his or her work relates to the work of others. Each person must also be conscious of the systematic pursuit of higher quality possibly at lower cost.

The third area concerns the body of knowledge. Each person must understand, to varying degrees, something about the subject matter with which members of the enterprise deal. For some people this simply means developing a mental taxonomy of key terms. It requires a deeper knowledge of relationships and meanings both within the enterprise and the outside world. This allows members of the enterprise to respond effectively to changes in trends and market conditions in their particular field, so as to provide the right kind of customer value even if circumstances may change.

If a business idea is to be successful, it has to deliver value and it has to deliver profits. Knowledge management can realize business value in several ways, eg productivity, improved customer service and innovation. (See Figure 3.1).

Knowledge management practice tended to come from a TQM perspective so it is interesting to compare the two. Knowledge management is concerned with how an organization can develop the practice of what it does so it can also develop an understanding of why it was done.

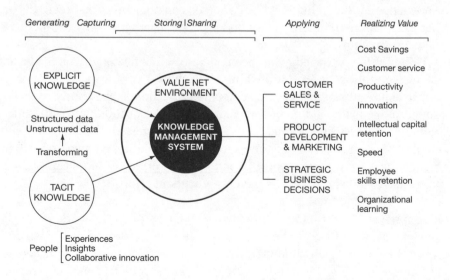

Figure 3.1   *The link between knowledge management and customer value*

TQM tended to look purely inwardly at the organization from the perspective of improving the quality or efficiency of current practices, so attention was focused not so much on what the organization knew but on how it did what it did. When an organization examines how it does things there is a tendency to turn off the strategic learning process, in other words, to neglect to ask 'Where should we be going?' TQM did not resolve the issue of whether the enterprise should be making that product or providing that service in the first place. It did not address the question of whether an organization was supplying the product because the market was there or whether the market was there because the organization was supplying it.

TQM is about asking 'What went wrong, how do we improve it, how do we learn from this failure, how do we go forward?' What it fails to tackle is the ability to recognize that if we do not know, we need to ask! The key competitive issue is how to mobilize the collective horsepower that is available in the organization. Too close a focus on quality can cause the enterprise to lose sight of the big picture. For example, one utility company that won an outstanding quality award concentrated its resources on power failures. It set up a big internal quality operation to ensure that power cuts were restored in an increasingly shorter timescale. What it forgot was that most consumers are not really interested in having their power re-supplied quickly after a failure. What they are really interested in is not losing power in the first place since even a momentary blackout may require them to reset all their domestic timers.

Siemens

After being able to access the knowledge and experts, we need to be able to exchange the knowledge and experts. Knowledge exchange isn't too difficult but we need to work on people exchange. We'll definitely develop our incentivization schemes towards more and more obligatory targets. Content-wise, we will concentrate on identifying best practice and sharing examples of what worked and what didn't. We will also make our solutions mobile by putting them on something like Palm Pilots. So you can have it with the customer when you hold your discussion in the hotel bar or whatever. Finally, we will further our ways of collaborating by setting up communities of practice sets, along with the required things to support them such as worldwide calendars, global polling, defined objectives and goals and a dedicated budget for research on this type of community.

Bob Metcalfe, the founder of 3Com, came up with an amazingly complex mathematical algorithm for understanding the power of a network of people. However, this algorithm highlights the simple fact that the power in any network is not merely connecting people. It is connecting through people to their knowledge networks that makes the difference.

TQM focused on areas like quality circles (QCs). It took the line 'We are the people responsible for the problem so let's fix it'. The term QC is derived from TQM's Japanese roots, at a time when Japanese companies were giving a strong emphasis to quality issues. Today enterprises are in an evolving market place and must consider problems from a far wider angle. This requires the quality question to be put in a different way across the business, asking 'Where does the wisdom come from?' This is the wisdom to fix something, to resolve something or to innovate. This wisdom may come from outside the business. It may come from something in the social environment. When James Dyson was looking at the issues around the vacuum cleaner he was inspired by a new way of looking at the device, away from any business context.

If there is a quality problem, organizations are most likely to get inspiration by asking where they can get explicit, documented knowledge. How do they recognize data that is apparently completely out of context? If all they are ever doing in a QC is looking at current practices and procedures, they are not going to perceive an 'out of box' fix. So knowledge management is really about drawing this into the value management of the business. It is bringing the combined knowledge resources of the enterprise to bear on both strategic and tactical business decisions.

PricewaterhouseCoopers

We're in quite a good position to talk to you as there is obviously knowledge management as a strategic consulting layer. It is also in some way related to relationship marketing, which we might call Web personalization, or relationship commerce specific to customer requirements, which is viewed as part of knowledge management. It's a matter of seeing it as part of the client's profile and content specific to individual requirements. So we have a top–down strategic management consultancy view of knowledge management. We have practitioners delivering anything from data mining to document management to Internet-based solutions to CRM and Siebel implementations (which focus on knowledge of client bases, etc) and then through to relationship commerce. So we've quite a broad spectrum of activities which fall under the knowledge management umbrella and it's all topped and tailed by the strategic management consultancy view.

Building a knowledge system is like undertaking a journey; you need a map to plan out your path and to determine possible alternative routes along the way. KPMG Consulting has suggested that this journey has five distinct stages; it is interesting to compare these with the quality stages identified by Crosby (1979):

1. **Knowledge chaotic.** The organization is unaware of the importance of knowledge to the achievement of its goals. Knowledge is therefore stored and managed in an *ad hoc* way across the organization. Accessing and retrieving this information is difficult and time consuming because no one knows where knowledge may be held. Systems may be incompatible. Processes for collecting the information may be ineffectual or non-existent. People may be reluctant to share information, or simply lack the time or incentive to do so. In terms of providing customer quality therefore, the cost of quality is unknown but the actual costs are probably in the region of 0–40 per cent of sales as members of the enterprise engage in frequent fire fighting. Since they do not know why problems are occurring they tend to address symptoms and not causes.

2. **Knowledge aware.** At this stage the enterprise recognizes the need to manage knowledge and some attempt is made to do so. The easiest and most attractive first stage in this process is cataloguing available knowledge sources, which involves identifying and documenting the sources of knowledge and establishing some sort of retrieval system so that it can be related to processes. However, awareness and implementation across the enterprise are not uniform and there may be issues of sharing the knowledge. In quality terms, costs are generally reported at around 5 per cent of sales but are probably running closer to 18 or 20 per cent. Since managers are just awakening to these issues they are supporting initiatives more theoretically than practically. Some functional titles have been designated and teams are established to resolve problems but actions are still very short term and are based more on exhortation than anything else.

3. **Knowledge enabled.** The actions taken in step two are slowly beginning to pay off and knowledge management is beginning to benefit the business. Standard procedures and tools are utilized across the enterprise. Knowledge resources have been inventoried, evaluated and classified and formal procedures are well established to maintain these. However, some cultural and technological barriers remain to be addressed. At the stage of enlightenment, management is beginning to support the quality of knowledge management more actively. Reported quality costs and actual costs are beginning to converge at 8 per cent and 12 per cent of sales revenue respectively. Knowledge management personnel report to top management and their leader is more actively involved in the management of the company. The belief that knowledge management is beginning to pay off and the value of knowledge management approaches is becoming more widespread. It therefore becomes possible to expand the activity on the basis of a systematic plan.

1. **Knowledge managed.** The framework of procedures and tools to discover, create, maintain and elicit knowledge have become more integrated. There is an overt recognition of the importance of the need to use the technology to facilitate and enable cultural processes to blossom. The knowledge strategy is reviewed and there is a shift away from hard to soft measures. The delicate balance between the need for formal processes and the need for informal facilitating processes is recognized so time for reflection and introspection are built into work flows. The cost of quality is now reported at 6 per cent of sales revenue and is probably closer to 8 per cent. At the stage of wisdom, managers are participating personally and provide leadership in knowledge management quality. At board level, an appointment with a title like chief knowledge officer may be made. The knowledge made available to the corporation is leveraged proactively, rather the reactively, so the company seems to be a step ahead of its competitors most of the time.

5. **Knowledge-centric.** The enterprise redefines itself in terms of a knowledge-based organization. It is able to demonstrate sustainable competitive advantage through the application and enhancement of its knowledge base which competitors find hard to replicate. Knowledge management procedures are an integral part of the organization and members of the enterprise accept them as part of their daily work. There is a robust technological backbone that allows knowledge to be mission critical to the enterprise. The assessment and improvement of the knowledge environment is a core activity. The value of knowledge to the organization is being measured and reported to stakeholders and is reflected in the organization's market worth. It is also being valued as the organization's intellectual capital. At the stage of certainty, the cost of quality in knowledge management is reported as 2–3 per cent of sales revenue and is actually running at that level. The importance of knowledge is recognized as necessary for corporate survival and growth. Many conventional organizational forms have been abandoned to allow greater autonomy, empowerment and choice over the nature of the work to be done.

If this looks like an impossible journey consider some evidence from the real world. The Palm Pilot invented by 3Com became an instant bestseller and achieved market dominance and high levels of customer loyalty. Despite technically superior products launched by Texas Instruments and Sharpe which were faster, had more features and were even, in some cases, cheaper, they were unable to shake the Palm Pilot's lead. Perhaps the fact that by May 2000 the Palm Pilot could connect and integrate with some 4,000 knowledge sources in different applications had something to do with it. In the service sector Microsoft was ranked 137th on the Fortune 500 list with about US $12 billion in sales and US $14 billion in assets. By comparison, the Ford Motor Corporation alone had US $155 billion in sales. Yet the market valuation of Microsoft, that pushed close to US $400 billion at one point, far exceeded the market valuation of General Motors, Ford and Mitsubishi combined. IBM's market valuation in 1999 was approximately twice its annual sales level of around US $78 billion.

Rolls-Royce

The organization is very much technology based with multiple projects running at the same time. The sharing of knowledge is critical and there is always pressure to bring in new types of technology. The sharing of knowledge from customers and ideas from other divisions of the company is also important. In addition, the company is taking a more global stance. At one time the only knowledge sharing that needed to be done was between the various divisions in Derby, Bristol, etc. Increasingly this is widening. Design issues in particular are being distributed to a wide range of companies throughout the world. Most of these projects are made up of a number of sub-systems and it is not unusual for each sub-system to be designed by a different organization. Clearly, each of these design teams needs to have common knowledge to ensure the most efficient management of each overall project.

In a knowledge-based economy, market valuation seems to be based much more closely on intellectual assets than on physical assets. These knowledge-based assets reflect areas such as brand recognition, industry vision, thought leadership, intellectual property, customer loyalty, innovation and what some analysts have even called dream evaluation – a belief by investors in the value of anticipated future, products and services. It is this dream evaluation that gave Amazon.com a market value of US $18 billion, against a reported loss of US $400 million in 1999. This is because the market recognized that Amazon had established a brand, a presence and a knowledge base that competitors would find very hard to match.

Knowledge management looks across the entire business – not only at sales to customers but also outside at the customer's customer. It provides the tools to examine how the value of the business is actually shaped and what the drivers are for shaping the value of the business. In making these strategic decisions it encourages a redefinition of the rationale for development and marketing. IBM provides a classic example. When it returned a massive corporate deficit back in 1993 it actually recorded a record sales year. The only problem was it that it cost some US $5 billion more to make everything that was being sold. IBM was able to sell everything it was making — no matter how much it cost. IBM is an organization that has access to probably more analysts, experts and industry observers than any other business in the Western World. Yet, despite all that expertise, all that drive, the company could not see that it was continuing down a route that was making an out-of-date product. From within, there did not seem to be a mechanism to question why it had adopted the market posture of the time. The market was moving away from the company but it could not see how to stop itself making a product that was ever more expensive, ever less profitable. The company could not break the silence across the business. It took a new CEO to break that silence, develop knowledge sharing and open up the questions.

TQM does not address those issues either. As already identified, it does not take a holistic view of the business. However, TQM had much to offer and it would be wholly mistaken to regard it as a business idea that failed. TQM was a stepping-stone to learn about the value of the knowledge that exists in the business, to learn where intuition and wisdom might reside. Its main value was to show where business strategy and decision-making should occur. It was a business practice adopted by the West as a classic copy of what was happening in Eastern markets where they were trying to fix a specific business issues. The West just adopted it as a panacea on the basis that if it were implemented across everything it would cure all problems.

HOW TO INSTITUTIONALIZE BEST PRACTICE

PricewaterhouseCoopers

I'll give you one example. Effectively writing up an assignment and noting things learnt as a case study. We are asked to do this at the end of every assignment and it is either posted internally or in the public domain.

The same people that failed with TQM will fail with knowledge management. Knowledge management is no more the panacea than TQM ever was. There are places where knowledge management will not have a role. To be successful, knowledge management must eventually take into account all aspects of the business strategy. In the short and medium term this means recognizing the key business issues of the here and now and trying to fix them. Taking a step back, knowledge management may even be concerned about what the business issue actually is and how the business should be positioned in relation to that issue. Managers should pose three fundamental questions to the individuals in the business:

- What do you know?
- What do you need to know?
- What is the best way of getting it?

The worth of these simple questions lies in the way they are asked. For example, suppose a market analyst was asked to explain what he or she knew about doing an analysis of some company data. The analyst would probably explain how he or she did it and probably would not have any qualms about telling the boss. If the question were broadened to 'What else do you need to know?' again, the analyst would present some perfectly well conceived, logically thought out ideas. Now suppose we added 'What would help you to do an analysis?' We would now get something quite different. This is a broad, open question. Taking the three questions above, the challenge is to ask the right ones, with the appropriate focus.

Rolls-Royce

I think I'd define, if that's the right word, knowledge using the analogy [of a] pilot's cockpit. Data could be the signals that come from the airwaves around the aircraft, the outer tube, air speed and so on. You can transform data into information by reducing and collating that data, ie by putting the data into context and displaying it in an understandable format, eg the dials in the cockpits. Knowledge is something rather different because knowledge is something that allows the pilot to take an action based on the information he [or she] is presented with. Therefore, our purpose is to bring something else to the data so that the pilot has an understanding of how the aircraft behaves and what he [or she] should do in particular circumstances. So knowledge is something different to data. Interestingly though, you can embed certain elements about knowledge into a system. You can build an auto-pilot mechanism and that auto-pilot will respond in a particular way, in particular circumstances.

There is a lot to be learnt from watching TV interviewers who work with children. These interviewers very quickly learnt the art of never asking a closed question, because if children can answer questions 'Yes' or 'No' they will and that makes for pretty poor television. For the same reasons, managers should never ask a closed question in an organization. Ask the open question 'What do you know about this?', which demands a response showing an individual's knowledge in the context of his or her job.

The starting point is to ask managers what knowledge they need about the context of their job. The follow-up question is 'What's the best way of getting the knowledge you need?' The knowledge management engineer will then start to align their knowledge productivity programmes around helping that manager. The aim would be to provide something that, on a Monday morning, will help managers get what they need to know. That may appear to be more like common sense than knowledge management. Most managers intuitively understand that this is how the enterprise should be working. In a TQM scenario, common sense is about making sure that the enterprise is exploiting the right capability at the right time to resolve the right issues. It is about moving the business performance forward. Knowledge management is about that business performance. It is about realizing value across the business releasing the untapped value that exists in every business so that it can come to the surface. Knowledge management is like a bottle of fizzy water. You take the cap off and it loves to fizz up – it is all there in the bottle, all you have to do is open it.

Nokia

I think it is remarkable that in Nokia we have been able to spread the spirit, throughout the whole organization. There certainly will be exceptions but overall I would say that knowledge management is there within the thinking of all the managers and all the team leaders and all the team members.

TRANSFER OF BEST PRACTICE

That we can build on each preceding stage in the journey to a knowledge-based organization is most easily recognized from the procedure of the TQM era of the 1980s mentioned earlier, the famous QCs. A QC comprised structured, voluntary work groups of around 6–8 people, usually from a particular work area (this concentration on a limited number of work areas is one of the several significant differences between a QC and a community of practice). Typically, a QC would meet for one hour or so on a weekly or fortnightly basis to discuss and resolve work related problems. The group identified the problems to be solved. The activity may have been facilitated by training, such as developing abilities in areas like problem solving and the implementation of change. The idea was to give employees themselves an opportunity to do something positive about the problems and issues they faced, rather than simply making suggestions for others in the organization. Although not established as a knowledge management tool, it is apparent that a QC recognized knowledge as a personal and a social property. QCs usually had little formal power but they often discussed things widely outside their official remit that gave rise to an exchange of knowledge.

BOC

About five years ago I was involved in a best operating practices initiative, which looked at things like, 'Malaysia can paint cylinders faster than anyone else in the world, so why can Malaysia paint cylinders faster?' You work out actually that it's a question of [the workers] being paid piecemeal, in their lunch hour, to do it. And you suddenly think, 'Ah now there's an idea!' So you tell the rest of the world. 'Hey! This is the way to get your cylinders painted faster.' Yeah, forget technology! So, some of this knowledge management is just a transfer of knowledge.

Quality in this sense means doing what we do better and in fact the American Productivity and Quality Centre (APQC) identified the transfer of best practice as the most important issue facing companies in its 1996 survey of emerging practices in knowledge management. The APQC itself is a little uncomfortable with the term 'best practice' since it can lead to arguments about the validity of the term 'best'. The word has a rather final connotation and seems to close off debate. What happens to be best depends largely on your point of view (and is changing as knowledge advances), what is best for one person, or enterprise, may not be best for another. In fact, AMP, the world's largest manufacturer of electrical and electronic interconnection devices which employees 40,000 people in 40 countries found that the label 'best practice' was somewhat counter productive. It came up with the term 'SDP' which stands for successfully demonstrated practices. To add creditability to these labels it established three clear criteria for successful demonstration:

- Has the SDP resulted in a measurable improvement?
- Has the SDP been recognized by internal and external experts?
- Has the SDP been recognized through business assessments and audit?

However, it must be acknowledged that the term 'better practice' has never really caught on so we will stick to the conventional usage.

In order to identify and institutionalize best practice Chevron Corporation recognized four levels, both in its corporate databases and in its best practice teams:

Level 1. Good idea – unproven and could make a positive impact on business performance. Makes sense intuitively and if substantiated by data this idea could be a candidate for implementation in one or more areas of activity.

Level 2. Good practice – this is a technique, method, procedure, or process that has been implemented and has improved business results for the enterprise usually by providing added value to customers. This is substantiated by data collected both in relation to the activity and by using a limited amount of comparative data from other organizations. This practice is a definite candidate for application in other areas and at other locations.

Level 3. Local best practice – this is good practice that has been determined to be the best approach for all or for a large part of the organization such as a department or operating division. There is considerable evidence to support this view based not only on an analysis of internal performance but also on a review of similar practices outside the company. This practice is applicable at most or all similar locations elsewhere in the corporation.

Level 4. Industry best practice – this has been demonstrated to be the best approach for all or large parts of the enterprise. It is based on both internal and external benchmarks including an analysis of performance data. The external benchmarking may be cross-sector and will extend beyond the organization's industry.

In terms of categorizing its processes at each of these four levels, Chevron allows contributors to decide for themselves if the practice is worth sharing and at what level it should be catalogued.

Buckman Labs

At first, our first electronic notice board was just an ordinary CompuServe forum. It had 22 sections and these sections were divided up according to our various areas of business, so that they became what are affectionately known as communities of practice. Everybody in the pulp and paper division knew that if they wanted to learn what was going on, or to help their associates around the world solve their problems, the quickest way to do it was to get into a community of practice.

We had the same technology available to all our Spanish, Italian, Portuguese associates who would ask questions in their own language because they were more comfortable doing that. If the question was not answered within 24 hours we had two people responsible for maintaining these communities of practice and they would translate the question from Spanish into English and post it in English.

SUMMARY

The quality management era taught us that a huge amount of knowledge tends to flow through informal networks that serve as internal knowledge markets. To take advantage of this knowledge, efforts need to be linked to the organization's business strategy. Formal knowledge management projects should extend the reach of knowledge markets and make them more efficient, but knowledge is socially constructed and may best be transferred through stories and interactive dialogue. Successful knowledge management projects are possible but require people to focus on the quality of the knowledge and of the transfer. In this respect technology does not change actual behaviour and access to knowledge sources does not itself add value. A knowledge management philosophy may require a change in the culture of the organization and depends substantially on each member's willingness to participate and the extent to which they trust fellow members and management.

4

Process orientation

Barclays Bank

The thing that really excites me is the idea of getting more and more buy-in from the different business areas. Once we manage to include more and more people on this knowledge gateway, we will be able to really open the roof on what we can achieve. However, I suppose you have to remember that things must evolve. You have to sort of move with the business and do things gently to get the buy-in. You're talking about changing cultures, changing organizational infrastructures and technology. You have to do it gently and try to pull all of these things together without conflict or strain.

Many years ago a man called Robert Townsend, a former chief executive of Avis Rent-A-Car, wrote a famous book called *Up the Organisation* (1970). In it he defines a consultant as someone who borrows your watch to tell you the time and then walks off with it. It is a great definition. Of course what it means is that consultants are better at learning, in other words acquiring knowledge, than the organizations that they work for. It also means that consultants are expecting to sell the same knowledge over and over again. The idea behind the quality circles that we discussed in the previous chapter was to improve existing practice. Quality management consultants will say that the benefits of these improvements are so great that the quality is effectively free. Many mangers have been heard to observe that they are under pressure to perform and that while there never seems to be the time or the resources to get things right the first time round, there always seem to be the time to go back and do it right after it has gone wrong. Has this changed over the years? Teece (1998) reported that the annual aggregate re-invention costs in the United States ranged from between US $2 billion and US $100 billion each year. Organizations are re-inventing solutions and repeating mistakes because they cannot identify or transfer best practices and experiential knowledge from one location to another or from one project to another. To test this, it is only necessary to do an informal survey of colleagues in your company by asking them the question "Have you ever worked on a project only to realize eventually that somebody else in the company has done exactly the same thing, at another time or place?" If this happens even once, it is clearly a waste of time and a certain measure that knowledge is not being transferred or shared.

BG

I think it's to do with something called bandwidth... Now I'm not a 'techie' but it is all about working differently, working smarter and things like on-line training, delivery of video, delivering conferences over the desk-top, so to speak. I think a key element would be our network capacity but equally, we have got to keep reinforcing the message to share information, share your knowledge. If you make a mistake you should tell people about it because we don't want to make too many more, especially if they're expensive. The trouble is it's a cultural minefield. I would suggest that in any organization it's difficult to talk about your mistakes. So we're trying to break that mould and start sharing knowledge.

Does this mean that somehow modern enterprises are becoming less good at capturing and storing information? Or course the answer to that is no but it brings us face to face with an important paradox in an information rich environment. Offer a child a strawberry ice cream and he or she may very well accept. Offer a child a choice of ice cream from the range of many available in an ice cream store and you present the child with an acute dilemma. More choices, more information, create more difficulty in resolving problems. In information terms it is apparent that at the individual level, whilst the amount of information that may be accessed from many internal and external sources has increased substantially, the attention span and the rate at which people can learn and absorb new knowledge is more or less fixed. So, if information sources expand and attention sources remain at more or less the same level, it follows that the attention that can be given to any one source is increasingly diminished.

Knowledge management is a means rather than an end. The focus must be on core business processes because the intention is to improve the enterprise's ability to perform these core processes and add value more effectively. These core processes must in turn concentrate on the creation and effective application of knowledge. Here lies the rub. It is quite easy to create knowledge sharing systems which are out of context or misaligned with the underlying core business processes. In other words, they sit to one side of what members of the enterprise actually do. An easy example might be something like a staff handbook which details all the policies and procedures in the organization that is given to every person on arrival and is probably read by almost nobody. That is not to say that something like a staff handbook cannot add value. Obviously if you take the trouble to read it you can save yourself some time in learning about the way we do things around here but it is sub-optimal. What most people do when they want to know how something is done in a particular firm is ask a manager or co-worker. You might be hard pushed to find someone poring over the Staff Handbook.

Another related issue is the capture of high quality knowledge. If knowledge management processes are not aligned with the main business processes or if the consistent capture of high quality knowledge requires significant additional effort over and beyond regular work, then most people will not bother to capture it. Without effective knowledge capture all other aspects of knowledge management are irrelevant. Obviously capturing good quality knowledge is the foundation of knowledge management. The trick is how to do it. The life cycle for knowledge management therefore looks something like this:

- The capture of good quality knowledge from external or internal sources.
- A method of codifying that knowledge is devised. Somehow the knowledge has to be classified and valued in terms of context, relevance and lifespan.
- A means of giving access to the knowledge then has to be created. This might be mechanical or it might be personal.
- All this is wasted if the knowledge is not actually used. There has to be a culture of searching out and personally importing available knowledge.
- The feedback loop then has to be completed as the knowledge worker adds value to existing knowledge by amending it through use.
- When knowledge has outlived its usefulness it must be removed from the knowledge base.

Many of these activities – acquiring, classifying and accessing knowledge – are similar to those of librarians. There are however some significant differences. Librarians are usually not impressed if people make notes in books or remove pages from them. Nor do librarians usually have any involvement in the way in which people use the knowledge that they obtain from their books.

The initial evaluation and continued enrichment of knowledge is a key aspect of knowledge management.

BPR caused companies to re-examine critically their traditional ways of doing things. By the late 1980s, information services in many organizations had reached the point where there was the potential for using the dynamic represented by the process networks themselves. Information connectivity allowed for radical new ways of doing things and even for the provision of new information-based products and services. BPR consultants were hired to go into organizations to try and identify where the potential for the most rapid advances might lie. As a result of these efforts, massive leaps in connectivity and the use of information were sometimes achieved. Sometimes, the exercise went horribly wrong and the net outcome was merely to disrupt the existing services. The problem lay in the view taken of the organization that, in the case of BPR, was very mechanistic (shades of scientific management again!). If an enterprise were to be envisaged like a clock, everything was fine. You can take a mechanical clock, disassemble it, oil the cogs and levers, replace worn parts and reassemble it. The result is a better clock. The trouble is that the model of the enterprise as a clock is probably not always appropriate. What if the enterprise is more like a cat? Once you have disassembled your cat, the chances of reassembling it and even ending up with a working cat are pretty slim. Cats probably make better analogies for organizations than clocks since enterprise members always have the potential to act in unexpected ways and to interact in even more unexpected ways. The problem therefore is how do you get the best out of a cat?

Cable & Wireless

I think that, within Cable & Wireless, the best future opportunities will occur when we establish a true coming together of all the parts of the organization. As an example, many people have no idea that Optus in Australia was part of Cable & Wireless. We now own 53 per cent of it and it's called Cable & Wireless Optus. Very few people knew that [the] Hong Kong [investment] was actually Cable & Wireless HKT. So, being able to tie into the Cable & Wireless name, using a single image, even where we don't have majority share-holdings, will be important. We've still got places like the Solomon Islands and Fiji, which are Cable & Wireless investments where operations are not clearly identified as being part of Cable & Wireless. Once we get the Cable & Wireless name on the different companies it is much easier to encourage Cable & Wireless thinking. You must get employees to relate to the company before you can actually start imposing Cable & Wireless thinking. Otherwise they will still see themselves as an employee of Hong Kong Telecom or whatever.

The answer is of course that organizations are both cats and clocks. Generally, high level managers, technical experts and researchers are treated like cats; they are allowed a great deal of freedom in how they do their work. This is supposed to allow them to be creative and inspirational. Other members of the enterprise are treated as if they were part of a clock. There are rules and procedures they are supposed to follow on the assumption that they will work better that way. This highlights the very different approaches used in re-engineering and knowledge management. Re-engineering is about making your clock work better based on the structured coordination of people and information. It tends to be a top–down approach that assumes that it is easy to codify value creation. To work well, it requires a certain predictability in the environment. Knowledge management focuses on effectiveness more than efficiency. It is bottom–up and assumes that managers can best foster knowledge by responding to the inventive, improvizational ways people actually get things done. It assumes that value-creating activities are not easy to pin down, partly because they do not all reside at the 'top'. It also assumes more turbulence and unpredictability in the environment.

From a knowledge management perspective, the potential losses of knowledge incurred in disassembling your cat and of the knowledge that resides in every part of the enterprise can be illustrated by the example of a water utility company, XYZ Water. It undertook a process study that looked at the working patterns of some of its engineers. The company had a large central office overlooking a major river in a city centre and that is where the engineers always used to meet and get their job cards. Indeed, at the start of every day they would get everything they needed. Apparently over and above the time spent travelling to the building, this took an average of 16 minutes every day when the engineers also had an opportunity to talk to each other about the jobs they had. They would then go out in their vans and fix whatever water engineers fix. The process people thought they had spotted an opportunity for improvement. First, the building was a prime piece of riverside real estate that was extremely valuable. The capital from this could be released. Second, at 16 minutes each day and with 500 or so water engineers, some 3.8 person/weeks every single day were being spent in meeting their managers and chatting to each for no apparent added value.

So a decision was made to sell the building and give all the engineers laptops onto which they could download their job cards electronically over the IT network. A seemingly classic re-engineering of a process based on information sharing. The building was sold, the laptops were issued, the engineers were trained to use them. Productivity promptly fell very sharply.

Initially, it was felt that this fall was due to settling in problems for the new process. Sure enough, after a few weeks, productivity started to creep back up but the improvement levelled off. It was never quite as good as it had been previously. However hope remained that overall the exercise would pay off.

Purely by chance, one of the company's executives happened to stop in a local café where he came across what seemed to be an XYZ Water notebook. The book turned out to be a notepad where the water engineers were writing messages to each other. The messages might concern arrangements for meetings or might be about problems the engineers were encountering in their work. In a way, it was like a bulletin board or a wallpaper exercise. One person would post a problem and others might add information about how to solve it. Or they might suggest people (other engineers) who had met similar problems or were knowledgeable about particular bits of equipment.

It seemed that the partial recovery in productivity after the re-engineering exercise was due not so much as to the bedding down of the new system but the discovery of this café and the starting of the book. The engineers had declared, 'Well, our office is gone, long live the new office'. That was how the business was working. In the process re-engineering environment, the value of knowledge had been overlooked, as had the value of the community of engineers as a team. By swapping stories, the engineers were exchanging knowledge, providing a directory service (to expert advice) and building a knowledge base.

Let's go back to the three basic questions an organization needs to ask its members – what do you know, what do you need to know and what is the best way of getting it? Invariably we find that an organization works on its human dynamic. A clue to the reality of this dynamic can be found in just about any e-mail system. How many times do you get within the replies to your e-mailed requests for information a message that contains a couple of attachments, a pointer to a Web site or to someone's name? This is the informal knowledge network in action, an electronic version of the XYZ Water notebook.

AstraZeneca

If there was ever a time when knowledge management would help it is now. As we're building and reforming our business processes, we need to be building in the ideas about sharing knowledge across the business. Knowledge management thinking comes into its own in situations like these because we're a company that has lengthy, complicated business processes and the hand-overs required for these are important.

It may be that no one is actually answering the original question that was posted. The message might read, 'Go and talk to Sarah, she knows something about this and there is a good Web site at this URL...'. What the respondents are actually doing is providing pointers that allow you to construct an answer for yourself, as you want it. In other words, they are allowing you to contextualize the information and turn it into knowledge and they are decomposing those pointers from their own knowledge, their background, their experience and from their wisdom. That was where BPR hit a brick wall. You can re-engineer processes for increased efficiency to a point where important sources of knowledge are squeezed out and their value to customers is actually decreased.

Siemens

I am ultimately responsible for its quality [the quality of knowledge], so if I feel it is poor then I must improve it! I only want people to find information when they specifically need and to find it fast. I want it already to be in context and for the systems to be intelligent enough to give only that information which is relevant to their type of project. Finally, I want it to help you to ultimately make good decisions. The major thing is to structure the information along the lines of a project. So, we asked people about the kinds of information they needed at different stages of their work or processes and structured the systems accordingly, using a wide range of domains.

Providing knowledge in a form that requires contextualization may seem irritating to some people. After all, when presented with a problem managers are usually in a hurry to get it fixed. However, the thinking behind it operates on the same principle as charitable aid. Give a man a fish and you feed him for one meal, teach a man to fish and you feed him for life. If you are given the tools to go away and you make your own conclusion, you end up learning a lot more than you would have if you had just been given the right answer. Most people are more than happy to participate in this process once they get past the initial irritation and recognize the underlying principle. The process actually gives lifelong learning by building a sustained lifetime learning model.

The process can be seen in another way in face-to-face meetings. Given a problem, people put a lot of energy into discovering if anyone knows how to solve it. Two minutes later, after a solution is offered, the problem owner might say 'Oh hang on, I didn't mean it quite like that, it's more like this'. People articulate things yet shape them relative to the context of the job they are doing, to their own background and experience. It is that shaping we are looking for when other people's wisdom and knowledge is put on the table. It is not me you want when you have a problem, it's my network. Reach through me to my network and you have access to my research ('problem solving') space. This provides a far more enriched and more developed learning environment. It is the difference between a short-term fix and a long-term solution. The holistic picture of the network progressively spreads out to colleagues and to peers in a kind of ripple effect. I may not know the answer to your question but given advice on where to look (where I would have looked) and how to contact other people who may help, I suddenly get a far quicker route to learning and improved understanding. This is simply because there are more people doing more research, coming at every problem from several different angles.

A telecomms company

My particular boss would frown upon it totally. I mean, he's the sort of guy that says his door's always open but he sits in an office with his secretary in front of him and her door shut. You'll ring his phone and it's diverted. You'll send him e-mail and if you ask a simple question like 'Could I see you this afternoon?', you get a two-page reply as to why his diary's so full and he's not available, without even asking what was the question. However, you then get sudden explosions about 'Why didn't you tell me about this?' 'Because you told me, if you remember, to get on with it, not to bother you because you were too busy, so I did'. People find that sort of attitude very, very difficult.

The importance of contextualizing answers can be illustrated by an example in the washing powder market. Some seven or eight years ago, researchers at a major pharmaceutical company developed the washing powder tablet. The chemists who developed the idea did not think much of it since they hardly regarded it as a technical challenge. They knew how to make washing soaps into nice granular format, they had been doing it for years and understood the chemistry through and through. Combining these products into a tablet was not new chemistry, just a reformation of stuff that already existed. Done it. Tick that box. Ideally, the chemists should have talked to the marketing people rather than prejudge whether the customers (lay people) would have the same conception of the product as they did.

Shortly afterwards the chemists in Unilever (a major rival) came up with the same idea. However, Unilever was able to connect the research chemists and their tablet with the marketing people who actually made the mind jump needed. They recognized the market potential of a good idea and stole a thumping great share of the market. The first pharmaceutical company is still trying to recover market share. This example underlines the well-known point that only one company can be first to market with a good idea. The trick is at least to make sure you have the option of being first if you want to. An exchange of knowledge between chemists, marketing people, customers and

63

others might have given company Λ a better view of the big picture and the potential that lay in their hands.

RECOGNIZING DIFFERENT TYPES OF KNOWLEDGE

Examples abound of senior managers who had access to knowledge but for one reason or another failed to act upon it. For armchair historians there is a constant delight in reading about generals who were provided with intelligence about the enemy's disposition yet failed decisively to act. Let us examine why this might happen by considering the four Rs:

R1. Recognize that there are different types of knowledge

Most texts on knowledge management will provide a handsome range of categories for cataloguing types of knowledge. The most well known distinction is that between tacit and explicit knowledge. But other forms of categorization are possible, for example:

- static knowledge;
- dynamic knowledge;
- declarative knowledge (knowledge of facts);
- procedural knowledge (knowledge of how to do things);
- knowledge that is abstract (in that it may apply to many situations);
- knowledge that is specific (in that it applies only to one situation).

All of these are very interesting and have their place and use. However, in each case it is probably the emotional overtones of the knowledge that are most important. This refers to things like attributes and values or derived concepts like rules. Knowledge from an important or trusted source such as a successful colleague or the boss maybe treated differently than knowledge from other sources. This is probably why the general fails to act. Either they don't trust the source or the knowledge that they are provided with does not fit with what they want to do.

R2. Recognize that there are different types of experts

Researchers in the field of artificial intelligence have been discovering this for some time. Experts may know things without knowing and may indeed find it difficult to communicate their expertise to others. People in the training or teaching business are usually better at making their knowledge explicit and sharing it with others. On the other hand, some experts find it very difficult to articulate exactly how they achieve results. This is why an Olympic athlete may not always make a good coach and why all good coaches are not Olympic gold medal holders. What the coach aims to do, dispassionately and without bias, is to take the essence of a process or a procedure and share it with others. Experts may skip over parts of the procedure that they consider unimportant, or may exaggerate those aspects that are particularly unique to themselves. In other words, there is a risk that they might attach emotional overtones that would confuse or obscure what is really important.

R3. Recognize that there are different ways of representing knowledge

Traditionally, knowledge in organizations is recorded in very formal ways such as in reports, manuals, computer databases and so on. When trying to communicate a difficult idea to someone, especially if they are not an expert in the field, an analogy, an anecdote or a diagram can make a critical difference both to understanding and to remembering. Knowledge managers make a great use of pictures, anecdotes and 'war stories'.

R4. Recognize different ways of using knowledge

Early management writers were concerned about the one best way to run an organization. It took a long time to realize that different people or different forms of organizations could achieve similar results by a variety of routes. For example, it is sometimes held that formalized, bureaucratic procedures are unresponsive and slow to change whereas highly organic organizations are nimble on their feet and flexible. In practice neither of these stereotypes is true in the absolute and a mixture of the two approaches is desirable. In the same way people, groups and communities will use an identical knowledge source in different ways. They may achieve similar or better results importing or personalizing the knowledge in this way. This means that the knowledge available within the enterprise must be accessible from a variety of directions and should seek to suggest a range of goals or uses to which it may be put. All knowledge is based on a set of assumptions and judgements and this some-times gets forgotten. In the soap powder example above, managers in one company failed to question the assumptions and judgements behind a particular piece of knowledge. As a result they lost a major market opportunity.

What is needed to achieve knowledge management take-off? It takes the same kind of things that is needed to get a space station into orbit, some tech-nology, a lot of expertise, a dedicated team and above all a shared enthusiasm and commitment. We can look at these four stages suggested by Quinn, Anderson and Thinklestein (1996).

KNOWLEDGE TAKE-OFF

1. **Know what.** Formal knowledge management procedures can help a great deal with this stage by capturing, cataloguing and making accessible the knowledge required to achieve certain corporate goals. At this point we have the music, the instruments and the musicians but we do not yet have an orchestra.
2. **Know how.** The second stage represents the ability to retrieve and use the knowledge at the right place and time. So, given the right kind of conductor, our orchestra can now play a symphony.
3. **Know why.** This is a long way from stage 2 and it involves changing the culture, beliefs and attitudes of members of the enterprise. In moving people along this route we must not only develop their problem-solving skills but also give them a deep knowledge of the complex cause and effect relationships that underpin their area of responsibility. This knowledge enables individuals to create leverage by using knowledge and by bringing with them the ability to deal with unknown interactions and unseen situations. Our orchestra members now know when they must play fast or slow, loud or soft to support and enhance other members of the orchestra, perhaps even to cover up for their mistakes. Organizations generally find this very difficult. The point is best illustrated by the privatization of the public sector activities that was fashionable in the 1980s and 1990s. Quite often, public sector corporations that required huge amounts of public subsidy suddenly became profitable when moved into the private sector. One reason behind this was that a huge amount of knowledge available to existing members of the organization, inhibited or constrained by the previous organizational form (usually political interference), could suddenly be used.
4. **Care why.** Of course the other reason that privatized industries were successful is that they enabled self-motivated creativity to be channelled into results. This level of knowledge management activity is the most difficult and problematic to sustain by any kind of formal procedures or structures. Going back to our military analogy, a general might call this morale or *esprit de corps*. Through recorded history it has been demonstrated repeatedly that highly motivated groups can often overcome significant material or resource disadvantages to achieve outstanding results. In commercial organizations we talk about corporate culture. It is probably a function of visionary leadership and the right kind of empowerment.

Hewlett-Packard

On the other side you have got the whole tacit bit and HP itself is actually built on layers and layers of tacit knowledge. And it's all built on layers and layers of personal relationships, which is really very important. Some of these fundamental cultural traits that I mentioned, about how we respect people, how we allow people to communicate, are encouraged and fostered. So these personal network relationships is where the real knowledge base is actually sitting.

THE INTERNET AND INTRANETS

Andersen

Technology is also important. I mean, if you're a global organization and you're going to share codified knowledge like we do in Andersen Consulting, you need a good technical infrastructure – maybe now you can use the Internet. Certainly, when we started doing it seriously six or seven years ago we couldn't use the Internet. So we built our own global technology infrastructure which is extremely stable, extremely well maintained and pretty expensive... I know from talking to clients and also talking to people in other management companies that we are better equipped on this side than most other companies are. I mean, we have reliable, global technology infrastructure just in terms of pipes and wires and networks. Also we have a common application platform, which is rolled out to the whole organization, so that everybody is using the same tools.

One very common tool used to store information is the database. Databases are full of information that has been distilled from the knowledge of members of the organization. The trouble is, the way in which they are structured and what they contain is usually determined by the 'cats' end of the enterprise on the assumption that the 'clocks' will use it. Problems of context and relevance quickly arise. The notebook used by the water engineers was a much more relevant 'knowledge base' than most formal databases. It was created by experts, assessed by peers and built up willingly. Making entries in the notebook exposed your expertise (or lack of it) to judgment by your peers. Other members of the group read it because they were interested in the knowledge it contained.

BG

Perhaps if I talk about how we manage our intranet. Again, we have a steering group, we have a management group and we have individual business units all championing their own parts of the intranet. We hold the thing together through common navigation. As an example, we call our intranet KITE because when you talk to people about putting things on the intranet, if you say that word quickly it could go to a 150 million people [on the Internet] as opposed to 16,500 employees! ... KITE stands for Knowledge and Information To Everyone... A KITE is also the British Safety symbol. Safety is paramount in our gas business. It's also environmentally friendly in terms of kite-flying and countryside and things like that. And there's also a pun in terms of if you want to tell somebody what to do, you tell them to go and fly a kite! So we can have a laugh as well. It works quite well. KITE is fundamental for our business. Within KITE and within our sort of structure, we exchange best practice. We make sure that if we're developing any applications it's done once and once only and that knowledge is then shared. There are several key applications on the Intranet, which really add value.

Basically, there is no easy way of linking the interest and content of a knowledge base with improved knowledge, learning, competitive position and business performance. Certainly content does not equate to access. Throughout Europe, the big supermarket chains are the largest resellers of confectionery. They sell more bars of chocolate than anyone else. Yet it is quite hard to find someone who will admit that they went into a supermarket with the sole purpose of buying a chocolate bar. In any case, such small purchases are more easily made from smaller shops or filling stations. People go into supermarkets for 'serious' shopping, attracted by the convenience, the prices, the product range and so on. The secret factor, the hidden, additional margin for the store is based on something you pick up on the way out.

AstraZeneca

Over the past year and a half I've been specializing in, focusing my attention on, building knowledge management through a company-wide intranet. When the merger came along, I saw that as an opportunity to actually use the energy that was needed to communicate with the business and focus using knowledge management principles to build that system. I don't just mean technology but the whole thing around it and deliver that for the business, to people. To keep them informed of the progress of the merger and so on. It's been very successful and now we've got a huge intranet following.

What is needed for intranets across all types of organization is to focus on the attraction factor. Just because someone has put the human resource management manual on the intranet, why should anyone read it? Just because it is now conveniently available in an electronic format compared to previously when it was there in hard copy? Perhaps no one ever touched it because there was no context to the information it contained. There was no attraction factor, nothing that an individual could get to that had any relevance to his or her job. Making it electronic will not change that. For an intranet, as with the Internet, what is needed is to make sure that you have an attraction factor to get people to come to the door. Otherwise, you have opened the store but no one will come along. What gets people through the door is access to the sort of knowledge that makes it easier and better for them to do their jobs. Once you have got them through the door, content designers then need to think about what they want users to access and where the value proposition lies. This in turn leads to decisions about where they might find this knowledge because intranets, like the Internet, need to offer portals, jumping off places to other sources of knowledge. This is the power of connectivity. Connectivity is like the chocolate bar in the supermarket. It may not represent the primary reason for using the intranet but it is an extra attraction whilst people are there. Whether the knowledge is shared by mentoring or by codification into a database, it is not the technology or even the mentor that people turn to, it is the access they can get through connectivity to a network. Suddenly the sheer power of connectivity becomes apparent. Whilst this is still about people and ideas, it produces shifts, sometimes parallel shifts, in productivity that process re-engineering found hard to deliver.

BP Amoco

Because there are just too many isolated databases and many of them are either too specific or too general, we developed a framework for trying to manage them in a more effective way. It really consists of an intranet site which will have the detail of the lessons learnt; it will have the verbatim quotes of people talking passionately about the benefits; it will have a dynamic link to people who have the knowledge today via the Connect directory and at the highest level and it will link to what you might call the distillation of the key learning points. So you'll have all the experience, the war stories, the post-project appraisals, the tools in there and you'll have the top 10 points that we've learnt as an organization about that particular theme. We've probably got about 20 or 30 of these little oases on the intranet at the moment which are knowledge-rich and quite powerful tools.

SUPPORTING TI IE KNOWLEDGE MANAGEMENT PROCESS

Siemens

With our global knowledge sharing network, Sharenet, we have chosen to focus on one of our key business processes, ie sales value creation, which is very close to our customers, rather than say our logistics or our research and development. But it is also about our competitors, our products and finding solutions. So you can see that, in a way, it cuts across all areas.

What is important about the technology that supports the knowledge management process is not what it can do but the way it is used. Both social and material technologies are relevant here. The easiest way to demonstrate this is to look at your own e-mail inbox. How many of the e-mails that you receive in a day or a week are concerned with customer value? How many are simply seeking information? How many are merely political in character, copying you onto a circulation list for the sake of form? How many are from the people who work in nearby offices, who could have much more easily come and spoken to you? The technologies to support knowledge management processes, therefore, should probably have the following characteristics:

- They should be well accepted by the community that has to use them.
- They should allow and support rich communication in a simple efficient way.
- They should have a way of conveying emotional overtones, such as opinions and biases.
- They should support informal communications and multiple ways of expressing ideas and thoughts.
- Above all, they should not be imposed, they should feel 'natural'. To give this a label, the technology should seem 'transparent'.

Barclays Bank

Our system allows you to hyperlink into all the documents on our network, into relevant intranet sites, Internet sites and e-mail addresses. I think the key to knowledge management is having a system that can point you to the right place and you can do a keyword search or find out where you need to go.

By the same token, the technology should cut across organizational boundaries and reflect shortcuts to results. A good example here might be a chart used by one company to record the status and progress of sales. Procedures required that this chart be marked up in different ways with different coloured pens. Internally it was known as a 'Picasso' because after a few days of use it looked very much like an abstract painting. After a few days of use, it also required some expertise in order to interpret its meaning. Members of the department used to resolve the problems of interpreting an advanced Picasso by simply picking up the telephone to get the information they needed from the person most likely to know.

Telecommunications company

I don't rely on it; I rely on my brain more than a computer. Give me a piece of paper any day. I was putting everything into an electronic organizer until I left it in a hotel in Geneva, dashing for a plane. I know where it is, it's in the drawer. I sent a fax on arrival in the UK to [the] hotel and they just didn't reply and I know it was there. So, every telephone number that I gathered over the last five years is sitting in that stupid organizer. I do have all the business cards I've ever collected somewhere in a drawer but there's hundreds of them.

SUMMARY

From a process perspective seven major themes can be identified:

- Generating new knowledge. Creating new knowledge provides process competence and a hard-to-copy competitive advantage.
- Actually using knowledge for decision-making.
- Embedding knowledge in products, services and processes. This should result in higher quality outcomes at lower costs than those of the competition but above all it must deliver value to the customer which is not available elsewhere.
- Facilitating knowledge growth – which we shall come back to later in the book.
- Transferring existing knowledge. This means recognizing the different types of knowledge that are needed and the kinds of people who might be good at capturing and sharing them.
- Integrating competitive intelligence.
- Aligning knowledge management processes with key business drivers.

It is apparent that the knowledge-enabled organization will have certain key characteristics. It will focus on customer satisfaction and on the capabilities and enablers that are required to produce that value. These will be translated into a focus on processes, collaborative and cross-functional work, localized decision making and a recognition of the need to share.

Andersen

So, if you want to innovate, if you want to be successful, you had better figure out how to make your knowledge-sharing activities a level playing field. It's the quality of ideas that count not the position of the author.

Most fundamentally, the organization will recognize the importance of a shared sense of values so that there is a close alignment between knowledge management and the achievement of the vision and values that the organization is setting out to achieve. In turn this will require high levels of trust and team-based collaborative work. There may well be a shared sense of responsibility and joint team-wide accountability. The rewards for sharing and for encouraging these processes need to be thought about very carefully. It is easily apparent that the level of trust and sharing that is required cannot simply be bought. Somehow or other, members of the organization must value these activities at a personal level.

5

Communities of practice and knowledge conversion

MODES OF KNOWLEDGE CONVERSION

Cable & Wireless

The development needs of the individual are identified by the individual and by the individual's manager and they negotiate on how those shortfalls in knowledge can be addressed. So it could be by training, it could be by shadowing, it could be by a change of role, it could be that an individual just cannot cope with pressure but they are still a good employee. Therefore it may be more applicable to transfer them to another position rather than let them struggle on and never achieve what they're trying to do. So everybody's treated as an individual, everybody is on effectively performance related pay. Some are on much higher grades of performance related pay than others but the performance of everybody is recognized at the end of the day.

Nokia

I would say that there are tremendous possibilities in Nokia, so we can provide a unique career opportunity. Anyone who has the ability to take more responsibility and develop their competencies is being given the opportunity to do this. I would say that this is even more important than the financial compensation. You can get responsibility exactly as much as you are willing and able to take, by upgrading your own competencies.

While some kinds of knowledge can be codified or recorded formally, very often using the knowledge in peoples' heads will prove the sole method of solving the most intractable and difficult problems. So, whilst the technology acts as an important enabler for storing knowledge and for facilitating communication, the culture and values which support knowledge management tend to be much more important. Unfortunately, developing this culture and sustaining those values is much more difficult than the task of developing the underlying knowledge-based technology. Sveiby (1997) categorized four modes of knowledge conversion.

Embodied to embodied knowledge

This is a process of sharing experiences, mental models and skills which requires socialization. The best example of a transfer of the embodied knowledge from one person to another is hundreds of years old. An apprentice working with a master learnt craftsmanship through observation, imitation and practice. Language alone is not sufficient to teach someone to become a master craftsman. Craftsmanship remains a part of many expert activities.

Embodied to represented knowledge

This is the process of articulating embodied knowledge in represented concepts through spoken words. The embodied knowledge can take the form of metaphors, models, concepts or equations which express, in a reduced or perhaps distorted form, the embodied knowledge of an individual. Cookery books are a good example of externalization in this way. A master chef may write down everything you need to know to create a particular dish but the act of writing will lose certain aspects of flair and creativity. Even pictures will have difficulty in capturing certain aspects of the knowledge required to create a dish, such as when the exact texture of a sauce is just right. The good news here is probably that there is a market for cookery books and TV cooking programmes for the foreseeable future as experts attempt to share an expertise that cannot really be shared through these media.

Represented to represented knowledge

Represented to represented knowledge produces combination. Different bodies of knowledge are combined through analysis, categorization and reconfiguration. This form of knowledge conversion takes place in universities and other formal educational establishments. The recent rapid growth of corporate universities is a recognition of the potential power of this form of knowledge conversion. The combination of many knowledge sources into a new format can yield new insights.

Represented to embodied knowledge

This represents the highest form of knowledge conversion since it results in internalization. One person is accepting another's represented knowledge as if it were his or her own. The person is trusting and using the knowledge. If it produces the desired results the person is in effect learning by doing. At the same time by adding his or her own experiences the person will enrich the knowledge. Learning by doing or simulations are good ways of encouraging internalization.

NEW WAYS OF DOING BUSINESS

Siemens

Our teams are working all over the world to restructure the business through knowledge management and where we need specific systems in place, to make that work, then we partner with IT people. However, because of the speed at which we need to react, if our own IT people aren't able to find a fast enough solution then we'll look outside for help. We rely of course on a global Intranet across the organization to ensure exchange of relevant information. However, we also work closely with HR, as something like an incentivized scheme for knowledge management can only work if we align it with existing HR practice such as core competencies, training and learning.

It is evident that successful knowledge management requires a fundamental change in the way most companies do business. At the heart of that change must be people. Knowledge only has value when it is given expression through use. Davis (1998) has identified four important groups.

Clearly the most important of these are **knowledge users.** If the knowledge is not used, then all the efforts by managers are worth nothing. Users are members of the enterprise who are involved in the day-to-day core business processes. In the end knowledge management is about enabling members of the enterprise to make a more effective contribution. The difficulty here is the lag effect in setting up the processes. To capture and share best practice takes time. Typically it does not contribute immediately to the successful achievement of outcomes nor to competitive success. What is more, it may not contribute most to the person who contributed the knowledge and this presents something of a challenge when encouraging knowledge capturing behaviours.

Addressing this challenge is the responsibility of the **knowledge managers**. For knowledge users to take advantage of available knowledge they must be trained to use the automated tools that are available to find and access knowledge. Users can also be trained to work with knowledge managers who will help them recognize where they might hold valuable expertise and how that can be contributed to the knowledge base. For this to be successful everyone must be using a common language. It is important that everyone is talking about the same thing when they use a particular word. This is known as a controlled vocabulary. Users have to learn this controlled vocabulary so that they can use it intuitively. Since the vocabulary will also evolve and change it must also provide feedback on the use of words and their meaning. Knowledge managers also have responsibility for the management of every day, line activities. The knowledge manager is also a knowledge user so he or she must identify areas in his or her field of activity that are candidates for additions to the knowledge base. Knowledge managers help to develop the controlled vocabulary and produce descriptors for each term. They decide the initial valuations of new knowledge components and help implement measures by which the performance of the knowledge base is assessed.

The **competency knowledge manager** focuses on the skills or capabilities in which the enterprise must excel to succeed. These critical success factors are not always self-evident. It is fairly evident that a boat builder must manage a range of competencies to do with the design and building of boats. However, regardless of how much expertise may reside in the organization in relation to steel work, power systems, hull design, fitting out and so on, all of these are wasted if the right kind of customer relationships are not established. A boat is a complex machine and very personal in character. Few customers are experts in the design and building of boats and so depend heavily on the boat builder. Acquiring and sustaining the trust of the customer is therefore crucial to the company's success, since word of mouth referral is very important in the industry. Although the example is a little unique the same issues apply in many businesses. The competency knowledge manager must therefore determine which knowledge components are currently relevant and which are required to support the scope of the business. He or she must work closely with an overall executive sponsor for each broad yet clearly defined competency scope. Competency knowledge managers then set security and ownership specifications for content and provide guidance on the accessibility of content as a function of the value of intellectual property. They also help determine the initial valuation of new knowledge components. Whilst competency knowledge managers are also users and knowledge managers they perform an important role in the analysis or synthesis of sub-sets of knowledge and approve modifications to the knowledge base within their area of responsibility.

Finally, there are **chief knowledge officers** (CKOs) who are responsible for the overall knowledge assets of the enterprise. The CKO has the ultimate, enterprise-wide responsibility for the controlled vocabulary and the knowledge directory and tackles the difficult issues associated with cross-enterprise processes. The easiest part of a CKO's job is to manage the technology infrastructure that facilitates effective knowledge management. This may well be largely a coordination role but sometimes the CKO is also the chief information officer. More importantly, however, the CKO is the facilitator of the knowledge-based enterprise. It is no accident that this role has been described last. The sort of organization structure required for effective knowledge management takes the form of an inverted pyramid. More senior mangers have responsibility for ensuring that each successive 'lower' level is knowledge-enabled so that people at the front line of the enterprise, those with the highest level of customer contact, are most easily empowered to leverage and exploit corporate knowledge assets.

Buckman Labs

We had a chap, D, who was manager in Singapore and he was developing and growing the company in Singapore. A very small company was opened in Indonesia and D needed to get that business. So he put a note on the forum saying he needed the best felt-cleaners that we have worldwide, where could he find them? He had seven responses from five countries within 24 hours. He got the business, not because the customer knew that he was relying on D's expertise but because he could rely on the sum total of expertise within Buckman. So, the resources of our company are not restricted to where you work, you bring them to bear where they're needed.

The issues around trust and commitment in both the traditional and the virtual enterprise are massive. Everyone needs a set of core values with which they can identify and these core values are things like trust, a common language and common objectives. Nowhere are these issues more central than in the area of communities of practice. Communities of practice are people based. The communities form, grow, change and they have been around in one form or another for a long time. The best-known communities of practice were the ancient guilds. In knowledge management parlance, guilds are not true communities of practice since they only involved one type of community, a single craft, or trade. Nevertheless, the example is useful because it illustrates what a community of practice does, it passes on wisdom or knowledge – in the case of guilds, from master to apprentice over hundreds of years.

Groupings of people with similar interests are very common of course. They may not be labelled formally as communities or even think of themselves that way but that is what they are. A group of residents may meet in the local pub to talk about community issues such as zoning regulations or environmental issues. A group of people with a common interest in snow skiing might exchange information and advice about routes, pistes and weather conditions. A spin-off from either of these might be business contacts and advice. Based on knowledge exchanged about Geneva as an entry port to Switzerland for skiing, travel advice and business contacts might be exchanged. This illustrates three types of informal communities but the same sort of networks exist in enterprises. Whilst they may be focused more round the water cooler or coffee lounge, people with common interests are going to come together to exchange useful knowledge. Understanding what those networks are and how they link to each other is a useful pointer to how knowledge might be generated and exchanged. The problem is therefore how to identify, develop and sustain these communities in a dynamic business world. One of the major shortcomings of TQM and the QC philosophy was its narrow focus on problem solving. A community of practice must be able to range across a number of corporate issues.

THE SOUND OF ONE HAND CLAPPING

In addition to being concerned with a range of business issues, a community of practice must sustain the interest of its own members. Thus as a manager you have the paradox of identifying and facilitating something that is very informal, that exists outside the formal organization structure. You cannot force people to join or participate in a community. Imagine holding a party, making person A responsible for the liquor and person B responsible for the mixers. A and B do not know each other, neither of them really know you and they do not actually care about the party. Clearly, you have made it very difficult to get the gin and tonics together. Apart from this, the point of the party is to have fun and this is unlikely unless the people invited can find some areas of common interest, at the very least as a social group or perhaps as people with a professional background.

Barclays Bank

Nine years ago we decided to have knowledge management meetings once a quarter but also our main aim was always to avoid duplication, promote best practice and then obviously to act as a forum where people of either specialization could get together and share ideas. Now, we still have those meetings but we use a presentation theatre and there's a least 100 people coming each time, under the umbrella of knowledge management. Additionally, I formed a committee two years ago, which meets on a monthly basis. The people who sit on that committee are the people that are the real doers, the influencers, the people who can make decisions within the organization. We send the minutes of all the meetings to the heads of the four business divisions and other senior executives that are obviously interested. The knowledge management working party has undoubtedly built on a lot of the strengths. Similarly, the work that we've done with the seminars involves a strong, dynamic group of people, who are very much committed to making sure that we can give the business exactly what it wants and give the business the flexibility to make things better, whichever area we're working in.

In professional terms, the community of practice must add value to what you do on a daily basis or give you something that you can take away to your workplace. Membership should make life a bit better otherwise you are not going to stay in the community. One of the early failings in the area of communities of practice was a determination by managers to turn the cat into a clock by seeking to shape and define the way networks and communities work. However, the community has to find its own level of intensity and interaction. It will not always be sustained in the same shape or form. Managers need to recognize that communities will follow a sort of life cycle. They will be born and will develop. Some will grow, others will die. A kind of rolling wave of formation and reformation can be observed. The enterprise has to offer a rich, fertile environment where the different communities that are formed within them can come together without being prescriptive. There is a common misunderstanding that you can help communities by identifying some of the roles that people might play within them but this is like instructing people how they will enjoy themselves at the party. To take an example from e-learning, lurkers (people who monitor an electronic seminar without actually contributing) may benefit greatly from observation. They may simply be at the pre-participation stage. Forcing them to be active or to undertake a certain role tends to drive them away. As in a community of practice, what you have to do is use a combination of push and pull techniques to try to lure such people to participate fully.

Procter & Gamble

It seems that in those cases, the people who are working in the teams are being won over by the enthusiasm of their team leader. In fact in one team, there is somebody at the coalface who has made it happen in that team through [his] pure belief that it's the right thing to do. I think he just sees it as the right thing to do and he's just embarrassed his colleagues into doing it, which is really powerful. What we haven't done yet, is go into a team that says we don't want to do it and completely turn them around. If the team leader isn't 100 per cent sold on it, then it's really difficult.

DEFINING COMMUNITIES OF PRACTICE

Communities of practice are defined as collections of individuals bound by informal relationships who share a similar work role in a common context. They are groups that:

- come together voluntarily for a shared purpose;
- have members that identify themselves as part of the community;
- repeatedly engage in activities with other members and communities;
- have interactions that last for an indeterminate period of time.

The term community highlights the personal basis upon which the relationships are formed. The boundaries of the community are fixed by common tasks, context and work interests rather than any organizational or geographic form. The word practice implies knowledge in action. It refers to the actual dynamic process by which individuals learn to do their jobs through task performance and interaction with others. We are therefore concerned with the day-to-day realities of work rather than formal policies and procedures. Communities of practice are characterized by a membership that is often fluid and self-organizing in nature. Nahapiet and Ghoshal (1998: 242) have written about this in terms of the social capital of the organization which they described as the 'sum of the actual and potential resources embedded within, available through and derived from the network of relationships possessed by an individual or a social unit'. They identify social capital as having three inter-related dimensions.

The **structural** dimension refers to the formation of informal networks that enable individuals to identify others with potential resources. These include relationships with both 'strong' ties (perhaps individuals who make regular contact with each other) and those with 'weak' ties (rather looser personal links). Basically, this portrays the need for people in organizations to reach out to others who may have resources which they themselves do not have at their disposal.

The **relational** dimension addresses issues around trust, shared norms and values, obligations and expectations. It describes the interpersonal dynamic. The best example of a unit with high social capital is a family. The social capital transmitted within a family is transferred through cultural mechanisms and is based on strong beliefs that the actions of one member will be reciprocated, that individuals will meet their expected obligations and that people will deal with each other honestly.

The **cognitive** dimension addresses the need for a common context and language to build social capital. We have touched on this earlier. Without a common vocabulary it is difficult to construct the necessary connections to create and foster social capital. Building this common context can be done either by explicit mechanisms such as manuals, databases, manuals and formal procedures or by tacit mechanisms such as stories, analogies and metaphors.

These three dimensions of social capital (structure, relationships and cognitions) influence the four variables that affect the creation and sharing of what has been called organizational knowledge. These four dimensions include, access (to people), the anticipation of value, the motivation of individuals to share and the ability of the organization to change in response to changes in its internal environment. To take our recent example further, if you have just robbed a bank, you might well use another family member to help you hide the loot and take their advice on how to launder the funds. All the benefits of social capital are illustrated by this example although, somewhat unfortunately, contrary to the benefit of society as a whole. Moving back into the corporate domain, the social capital of companies like Nokia and Microsoft can be valued partly through the differences between their capital valuation and their market valuation. In both cases, powerful communities are constantly networking with each other to share ideas for products and services, solve problems and change the shape of the company.

One of the tools that has been developed by IBM to study the effects of communities of practice is organizational network analysis. This provides a formal analytical method that can be applied to a department or a division of a company and analyses the effects of 'natural' communities of practice. It is based on asking a small number of simple questions to between 50 and 100 people in relation to an issue or topic that has relevance to them. The first step is to enquire about the sort of conversations people have with each other within or outside the work place (in connection with their jobs). For example, a common theme may emerge in a design area. Three or four simple questions then allow the analyst to determine the structure of the community. These could be questions like: 'Who do you go to for expert advice on design? Who do you talk to normally? Who do you telephone on a Friday night when you have got a big design problem?'

NatWest

The third element [of our strategy] was the community approach and was quite revolutionary for 1997. It's something I've continued to this day actually in terms of community building. We asked each area to nominate a knowledge coordinator, ie somebody who knows what was happening and could pull it all together. So if you couldn't find an expert in the expertise directory, you'd phone the knowledge coordinator and they'd be able to put you in touch with the right person. Then we decided to form a community of knowledge coordinators, with about 100 people taking part. We asked Larry Prusak to talk to them and make them feel important. These were not senior people as such but were people, who had been around, knew everyone and could put their fingers on the right information. That is one hell of a skill as you've got to move fast. You need to know the answer quickly if you've got a corporate client on the other end of the line. The thing that really emerged was that, by getting these people altogether in a room as a community, you form a network of networkers. These people were the best networkers in their product areas. I've gone on to build quite vibrant communities across the board and have now got 250 people in an operations community and nearly 100 in a wider knowledge management community.

When simple questions are asked to determine the structure of a community, the answers allow communication paths to be identified. The sort of 'spider's web' of connections (or sociogram) shown in Figure 5.1 was first developed in the area of sociometrics. Sociograms are often quite fascinating from a management point of view as they help identify the key knowledge flows – they show who talks to whom, who they need to talk to and how often they talk to someone. They also show which conversations are uni-directional and which bi-directional. A sociogram might identify people who just do not get spoken to. This could be an important finding if that person happens to be someone who is an expert on design. If no one talks to them, much expertise and knowledge is lost to the company. This is what Lew Platt, former CEO of Hewlett-Packard meant when he used the now well-known phrase 'if only we knew what we know'. If no one talks to the expert holders of knowledge, you are never going to tap into your most valuable sources of knowledge.

The key benefits of ONA include:

- More efficient transfer of knowledge

- Lower internal transaction costs

- Greater collaboration and cooperation

- Greater ability to respond and adapt

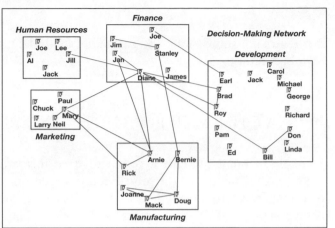

Figure 5.1 *Organizational Network Analysis (ONA) used to disclose knowledge flows*

Within many communities, someone will undertake to be what sociologists call the gatekeeper role in the group. This person acts as a kind of facilitator cum post person cum *Yellow Pages* cum social secretary; he or she receives a huge amount of e-mail and probably has a host of stickers reminding him or herself to phone X or e-mail Y. Most organizations have someone who is an extraordinary communicator, the naturally recognized broker of knowledge to whom people refer first on a wide variety of topics, even those outside the person's primary area of expertise. This person is in effect a classic knowledge broker but can equally well become a knowledge blocker if he or she withdraws support. Another important role is of course that of subject matter expert. There are usually people that can be identified from the sociogram as natural communicators and natural subject matter experts.

With much enterprise knowledge residing in informal communities, the development of multiple communities of practice is crucial to ensure the scaling of common language and practices. Leveraging multiple communities has a demonstrable, positive impact on business results. It can:

- improve asset reuse, increase business responsiveness, foster employee retention and satisfaction;
- play a critical role in building informal networks, trust and common language to share and apply knowledge effectively;

- help build and leverage deep functional skills necessary for organizations to succeed.

Experiences of propagating and sustaining multiple communities of practice show high return.

A VOLUNTEER IS WORTH TEN PRESSED MEN

A couple of hundred years ago, navies used to recruit their sailors using press gangs. This usually involved being struck on the head with a blunt instrument to awaken many hours later, miles out to sea, facing the prospect of several years of life-threatening hard labour. That some of these pressed men were less than happy members of the ship's crew is hardly surprising. Of course, to survive, they had to cooperate as active members of the crew. You cannot sink just part of a ship. Nevertheless, in every navy, volunteers are regarded as more useful than conscripts because they participate in what is needed more fully.

Swiss Re

We like people to put themselves forward to be part of a team. We were involved in a project two years ago, in which Arthur Andersen supported us and I'd definitely say that there's a certain sort of similarity between their communities and ours. We have individuals with assigned responsibility to be knowledge managers. They were volunteers originally but they had to be volunteers with approval from their line managers because they mostly sit outside of our team in other global positions and are asked to commit three hours a week specifically to support the wider knowledge network. There's a total of ten communities so far. We do a lot of work around information management, projects around electronic libraries and of course, we're a very large Lotus Notes user as a group. We have a number of common technology standards, eg we're all Microsoft Office users. We have a very strong corporate identity which again sort of influences people into thinking globally. Also, we ran a seminar earlier this year to bring together the experts physically and build an opportunity to share knowledge, experience and to meet people. We found this was particularly useful in terms of giving a good foundation for the knowledge communities. Face-to-face contact is so important. If you get an e-mail from somebody you've never heard of, whilst you don't deliberately ignore [the sender], they don't register against the other 50 [people] that you do know.

So it is with communities of practice. Some members of the enterprise are simply there to do a job. Others are looking for fulfilment in their work. They talk to colleagues about work problems and how to solve them. They have a genuine interest in what they are doing. This interest is clearly not confined to the top levels of the organization. A community of practice simply tries to channel this interest for the good of the organization. In effect, the organization seeks, through communities, to channel a stream that is flowing to the sea anyway, through a mill wheel or a turbine so as to generate another benefit as a by-product.

Members of the group might be allowed an extra 30 minutes each week within their work space for thinking time. Consider the impact on efficient transfer of knowledge if the process was semi-formalized in this way. In addition to a little time, all that is needed is to recognize the community and broadcast its existence around other parts of the organization. So instead of someone having to search for subject experts in, say, design across a large organization, or instead of speculating whether anyone has ever thought about detergent tablets, that person will know who to talk to. He or she will connect to the community of practice, probably through its gatekeeper, who may not necessarily be the subject expert but will have contacts to experts and also to the gatekeeper of other relevant communities. This is the person that may not know the answer to your problem but knows someone who does! Whilst a manager may know someone in the formal organization, real or virtual, the gatekeeper's contact inspires higher trust. The manager might need to make three or four phone calls before finding someone who really has the interest, time and capability to bring some ideas to bear on the problem. If you can cut through three of those phone calls and get straight to the community of practice then not only are internal transaction costs reduced but the prospects for a relevant solution are increased.

BUILDING ON SOCIAL CAPITAL

Improving flexibility, agility, and the organization's ability to respond to problems is the central benefit from improvements in the performance of a community of practice. The value that the enterprise gets out of this improvement is huge in terms of developing the new human resource environment in today's business. What those communities will do, very quickly, is act as filters of ideas, prioritize problems and start to identify intellectual property (IP) that, in the case of our example, is relevant to design. Indeed, this is the best way of getting to the IP in any organization.

To capitalize on IP a community of practice should be formed of subject matter experts who have been inside the company for approximately a couple of years along with communicators who have been inside the company for a long time, maybe ten years or more, and who know the social network. Perhaps someone who has recently been employed from a competitor and is therefore still connected to external networks will help. This person will know what others in the outside world are doing. Internal experts will be connected to their own professional groups which may be also outside the enterprise. Employees or virtual participants in the enterprise may be talking to customers or to people whose functional area is apparently some way removed from design. In other words, with a mix of people and perspectives the connectivity of the community can be very extensive, maybe too extensive to be mapped or formalized. However, together the community provides an energy like the parts of an engine. In an engine, different companies assemble components, third parties supply fuel, and customers use them for different purposes. The dynamic of the whole provides motive power.

The elements of social capital are shown in Figure 5.2

Companies that support effective communities of practice tend to recognize these dimensions intuitively. As in any situation, a working model is enormously useful in helping to channel ideas and activity. This focuses managers'

Structural • The properties of informal networks	• How is the network configured? • How does the network provide access to resources? • How readily can it reconfigure itself for new purposes?
Relational • The interpersonal dynamics within informal networks	• Do people operate on the premise that others are well-intentioned and competent? • Is there a common understanding of expected behaviors and obligations? • To what extent do people identify with the network?
Cognitive • The context in which network events are understood	• To what extent is a common 'language' used by network members? • What are the shared stories/narratives that form the context?

Source: Nahapiet, J and Ghoshal, S (1998)

Figure 5.2 *Three primary dimensions of 'social capital' in communities.*

thinking on where they can most usefully facilitate the formation of these communities. The communities' organic, fluid nature is easily destroyed by formal interventions. The copier company and the water utility examples given earlier illustrate how an apparently sensible process change initiative can actually create a negative impact if it does not take the value of social capital into account. Using this framework, management might therefore consider:

- What are the opportunities to provide access to other resources in the network?
- What are the interpersonal dynamics, how does the network come together?
- Is there a common understanding and a common language in use?
- How does the community share knowledge (through stories or whatever)?
- What is the context for the community (what are the members interested in, why do they meet)?

It is then possible to enhance, develop and build. Once an organic community is working there are tools that can be used to accelerate its growth. This is an interesting phase. An ability to nurture the structure of the networks distinguishes those organizations in which communities do well and those in which they do poorly. A technique that can be used to judge the relational strengths of communities is known as dispositional surveys. An output from such a survey is shown in Figure 5.3.

The technique uses a simple questionnaire to try to establish what the values and norms are amongst the community and whether these are recognized. It seeks to understand the life cycle position in terms of where networks of relationships are now and asks members where they want to be. It studies the slack, in terms of what might be called 'space for reflection and introspection' when new ideas and practices can be absorbed and internalized. It examines the perceived equity (the return) and the obligations (the investment). The answers to the questions are reflected back and used as a basis for exploring where the community might develop.

Once a common understanding of where the community is and what it is doing is established, this can be compared to an idealized or desired position. The manager, acting as a facilitator, can seek to suggest areas where further investment of time and effort might produce greater membership rewards in terms of knowledge sharing. Scope and stretch must also be taken into account – scope in terms of the range of topics and stories which the community exchanges, stretch in terms of the direction of rate of development. Some sensitivity is called for here since newly formed or less robust communities are less well placed to put a strain on relationships.

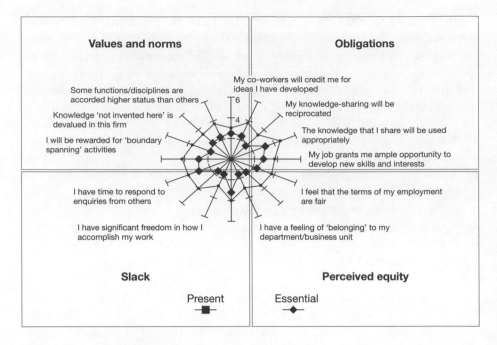

Figure 5.3 *Results of a disposition survey*

On the cognitive side, it is then possible to start to work on expertise directories. This is, unfortunately, a somewhat over promoted aspect of communities of practice. Since it is observable and 'measurable' some formal store or repository of knowledge makes an attractive first step in a knowledge management programme. One of the easiest and most popular of these repositories is a so-called 'Yellow Pages' exercise. This is an internal directory of expertise and is supposed to communicate who knows what and where the experts are to be found. Unfortunately, this takes us back to the manager's first free-fall parachuting exercise, when he or she was accompanied only by a parachute and a manual, as if the 'Yellow Pages' are going to pop out at 100 metres and save the company by telling everyone who all the experts are. Communities know the experts and identify them organically. In practice, expertise can be in a vast number of different areas, according to the nature of the problem. Trying to prejudge where solutions or creativity are to be found by trying to build an expertise directory, with expert categories, somewhat defeats the purpose.

Most managers will have a conception of which experts they need to run a business and what the shape of business might be. The difficulty with unexpected events is that no one expected them. Napoleon once pointed out that a general who set up to fight a battle according to a fixed plan was doomed to lose. Battles, like competitive environments, rarely run to plan. The formal organization, which has to locate people positionally against certain roles, may not be well placed to solve the problems that nobody envisaged when the structure was designed. Too often, organizations seek to prescribe roles and relationships. These are often based on what happened in the past (yesterday's battles) and sometimes bear no relation to where the business really needs to be. Many companies now operating in the virtual market place still have someone with communication manager tattooed on his or her forehead. These communications managers will try to understand who knows what and what the pattern or flow of information might be between different groups. However, they are working from outside the existing communities. Equipped with a hammer, all they want to know is how big is the nail. This may have no relevance to what the community perceives as important and what the organization then needs to do to move in the right direction. They are actually blocking the network by creating the impression that an open exchange of knowledge is taking place because some sort of directory has been drawn up and published.

This brings us back to Peter Drucker's comment in the 1950s (mentioned in Chapter 1) that all the unread, unused reports gathering dust on company shelves probably exceeded the number of books held by all the world's libraries. Like any manual – or database – a directory is of no value if it has more form than substance, if nobody uses it. The 'Yellow Pages' exercise runs the risk that it will remove the apparent need for broadcasting knowledge, doing things and building solutions together as a community.

The cognitive dimension of communitites may be developed by atttending to 'sense-making' activities:

- expertise guides – glossaries to key vocabulary, and personal competencies;
- knowledge coordinator roles – who and where are the experts?
- network events – bringing together participants as a community;
- story telling – the collection of anecdotes and significant 'teaching' stories.

In practice, most businesses do not have unresolved problems though every business has goals that it works towards and resolves. Organizations define the problem, investigate and build solutions. It may take time or it may be something that the organization can resolve quickly. However, in every business there are always unsung heroes who work together to fix problems. There is always the person that worked over the weekend, or the one who was in the office until 2 or 3 o'clock in the morning. Businesses are absolutely full of anecdotes and rich stories of what it took to get the business working. With dispositional analysis there is a discipline that can decompose these values, break the values down into rules and then recompose them such that they can be reclaimed by the business. The beauty of the approach is that they are then in alignment with the rules and values of the business. They have come out of the community and are ploughed back into the community to enrich it.

FOSTERING COMMUNITIES OF PRACTICE

In this section we look at the implications for managers of fostering communities of practice.

Communities of practice can play an instrumental role in leveraging knowledge. Some useful guidelines for managers seeking to increase the level of social capital via these communities of practice have been provided by Prusak and Lesser (1999):

- Identify communities of practice that influence critical goals within the organization. An organization of any size will contain a large number of communities. In choosing communities to which resources could be channelled it is probably most useful to select those that are most closely aligned with critical success factors. For example, a pharmaceutical company might support a community of practice to focus on regulatory approval issues.
- Provide communities with the opportunity to meet face to face. Electronic communications are good facilitating tools but they do lack a certain richness of communication which face-to-face contact allows. When meeting with a group face to face, body language, facial expression and even tone of voice carry important messages, all of which are lost by electronic tools. Allowing people to meet enables them to build a network of contacts within the community more quickly and facilitates the sharing of knowledge and the building of trust. That is not to say that the community will not grow without face-to-face contact but the development may be slower.
- Provide tools that enable the community to identify new members and maintain contact with existing members. This is where use of technology is vital. Tools such as Web pages, directories of expertise and knowledge maps can help individuals locate others with similar interests and experiences. At the same time, collaborative tools such as chat rooms and video-conferences can help foster interactions. The knowledge base itself plays an important role in helping community members maintain and refine their stock of knowledge.

- Identify key experts within the community and enable them to provide support to the larger group. Experts are community leaders and their leading position within the community may not correspond to their formal position within the organization. These experts usually provide organizational wisdom but they also act as directories to other individuals who may have even more relevant knowledge. Giving these experts more time and resources to create and share community knowledge efficiently will strengthen their role.

- Measure results. If we use expressions like social capital or intellectual capital, this implies that we are expecting some sort of return on the investment. The investment will take many forms, not only in direct expenditure on technology but also in terms of time and facilities for meetings. Some sort of dividend must be identified and monitored in relation to these investments and we shall return to this point when considering IP issues.

MANAGING INTELLECTUAL CAPITAL

Siemens

Definitely within the top management it is regarded as one of the main priorities and this can be proved by the fact that a lot of the decisions made by our CEO have been changed to fit in with knowledge management. For example, he changed the whole incentivization scheme across 160 countries to include things such as 'revenue generated due to international knowledge sharing' alongside the classic measurables.

There are a number of well-known tools for measuring intellectual capital, perhaps the most famous of which is that developed by Skandia in the production of its score card. The APQC have produced an interesting knowledge management assessment tool that looks at five main elements. These are: the knowledge management process, leadership, culture, technology and measurement. The assessments are associated with a scoring system that allows an enterprise to profile both its current position and its progress and was developed in conjunction with the consulting firm Arthur Andersen in 1995. Telecomms giant Ericsson has designed an exciting Web-based application which it calls the cockpit communicator (Barladi, 1999). In developing the tool Ericsson wanted to focus on value creation and therefore set out successfully to develop a competitive consultancy service for use by external as well as internal users. This produces a visible display screen that can be read from the Internet giving a kind of cockpit like display of dials measuring five areas:

- Process – which measures implementation against a plan.
- Financial – which measures the degree of consulting utilization directly linked to invoicing value.
- Employees – which measures the number of employees according to plan and incorporates an employee satisfaction index.
- Customers – which reflects customer satisfaction in relation to service levels.
- Innovation – which is a measure of a number of new services and the speed at which they have been produced.

This system was devised in collaboration with Professor Göran Roos from IMD in Switzerland. It not only provides a continuous measure of progress on the road to a knowledge-enabled organization but also helps to emphasize the importance of understanding and caring for the company's intellectual capital.

Cap Gemini

I guess that internally there are several things that need to be in place to enable effective knowledge management. The most important and fundamentally most important factor for knowledge management within our organization is that the Chief Executive of Cap Gemini Global Group and the Chief Executive of Cap Gemini UK both passionately and fundamentally believe in the need to have effective knowledge management within this organization. They are widely published internally and externally on this subject and have made it very clear to our organization that it is a core part of our future strategy and articulated how it fits. So that I guess is the most important thing. That the senior management of this company realizes that knowledge management is vitally important to our success.

THE IMPORTANCE OF CULTURE AND TRUST

BOC

We had a global team to decide what the best practice was and make sure everyone implemented it. Some of that was software scheduling. There are two scheduling packages that everyone in the BOC group globally now uses. It's as simple as that. It's surprising sometimes, you get people who do the same job in different parts of the world round the table and there are some really simple things in common.

Most knowledge management experts will acknowledge that technology contributes about 15 per cent of the solution for a knowledge-enabled enterprise. However, this is a very important 15 per cent, a point easily demonstrated by trying to implement a knowledge management programme without IT. The right technology to create infrastructure and provide facilitating access to people with information is critical for success. It is not in itself sufficient however.

Access to people with knowledge is more important. Organizational and human dynamics – probably better described as corporate culture – are ignored at your peril. Goffee and Jones (1996) describe culture as 'a habitual way of behaving and acting, often motivated from deeply engrained presumptions about the right way to act.' What this really means is that a corporate culture refers to a set of behaviours or qualities that are valued not because they are enforced from outside or even from within but simply because that is the way that influential members of the enterprise prefer them to happen. Culture is powerful because it is intimate. If employees are uncomfortable with corporate culture, then it is unlikely that they will be happy in their work. On the other hand, if they find a corporate culture that suits them, consensus building is streamlined, goals are internalized and it is easier to achieve consistent results.

BG

Culture is massively important. I mean the old days of 'knowledge is power', 'knowledge is personal' are not understood any more in this organization. It is 'knowledge is for sharing', 'knowledge is for adding value', for the organization, to the organization. It's very difficult to actually help people to understand that because there is still a great tendency if you share something to think, 'Why should I empty the contents of my head because you could then do without me?' So that is a major difficulty in terms of the cultural shift. Again, we've got some things under way where we're trying to help people with that one. And equally the connectivity, the physical networking are key elements as well.

The culture within an enterprise develops over time from preferences and styles. One of the most well-known books in this area was written in the mid-1950s by W H White. Called *The Organisation Man* it referred to the experience of working for IBM in that period. At one time White was an IBM employee. He resigned when he discovered one morning on opening his drawer, that he owned 16 white shirts and 16 pairs of charcoal grey socks in order to conform to the corporate dress code of the day. He suddenly recognized the power of acculturization – the process by which organizations sustain and reinforce culture. People who conform to the culture are more likely to be recruited. Once recruited they are more likely to be promoted. People who challenge or reject the culture are regarded as misfits. Corporate culture is a very powerful mechanism and the danger of these forces is easily understood if the culture in some way becomes unsuitable for the environment in which the company is operating. In the early 1990s, IBM reinvented itself, changing its culture dramatically in order to adapt to a market environment that required a more fluid and responsive form.

Barclays Bank

There are undoubtedly barriers with implementing anything new. Whether it's putting up new wallpaper in an office or something less tangible, it doesn't matter. We undoubtedly have had the normal cultural 'blockers' if you like. The 'not invented here' syndrome, wider cultural issues including things like blaming and shaming and of course techno phobia. Hopefully though, most of those things are out of the way now. What I'm trying to say is that you have to take into account all of these things before you can even begin to start thinking how you're going to move forward. Making sure that we completely build on that absolutely superb culture that we have, being one of the biggest and best banks in the world. That, in itself, is a damned good motivator to make sure we stay the best.

It is easy to make the mistake of stereotyping an organization culture and of believing that the same culture will suit all organizations that are engaged in similar work. In a survey carried out by the Haas School of Business on the University of California's Berkeley Campus, it was found that employees of consulting firm Delloite Touche voted informality to be of the greatest importance to their firm from a list of 54 characteristics. In the same study, employees at Arthur Andersen ranked informality as number 54. In seeking to measure cultures, Goffee and Jones classified cultures as high or low on two axes, sociability and solidarity. Students of management might recognize in this shades of the Blake and Mouton (1978) managerial grid first published in the 1960s and later republished as the 'new' managerial grid. Blake and Mouton used two dimensions called concern for people (sociability) and concern for production (solidarity). In itself, this is perhaps a good illustration of the benefits of using what is already known! The Goffee and Jones taxonomy creates the four classes of corporate culture, shown in Figure 5.4.

Sociability refers to the extent to which people are friendly with each other, a defining characteristic that is relatively constant over time. Solidarity, on the other hand, is a more formal property that does not have to be sustained by face-to-face relationships. It arises when people have shared interests in common. To sustain a community of practice requires both high sociability

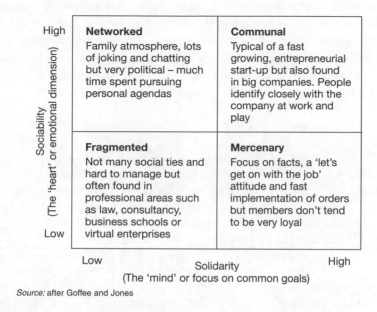

Source: after Goffee and Jones

Figure 5.4   *Two dimensions: four cultures*

and high solidarity. There is no reason to suppose that one of these cultures is somehow best for all organizations or indeed even for the same organization over a long period of time. The real test of the culture is whether it does the job. A highly sociable culture may slow down decision making at a time when rapid decisions are needed. At the other extreme, rigid management controls can actually prevent employees from making the best decision for a particular circumstance or can even cause employees to 'turn off' completely. Most analysts agree that it is important not to be prescriptive about culture. Over the years various aspects of organizational life have been proposed as the key to competitive advantage and corporate success. What is now recognized in every case is that all of these ideas, from supply chain management through to global reach, are merely entry prices for joining the game because all of them can be copied by the competition.

Ray Kurzweil, a pioneer in the field of voice recognition systems, observed that most of the wealth being created today is in the form of knowledge products with no corresponding material form, so, increasingly, natural resources are becoming less important. The route to creating wealth is based on the ability to create knowledge. Along the same lines, the well-known management writer Don Tapscott has pointed out that half the shares of Microsoft were purchased with traditional capital, ie money, but the other half were bought with intellectual capital. In other words members of the company were given shares in exchange for their knowledge and work. Tapscott believes that as the e-business revolution progresses, networks of suppliers and customers will become even more complex. Virtual enterprises may well make arrangements to share in and develop each other's human capital in order to create wealth through customer value services.

Cable & Wireless

Cable & Wireless is actually 70 companies and the culture of those 70 companies will not just depend on the Cable & Wireless stakeholding, it will depend on who is the dominant stakeholder in each location, whether that is an American organization, an Australian organization, a Middle East organization. Take, for example, the Solomon Islands where the government have a 51 per cent stake… It is a very difficult thing to successfully impose a Cable & Wireless culture. The employee factors are determined primarily by the country not by Cable & Wireless. It's only when we have, say, 60 per cent shareholding that we can actually develop a Cable & Wireless culture. So, if we had 43,000 employees fully owned by Cable & Wireless, life would much different to what it is at the moment, where we have to cope with differing cultures. The way we cope with them is to take the training to the country itself, which obviously limits [the employees'] ability to gain experiences from other countries.

THE ROLE OF THE CKO

Siemens

We also have about 5,000 people involved in our Web-based project called Sharenet globally across almost 50 countries, which is certainly known by everybody within the organization as a whole… We have about 100 knowledge management projects in motion at the moment… The way that we have introduced Sharenet is definitely through a top–down approach. It was started because top management felt there would be a great deal of added value and cost savings. We were prepared in this way to invest heavily in it. However, it was rolled out by getting 40 sales and marketing people from all over the world together and asking for their ideas, from the grass roots level. Similarly, we have a corporate knowledge management community which involves all Siemens divisions. This also uses a grass roots approach with top management support in the shape of a CKO and a dedicated team of 12 members.

The appointment of a CKO, possibly associated with the appointment of a Chief Learning Officer (CLO), is a step in the direction of formal culture change, since capturing case studies, best practice and even metaphors in an archive can be costly and time consuming. CKOs act as intermediaries between employees and knowledge. This is really an attempt to accelerate cultural transformation. The roles of the CKO and the CLO are still evolving. Typically, they have been in post for around three years. This is a new strategic, formal or informal role for HR people or former CIOs. It is a senior role, with teeth. Typically the postholders are good operations managers, excellent networkers and successful doers with a healthy scepticism of technology. Actually they can come from a variety of backgrounds such as consulting, academic, financial, marketing and technical but HR is common, especially for CLOs. Their job is to foster the growth of the knowledge organization. What they do not do is concern themselves with finance, funding and short-term issues. Mostly they use a relatively small staff and perhaps not an enormous resource base to begin with. The need for resources (and pressure for results) grows with time.

WHAT DO CKOs DO?

Typically a CKO will:

- align and integrate diverse functions;
- use previous best practice or design benchmarking strategies;
- develop a culture of organizational learning;
- have a customer service orientation;
- identify critical areas for improvement through needs or gap analysis;
- manage the capture, sharing and retention of activities;
- leverage corporate-wide learning;
- establish partnerships with senior managers;
- be a visionary champion for organizational learning and knowledge management.

The difference between a CKO and a CLO is that CLOs have a greater tendency to come from HR backgrounds. However, a CLO is not just a glorified training officer. Most CLOs have strong backgrounds in learning strategies and a strong orientation to setting and reaching business goals. They are committed to the strategic integration of organizational and individual learning at all levels and across all functional silos. Often a primary thrust is to shift the organizational mindset from training to continuous learning and human performance improvement.

A big five consultancy

I observe two kinds of CKOs and CLOs. Let me differentiate. From what I see, the CKO role tends often to have a heritage of coming out of technology. The CLO role is often more heavily linked with coming out of the training and HR side, to the extent that it depends on the push of the organization, what the impetus has been and why they're trying to think of knowledge in a more serious way. Generally, what I'm observing is that there are two kinds of candidates. There's a growing collection of people who are seen as being senior professionals in the knowledge management area who are getting recruited into being CKO or CLO for an organization. I don't know anybody who's moving around for under US $150,000 or US $200,000. The other thing I'm observing is that quite a few organizations are saying how important knowledge management is but rather than bringing an outsider in for the chief knowledge management role, they are actually taking somebody who is a respected senior manager already within the organization and making knowledge a key part of their responsibility. For example, an investment bank might take one of their top five people and say 'You've got to wear the knowledge hat and make things happen'. I think that a lot of the logic for acting that way is due to the fact that many of the things you're trying to drive as a CKO or CLO require a pretty insightful understanding of the organization itself, what makes it tick and knowing how you can make things happen using a whole network of people. They're not generally the kind of positions where you've got a lot of formal authority and therefore you've got to work laterally and generate sponsorships for initiatives and so on. Therefore, it's my observation that these inside candidates, if chosen carefully, are the ones that are most likely to be successful.

SUMMARY

Communities of practice add value to organizations in several important ways:

- They help to drive strategy. If communities of practice are small and fragmented their impact is lessened. Providing resources to facilitate the formation and maintenance of communities of practice will not only increase the number but will also increase their potential contribution to strategic direction.
- They start new lines of business. In some organizations, such as IBM, the community of practice is so powerful that it even organizes its own conferences and meetings. In this way its acts like a kind of petri dish for entrepreneurial insights that shape strategy and enhance reputation.

- They solve problems quickly. Members of a community of practice know who to ask for help with a problem and how to ask the right kind of question so that others can quickly understand and focus on the heart of the issue.
- They transfer best practice. There are several well-cited examples of this in industries ranging from car manufacturers, through pharmaceuticals, to oil refining, where the application of best practice has saved massive investments, by avoiding the need for investing in a new plant.
- They develop professional skills. Prusak and Davenport (1998) recorded a fall of 24 per cent in mortality rates by a group of heart surgeons in New England who got together as a community of practice to exchange ideas about patient care and operating techniques.
- They help companies recruit and retain talent. Membership of a community is voluntary and personal. People join and stay because of the personal rewards and this gives them an additional reason for remaining within the enterprise. (Wenger and Snyder, 2000.)

6

Transparent marketing

Andersen

[Knowledge] is what we sell. We sell it through people. Engagements with clients are, have always been our main business model. Clients come to us and we design solutions and projects to deliver those solutions. Then a bunch of people from our organization go and work with the client and deliver those solutions. So... people are our delivery vehicle but the raw product of what we're selling is knowledge or know-how. So it's absolutely critical that we manage what we know.

Transparent marketing looks across the whole spectrum of supply through to the customer. The basis of customer relationship marketing is that of having transparent knowledge across this complete environment. It requires some courage and determination on the part of any enterprise to open itself up in this way to its customer base. However true relationship marketing recognizes that power is passing from suppliers to very well informed customers who will make their own decisions about what to buy and when.

In today's wired environment, there is a huge amount of information available to both customers and suppliers. Not only over the Internet but also over PDAs, mobile phones and digital TVs. Some suppliers are acting as brokers against their own products. For example, a Web site operated by one major car manufacturer lists alternative and competitive dealer prices on its cars. Organizations are sometimes creaking under the competitive pressure. At the same time, enterprises are re-aligning themselves with mergers, alliances and takeovers to position themselves better in the value chain, moving out of some processes and into others. They are making political decisions as to which processes are core and which are merely supporting. As a result, enterprises need to be much more finely attuned to what is happening in both the customer and the supplier environments. A structure that was devised 10 years ago with a view to streamlining procedures, or even one that has been re-engineered for efficiency, is potentially competitively weak when effectiveness is the priority.

In order to compete, it is necessary to look through both your suppliers and your customers to take an overview of the complete value chain. Only by taking a holistic view of the market is it possible to understand what is happening. The aim is to learn how to extend communities of practice to include suppliers, contractors and even competitors. What might be regarded now as the greatest source of competitive knowledge within one organization, not disclosed to anyone except by internal confidential memos, will appear tomorrow on the Internet. Now the whole world can see, use and exploit an idea that may have started in your organization. Indeed, the idea may be more accessible to the outside world in this way than to the people in your own company. Therefore, the perception of where your competitive edge lies is changing dynamically in front of your eyes. To keep abreast of this competitive landscape it is important to talk to your suppliers and your customers, so as to involve them as part of one of your communities of practice.

There has been a great deal of talk about customer relationship marketing as if it were a single entity. It is not an entity at all. It has many facets. One of these is about customer knowledge. It is about who is doing what, what is needed, what is important and basically who knows what. It is about knowledge fundamentals. If organizations seek to establish a more knowledge-attuned, transparent marketing approach, they are less likely to be surprised by competitive actions or even hostile takeovers. The situation will become far more open and companies will be able to predict and shape their competitive landscape more effectively. They will also be able to position their products and services in relation to other offerings more collaboratively, reducing the effects of destructive competition of the sort that serves consumers only in the short run. This will allow them to identify profitable niches, thus essentially avoiding competition, more effectively. Had companies like the British car manufacturer Rover been able to do this, not only would they have seen more clearly where their competitive position was weak, but, more importantly, they might have been able to see where their value added lay in the market place. Despite having at least one acclaimed model in the late 90s with the Rover 75, the manufacturer was somehow unable to leverage their value-added proposition, which is partly why BMW eventually decided it had to withdraw their support for the firm.

BOC

And then there's knowledge management of customers. Whilst I'd say that we're not doing knowledge management, we've done a heck of a lot of work on improving our knowledge of customers. I know that W, our VP in the States, has presented a knowledge management conference, although we never called it knowledge management at the time. Instead, we called it 'getting closer to your customer!' In the States they've installed a system called Orem and so there are a lot of tools that are coming out now to really understand your customers better.

In the previous chapter we commented on the changing relationship between members of the enterprise and the enterprise itself. We pointed out that not only do members increase the wealth of the enterprise, primarily through the creation of knowledge but that they can exchange their knowledge for a share in the enterprise by trading knowledge for equity instead of money. You can observe this in new, entrepreneurial start-ups where members of the start-up team trade their ideas and effort not for a salary so much as for a share in the enterprise's growing wealth. Perhaps Microsoft is the best example of an organization that has employed this approach most successfully. It has encouraged bright, creative software engineers to contribute ideas in exchange for equity. These changes in the relationship between the enterprise and its members are also reflected externally. It is therefore useful to look at knowledge management as it affects two important relationships, those with customers and those with other suppliers.

Procter & Gamble

We would see you as a consumer and our customer as say, Tesco but we have to be flexible with our language because we do call our consumers customers as well. We spend an absolute fortune getting knowledge about the consumer, so we know everything about everybody. I think we know everything about a ridiculously high number of people. We are embarking on collaborative projects with customers like Tesco, Sainsbury, Asda and some others, where we actually have linked technology. But what we're looking at in future is how can we use the knowledge between partner companies to provide a seamless supply chain to our customers.

BUILDING COMMUNITIES OF CUSTOMERS AND SUPPLIERS

If we refer back to the three dimensions of social capital from Nahapiet and Ghoshal (1998), we need to add a fourth in order to sustain knowledge-based communities which link customers and suppliers.

THE STRUCTURAL DIMENSION

The structural dimension refers to the formation of informal networks that enable individuals to identify others who may be able to help them. A community of practice provides an opportunity for people to develop a network of individuals with similar interests. It therefore acts as a kind of clearing house that is particularly valuable as the organization grows and becomes increasingly 'virtual'. The structural dimension also acts as reference mechanism that enables individuals to evaluate the knowledge of others without having to contact each person. This aspect is particularly useful for new members of the organization as it allows them to contact people both within and outside the enterprise who may hold useful knowledge which may help in the performance of their changing roles.

THE RELATIONAL DIMENSION

Relationships are necessarily two-way and therefore a community of practice can only flourish when people believe that their actions will obtain a response and that others will meet their expected obligations. In this instance the trust-worthiness and commitment of other members of the community is para-mount. These are the building blocks that form the currency of the community. Value grows as a function of trust. As the dependence on others is rewarded so members are bound more closely to the community.

THE COGNITIVE DIMENSION

This refers to the common context and language needed, what we have called earlier a common vocabulary. There is of course a formal vocabulary built around documents, procedure manuals and memos. However, there is also a vernacular that is shaped by the actual terminology used by group members in everyday work conversations. Like the 'Picasso' mentioned earlier. As in any group formation process, communities develop their own set of norms and values to which group members are expected to conform. The stories built around these norms of behaviour, that reward some actions and punish others, provide the community with its continuity. They may be remembered long after the individuals who triggered the story have left the community. Customer stories are most easily visible through the activities of 'user groups' which are often established by customers of software companies. User groups exchange stories about tricks of the trade (best practice ideas to make the software perform to its best), describe how to overcome problems or work around problems and work together to encourage the supplier to modify their software to improve its functionality and its usability. Owner clubs set up by car manufacturers are another example. Here the manufacturer seeks to extend use of the product by harnessing the enthusiasm of customers in a common cause.

SUPPLIER RELATIONSHIPS

Closer links with suppliers provide unique opportunities to leverage the strength of the enterprise with the help of partners. As John Browne, Chief Executive of British Petroleum, observed: 'Any organization that thinks it does everything the best and need not learn from others is incredibly arrogant and foolish… You have to recognize that others may actually know more than you do about something – and that you can learn from them.'

The link with a partner in the supply chain can take the form of a bridge or a window. If it is simply a bridge, the possibility of a connection exists but people may choose not to cross. If is it a window then the possibility exists for bringing together different skills and knowledge bases to create a unique learning opportunity. The distinction is important. Alliances necessarily refer to some pooling of resources and the more limited and restricted the nature of the alliance the less likely it is to endure. In one of the many paradoxes of the knowledge management area, it is also true that where the alliance provides for knowledge sharing, once knowledge transfer has taken place the alliance is once again vulnerable. In management terms therefore, it is important to tread the fine line between knowledge sharing and knowledge creation. If the alliance results in the continuous creation of new knowledge that is of value to customers, then the supply chain is immeasurably strengthened.

The very formation of an alliance is an acknowledgement that the partner has useful knowledge, otherwise there would be no reason to form the alliance. It may also be assumed that this alliance knowledge has a value to both partners outside the alliance. For example, BP has acknowledged that it learnt about operating refineries and marketing lubricants from Mobil and about deep water drilling from Shell. Curiously, firms involved in alliances some-times fail to address the knowledge management issues explicitly. This can occur for a number of reasons. It may be that one partner in the alliance recog-nizes its continuing dependence or subordination on the other firm because it has no wish to enter that area of activity. It may be that one partner sees the objectives in very limited terms, such as a short-term financial gain, or it may be quite simply that one partner is using the alliance as a substitute for knowledge acquisition on which it places a relatively low value.

SUSTAINING THE KNOWLEDGE-BASED ALLIANCE

The factors affecting the likely success of a knowledge-based alliance are well described by Inkpen (1998), who sets out two broad areas which affect the likely success of an alliance, the accessibility of alliance knowledge and the protectiveness of alliance partners. If one or all of the enterprises in the alliance are reluctant to share knowledge because they fear that the effects of knowledge spilling over might create a potential competitor, then clearly there is little prospect of a long-term link. In this scenario two partners might set up a third, joint venture enterprise which acts as a kind of fire wall and prevents the transfer of knowledge from one to the other. This is usually a short-term action so that eventually the joint venture is either taken over by one of the partners or disbanded.

THE CLIMATE OF TRUST

Buckman Labs

I would disagree... that trust has to be earned. I worked for Shell for 20 years and I moved to Brazil for 3 years. Now, if I'd had to wait to develop a relationship with my Brazilian colleagues to determine whether I could trust them or not, I would be on my way out. So, what you really have to do is sum the person up very quickly and say 'I'm going to trust you' or 'I'm not'. You make mistakes but then that's life.

As with individual areas of knowledge sharing, trust is critical. Trust reflects the belief that a partner's word or promise is reliable and that partners will fulfil their obligations in the relationship. Trust is probably a personal property and cannot be fostered at the corporate level. It depends on personal relation-ships. Even where two partners set out to be very protective, it may be that over time individual relationships between managers will build trust and under standing. As they seek to work more closely together, so knowledge transfer will increase. Of course this can lead to some interesting effects. Middle managers may develop a bond of trust, a community of practice almost, which is not shared at the senior management level. This can result in some very mixed messages. On the other hand, where trust is absent, it is difficult to believe in the value of information being exchanged. It is interesting to observe this effect in joint ventures, especially where they are cross cultural in char acter and therefore perhaps more easily visible. At a senior level there may be some lack of trust between the members of the joint venture as they probe their way towards different business objectives. However, at middle management level, where there is a day-to-day requirement to ensure that the business meets the needs of customers, middle managers might grow to trust each other as they come together to solve operational problems.

THE TACITNESS OF ALLIANCE KNOWLEDGE

Embodied knowledge of course is not easily visible. It is also hard to formalize and that can make it difficult to share. On the other hand, represented knowledge is systematic and easily communicated. It is interesting to note that in joint ventures Western firms often set out to exchange explicit knowledge whereas Eastern firms are often more interested in tacit knowledge. The more embodied the knowledge, the more difficult it is to acquire but at the same time the greater the likelihood that knowledge is valuable. Represented knowledge can of course be created through analytical skills and concrete forms of oral and visual presentation. It focuses more on the 'what' to some extent than on the 'how' but much less on the 'why' and not at all on the 'why care?'

PAST EXPERIENCE OF WORKING TOGETHER

Established partners have already gone through the relationship-building process and will have experienced learning from each other. The relationship is therefore more likely to be regarded as more tenable because it is assumed to be more productive. An important point here is that the acquisition of knowledge is a cumulative process and therefore learning performance is enhanced in this environment. Prior knowledge permits the effective utilization of new knowledge in a synergistic way, knowledge begets knowledge, so that existing knowledge facilitates the use of other knowledge. In other words, as you get smarter so your ability to get even smarter increases!

KNOWLEDGE ACQUISITION EFFECTIVENESS

Inkpen (1998) identifies three levels of knowledge acquisition. At the individual level the critical process is interpreting, at the group level, integrating and at the organizational level, integrating and institutionalizing. Nonaka (1994), one of the founding fathers of the knowledge management era, developed the concept of a spiral of knowledge creation. In the spiral, knowledge moves upwards in an organization, starting at the individual level and then moving to the group and finally to the firm level. As it spirals upwards, individuals interact with each other and with their enterprises. It is these interactions or connections that form the basis of value. The key challenge for firms in supplier relationships is to create an environment that fosters this kind of knowledge-sharing movement across the two enterprises. For knowledge to be acquired there must be knowledge connections at different organizational levels through both formal and informal relationships, between individuals and groups. An ideal forum for this kind of exchange would of course be a community of practice, where knowledge that connects with other knowledge can be discussed, debated and discarded as required. There are four generic management processes that can create a knowledge connection between partners in an alliance:

- Personnel transfers between the alliance and the parents, in other words, an exchange in managers.
- Technology sharing at the explicit level.
- Interactions between the partners in the form of visits or tours.
- Tacit knowledge transfer. Although transfers of personnel could be associated with explicit knowledge, clearly they are going to be a very effective means of gaining tacit knowledge.

SUPPLIER KNOWLEDGE

Between suppliers, effective knowledge acquisition depends on four factors.

Flexible learning objectives

What knowledge management is certainly concerned with is understanding how we know what we know. It seems to be generally accepted that we certainly do not understand what we don't know! We have referred earlier to the example of boat building, in which at one level the explicit knowledge about the technology of boat building may seem to be the most critical factor, whereas in practice, customer relationship management might well be more central to the success of the firm. A great deal depends on how the learning objectives are set. If the initial learning objectives are not correctly focused and management is unwilling or unable to adjust the objective then knowledge management efforts may be ineffective. Quite simply, if one partner in the alliance sets out to acquire knowledge that is not central to success, then the absence of good business performance may cause it to lose interest in the relationship.

Leadership commitment

Leadership commitment is required for all areas of knowledge management but obviously in the more uncertain area of relationships between suppliers there must be at least one strong champion of knowledge creation in a leadership position. If there is a meeting of minds at chief executive level then there is a great deal of encouragement for knowledge creation and sharing between the two suppliers.

Performance myopia

This really refers to the opposite of the condition just described. If one or both of the partners in the relationship have very limited, narrow objectives, focused on some aspect of performance or on financial objectives, then nurturing a knowledge exchange will be very much secondary matter. This creates a very difficult situation because the acquisition of knowledge in itself is a confusing and difficult experience, so that the failure to exploit learning opportunities more rapidly encourages the conclusion that the alliance or partnership is not working.

Cultural alignment between partners

As with trust so with culture. A cultural mismatch, a lack of alignment between different organizational cultures, makes the transfer of knowledge more difficult. A culture that is perceived as more alien, in other words which does not conform at all to 'the way we do things around here', may seem to have nothing to offer.

Swiss Re

The way managers and senior managers act obviously influences the way their people will react. And then there's all the issues around trust. If I give something to somebody, am I happy that it's not going to backfire? Am I going to give all the time and not get anything back? I found a fantastic postcard that I'm going to scan and put around our community. It's a picture of a big elephant and a little mouse, hiding their private parts. It goes, 'You show me yours and I'll show you mine!' This can be quite an issue when dealing in markets at different stages of development. For example, you could have a very developed market in Europe and then say, an Asian market where things are many years behind. There is the potential for a very unequal flow of information, with people saying, 'Well, what's in it for me?'

At first glance, it may seem that any relationship between suppliers that is based on the creation and exchange of knowledge is doomed to failure. The contribution of each enterprise in the alliance is rarely going to be equal. One may always seem to offer more than the other, although these roles may be reversed periodically. Too fickle an approach to enterprise relationships can have the same effect as too fickle an approach to personal relationships. A 'strong' partner, who therefore has the greater bargaining power, may find it increasingly difficult to form alliances if it terminates ventures that are apparently of no further use.

CUSTOMER KNOWLEDGE

Reckitt & Colman

I think it basically splits into two camps. The two most important functions within Reckitt & Colman are the marketing function and the supply chain function. Our knowledge really organizes itself around these two and they hinge on us knowing what customers want. Then, having developed this item, [the issue is] how do we get the products out to the customers when they want [them]?

With the rise to prominence of database marketing methods in the last decade or so, the importance of customer retention linked to maximizing 'share of wallet' has become well established. Determining the lifetime value of a customer can only be achieved if the supplier has a deep knowledge of customer motivations. This includes an understanding of trigger events that are likely to change purchasing behaviour radically. Trigger events such as a change of job might cause a customer to switch from buying self-assembly furniture packs to weekend holiday breaks. The emphasis on database marketing, a term which refers to the driving technology behind relationship management processes for business to customer markets in which thousands or millions of customers might be active, has sometimes obscured the importance of the underlying relationship concepts. These are fully explored in Gamble, Stone and Woodcock (1999) but we can pick out the most important ideas relating to the management of knowledge.

Ericsson

Take, as an example, customer information. This is put in a global folder in Outlook Exchange. We are looking at such things as where do they get their information from, does it do the job, would it be better to interlink these systems, etc?

Effective knowledge management can make a significant difference to the relationship-marketing platform. In the business-to-consumer market, effective relationship management can transform the value of a customer for a single burger meal from 50 cents to US $50,000 if a lifetime relationship is considered. In business-to-business markets, a relationship that results in a reduction in the number of suppliers can increase value for both parties so that not only is the size of orders increased but also the cost savings achieved are passed to the corresponding partner. In both cases, involving the customer, either business or consumer, in the provision of goods or services can result in higher sales. This is achieved by using the customer's knowledge.

Customer knowledge management can be considered in four dimensions:

- Structural. This refers to the technology behind the customer database and the knowledge management repository.
- Economic. This refers to the strategic direction and the creation of benefits and is concerned with the measurement of intellectual capital.
- Inter-organizational. This refers to the management of team and individual motivations and the establishment of the learning culture. This aspect of the process provides for and facilitates knowledge creation.
- Social. This refers to knowledge communities, communications and customer contact strategy.

KNOWLEDGE PROCESSES

If knowledge creation is a necessary condition for the creation of wealth, a company can be viewed as consisting of three knowledge processes.

The generative process

The generative process, in which knowledge is created, comprises all the usual marketing, operational and logistic activities by which products and services are created and sold. From a management point of view, knowledge is transferred in two ways. The first of these is as migratory knowledge. In some senses this transfer of knowledge is very superficial and refers to the knowledge that is reflected in the product or service. Like any reflection, if you take away the mirror, the image is lost. There is an element of migratory knowledge in many products; for example fax machines or PCs. In buying the PC, the customer is benefiting from the knowledge of those who made the device. Very little of that knowledge is transferred to the customer in terms of usage. A skilled person can unlock that knowledge by reverse engineering the product. Well-known examples of reverse engineering can be found in the automobile, computer and even the fashion industries. Legal protections for this kind of knowledge are fairly limited and are very expensive to defend.

The second form of knowledge transfer is through embedded knowledge. In the previous section on partnering and alliances, it was this embedded knowledge which was at issue between the two parties. Consultancies, in particular, seek to trade on embedded knowledge. They aim to set up systems and relationships within their own organizations that allow for the rapid transfer of knowledge between members. They seek to add to this knowledge base by acquiring the embedded knowledge of their clients and they seek to retain their consultancies by creating the sort of communities in which expertise and knowledge can grow. Broadly, two approaches seem to be adopted (Hansen, Nohria and Tierney, 1999) and each of these has its place for the management of customer knowledge. The first is based on a codification strategy which, as the name implies, seeks to categorize and codify knowledge which is stored in databases where it can be accessed easily and quickly by anyone in the company. These are summarized in Table 6.1.

The codification strategy produces significant efficiencies. For example, Andersen Consulting and Ernst and Young, firms which use the codification strategy, enjoyed growth rates of 20 per cent each year in the latter part of the 1990s by pricing out their consultants at around US $600 each day. These companies can hire new graduates and train them rapidly in the use of stan-

Table 6.1 *Summary of two knowledge management strategies*
Source: based on Hansen, Nohria and Tuerney, 1999

Knowledge Management Strategies

CODIFICATION		PERSONALIZATION
High quality, reliable and fast implementation of information systems by re-using codified knowledge	**Competitive Strategy**	Creative, analytically rigorous approach to problems based on individual expertise
Re-use economics Invest once in a knowledge asset and re-use it many times. Focus on accessibility and re-use with big economies of scale in relation to high volumes	**Economic Model**	Expert economics Produce highly customized, individual solutions to problems based on small teams. Focus on value added and high margins.
People-to-knowledge base Develop an electronic document system with standard methods of codifying and re-using knowledge. Powerful indexing and search facilities are important.	**Knowledge Management**	People-to-people base Encourage and facilitate the development of networks for information sharing. Mentoring and asking for help are encouraged so as to share best practice. Culture fit is important.
Information storage, retrieval and dissemination Big investment in IT so as to enable the management of large databases. Big investment in cross-indexing and data cleaning.	**Information Technology**	Communications focus Moderate investment in IT so as to produce an efficient network and easy exchange of ideas.
Technical orientation, team players Employ university graduates with first class degrees. Train in groups, possibly using distance learning but with a strong emphasis on standard methods and team orientation. Reward people for using and contributing to the database.	**Human Resources**	Creative problem solvers Employ university graduates with advanced degrees, preferably MBAs. Seek out people who are creative problem solvers with a high tolerance for ambiguity. Training through one-to-one or one-to-few mentoring. Reward people for sharing knowledge directly with others.

dardized methods of information search and retrieval. By contrast, McKinsey, BCG and Bain tend to recruit much more selectively (and expensively), often after several interviews with senior partners and consultants. Cultural fit is taken very seriously and subsequent training is based on a system of personal mentoring. Thus, the second strategy, personalization, requires knowledge to be passed along on a one-to-one basis so as to create a different kind of individual value for customers. These firms offer highly customized solutions billed at an average of just over US $2,000 each day.

Interestingly enough, such transfers of embodied knowledge has produced another knowledge management paradox called a competitive cluster. Michael Porter, who observed that, in an electronic age, globalization of itself offered no particular competitive advantage, coined the term competitive cluster. He suggests that where a cluster existed such advantage could not only be maintained but could grow. Porter gave the example of the wine growing region of the Napa Valley or the textile-manufacturing region of Northern Italy. Developing embedded knowledge requires extensive relationships and networks. Where companies engaged in related areas of the supply chain are located in geographic proximity, members of those organizations can easily meet and exchange ideas. In other words they can develop inter-organizational communities of practice. It is perhaps no surprise that a cluster of supplier organizations have opened offices around Wal-Mart's head quarters in Arkansas.

The productive process

This is concerned with transforming knowledge into products and services. Through this process value is created. Probably the leading thinker in this field is Peter Senge, who identified the five disciplines necessary to succeed in continuous learning. These were: individual learning; guiding concepts and mental frameworks; leadership; shared values and visions; team learning; and finally the ability to see the whole. Team learning makes knowledge development possible in a way that individuals cannot achieve on their own. Senge points out that the main requisite for team learning is the ability to interact, which reinforces Porter's argument for the importance of geographic proximity on the growth of competitive clusters. It is interesting to speculate as to whether virtual communities, facilitated by groupware such as Lotus Notes, can produce the same effects.

The representative process

This area is concerned with the relationship between the company and its customers. The essence of this relationship is a dialogue, a two-way exchange of information and knowledge. It is fairly obvious that a supplier can benefit from a deeper knowledge of customers. It is sometimes forgotten that customers can benefit even more from a deeper knowledge of suppliers. E-commerce has passed significant amounts of power from the supplier to the customer. Increasingly, customers can choose not only what to buy but when and how they may wish to buy it. Sometimes this is not as easy as it may at first appear. With the arrival of travel services on the Internet in the late 1990s, many commentators confidently forecast the demise of the neighbourhood travel agent. In fact, with the exception of what might be called 'commodity travel'(low cost, point-to-point journeys), travel agents seem to have prospered. The task of buying an airline ticket between two cities can produce a very complex transaction, through a morass of fare structures and timetables. If customers understand how the supplier's reservation system works, they can achieve their goal much more rapidly and efficiently. As they learn more about the supplier's procedures, so they are more likely to trade with that particular company but this involves a great deal of learning and takes time. The triggering event that might cause them to switch away would be a loss of trust, even if it were not the supplier's fault. The customer might not have allowed enough time to make a connection or might not have read properly the conditions under which a fare was offered. This sort of knowledge, acquired on a daily basis by a travel agent, represents an important source of added value which the agent can repay to the customer in terms of time and confidence. It may actually be quicker to use an agent because the agent knows how to use the supplier's system efficiently and travellers can be more confident that their travel arrangements are more likely to be in line with their needs.

A loss of trust happens surprisingly frequently in the financial services sector, where financial products that appear to offer good value at first sight, subsequently reveal themselves to have created significant commercial disadvantages for the customer. In the UK a good example of this was the private pensions industry where it was found that pension providers had misrepresented and mis-sold personal pensions to the disadvantage of hundreds of thousands of households.

If trust can be established, customers will be more open about their needs and intentions. This can pay off handsomely. In one business sector, some 77 per cent of scientific instruments were actually designed and developed by customers (Gummesson, 1999: 136).

Where customers share such knowledge, they increase the intellectual property owned by the supplier. The power of this kind of activity has long been recognized by two acronyms, WOMing and SUGing. WOM stands for 'word of mouth' as in one person recommending a product to another, and SUG refers to 'selling under guise' as in an advertorial or infomercial.

Advertorials or infomercials are journalistic pieces, invariably labelled (some-where) as advertisements but which are written in the style of an editorial or serious informative piece. Both of these activities refer to the power of personal recommendation. Customers who deal with responsive and knowledgeable suppliers are more likely to attract and encourage other customers to trade.

PRINCIPLES OF MANAGING CUSTOMER KNOWLEDGE

Four basic principles can be applied to the management of customer knowledge:

Make it valuable

Clearly, the most advantageous areas will be those that focus on embedded knowledge. Examples might include customer support knowledge, design knowledge and knowledge of competitive bids. The GE database referred to in Chapter 1 is an excellent example of embedded knowledge. The pay-off for this activity must be visible in both the short and the long term. Short-term pay-offs are usually useful for encouraging long-term management commitment!

Make it rare

The idea here is to focus on areas of knowledge that give you an edge over the competition. A careful bench marking study of competitor activity might reveal areas in which they are weak. A knowledge-based service targeted at this weakness will produce a significant competitive advantage. One example might be to take one of the performance metrics for measuring customer rela-tionships to a very high level. A direct selling operation might therefore follow dispatch with a personal call to the customer to ensure that the product has been safely received and is performing properly. This customer contact also provides an opportunity for acquiring some knowledge about the customer's planned use for the product. Good customer support might then include acknowledging receipt of a customer product questionnaire and a further follow-up call to ensure that any usage problems have been resolved. Some care is needed at this point because what you measure is what you will get. The wrong measures can produce exactly the opposite effect of that which was intended. Call centres are one good example. Very fast responses to customer contacts, by answering the telephone in one or two rings, rather than adding customer value can actually be disconcerting to the caller, since most people compose their thoughts while the telephone is ringing and expect to have time to do that. The very fast response can therefore actually restrict feedback because the customer has not had time to prepare properly what he or she wanted to say. It can create the impression of a problem solved when all that has happened is a problem stifled so that important customer feedback (shared knowledge) is lost. Similarly, productivity measures that force agents to handle high volumes of calls rapidly, will probably frustrate both call centre agents and customers whilst satisfying neither.

Make it hard to copy

Sharing knowledge with your customer can provide an unassailable competitive position which competitors can find hard to understand. For example, in the utility sector it is common to segment customers as either domestic or business. Within this segmentation, however, is hidden a multitude of behaviours. A laundromat, a restaurant and a hospital are all business consumers of electricity but their needs are entirely different. Continuity of supply would be very important to one, low cost energy might be very important to another. Failing to recognize the crossover effect between two market segments can produce problems. In the late 1990s British Airways declared a strategy of concentrating on its business passengers to the implied (but not intended) disregard of its economy passengers. Of course in practice it needed both categories of customer but it overlooked the fact that many of its business class passengers also flew economy from time to time. Making them feel like second-class economy passengers could have lost the airline some valuable business class fares.

Make it hard to substitute

Any migratory knowledge, technical or process can be copied. Some of the best examples of both knowledge and relationship management stretch back a long way with examples like Tupperware or Avon. Simply making life easier for the customer can cement the marketing relationship. This can only be done with knowledge of the customers' needs and behaviours. In the UK, moving house is considered to be the most traumatic life event that can be experienced, after bereavement or divorce. This is because the legalities and logistics of moving house are fraught with difficulties and complexities. In France or the United States by contrast, real-estate agents will happily undertake a range of tasks to make the buyer's life easier, from making transfers of city taxes, to setting up telephones or even putting householders in contact with good schools for their children. In order to do this the real-estate agent must have a good network of relationships across both a physical and a knowledge community.

Procter & Gamble

It's fairly straightforward because we've got Lotus Notes and that's just fantastic for sharing knowledge. For our critical business processes we have a person that is responsible for owning the knowledge in that area. We've actually just started a project all based around the consumer. I have one guy whose job is knowing everything about the consumer. He's got absolutely tons of knowledge in his head and his team, a team of about ten, who are all experts in different aspects of shop psychology, through to designing the perfect shelf layout in the shop.

SUMMARY

Partnerships and alliances between suppliers are increasingly becoming a fact of life in the world of e-commerce and elsewhere. Whilst an alliance that is complementary may well serve a short-term goal efficiently, longer-term alliances of mutual benefit offer better prospects for the exchange and creation of knowledge. Since knowledge is a potential source of future wealth, supplier relationships should be approached carefully and with an open mind.

Customers are a particularly important source of knowledge since only they really understand what value they might be seeking from a product or service. Their experiences in using the product or service can help to make it better. If a supplier is unwilling to respond to customer experiences, in a world where power has passed substantially from suppliers to customers, buyers will simply switch their allegiance to a competitor. It is therefore vital that suppliers seek to establish with customers a knowledge-sharing activity. Like any community of practice, this needs to be nurtured very carefully. If trust is lost or destroyed, customers will withdraw from the community. However, the effective deployment of a sound relationship marketing model, coupled with the use of key knowledge management ideas, can ensure that both customers and suppliers benefit equally from an exchange of knowledge.

7

The knowledge management matrix

POSITIONING THE KNOWLEDGE MANAGEMENT STRATEGY

A favourite definition of strategy is that offered by Igor Ansoff many years ago in his well-used book on corporate strategy. 'Strategy is when you are out of ammunition but keep on firing so the enemy don't find out'. The most interesting aspect of this is that many companies use it in practice as a working definition! It owes its roots to the 'Don't just stand there, do something' school of management, on the assumption that any sign of activity will give the illusion of progress.

The trouble is that in the field of knowledge management this simply will not do. It only takes a few questions to realize that the absence of a clear knowledge management strategy, coupled with an undirected knowledge management initiative, will probably only make things worse. For example:

- How do we know whether the stock of knowledge is increasing? If it is increasing, how is this happening?
- How can we ensure that the stock of knowledge continues to increase?
- How useful is new knowledge to the goals of the enterprise?
- How durable is this new knowledge? Do the competition have it also? How long will it take them to get it?
- Are there things that the competition knows that we do not? Can we imitate the competition? Can we acquire it?
- Taking the total stock of what can be known both by us and the competition, can we leverage it in some special way to gain a competitive advantage?

Procter & Gamble

Yes, we're writing [our strategy] now. We have actually had a strategy for about a year but it's been a very un-Procter strategy in that we just started working on it and we didn't really have an absolute end point in mind. We started off very basically, giving everybody shared spaces by team. Then we came up with a global share-and-reapply approach, allowing us to jump from team level to global level. At first, it didn't work particularly well. It worked reasonably well within a team but then it got messy. That was around August 1998. In December 1998, we introduced a lower level of shared space, which was a UK and Ireland shared space. This actually worked really well because that's when we started working on business processes and building it into how we work. We haven't cracked the global perspective yet.

It is quickly apparent that increasing the total stock of knowledge without prioritization may simply make matters worse. This takes us back to the hose pipe analogy we used earlier. If the knowledge hose is turned on with no one to point it in the right direction, like an undirected garden hose it will spray around everywhere and just dampen everyone's enthusiasm. What could be known and used will grow without structure, increasing pressure on all enterprise members to somehow do better but without guidance or support. Providing a knowledge access tool without training can increase this pressure off the scale.

To determine the strategic k-spot, the current state of the organization can be considered against two measures. The first measure is what proportion of all codified knowledge do we have, especially compared to our key competitors? The second is what proportion of all our knowledge is embedded or tacit? Presented as a matrix, this will produce the four broad strategic areas shown in Figure 7.1. It is useful to consider these four positioning choices.

The matrix in Figure 7.1 is based on an idea first offered by Hall and Andriani (1998). In the upper section of the diagram, strategic positions A and B represent areas which hold the most promise for producing ground-breaking results. Positions C and D represent the areas where the support of a knowledge management system and an effective strategy are most needed. Positions B and D represent the best cases for knowledge management, where there is the strongest need. These should be the focus for strategic action.

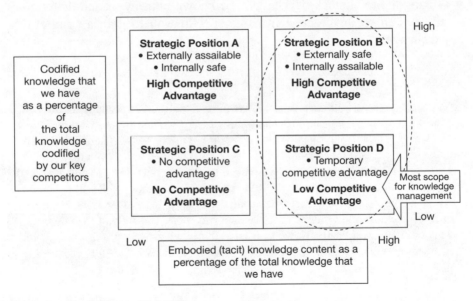

Source: based on Hall and Andriani, 1998

Figure 7.1 *Determining the strategic K-spot*

Position A

Here, the level of represented knowledge is high and the embodied content is low. In other words the companies' competitors do not have much more knowledge than they have. This is perhaps the best case for starting knowledge management activities, particularly in companies that have a strong leaning towards codification. Most companies with an existing knowledge management programme probably fall within this quadrant. They are internally safe but externally vulnerable. If competing companies manage to obtain any portion of this readily applicable and explicitly codified knowledge they can use it to their advantage. Probably in this sort of situation a key concern is to make sure that knowledge does not walk out of the door.

Position B

Companies in this category have managed to make explicit some portion of their knowledge but this is a relatively small percentage of what their competitors have. In this situation the tacit content of knowledge is very high which is an excellent scenario for a knowledge management initiative. Technology could be a major if not crucial saviour here and a well-funded knowledge management programme would be in order to try to capture the knowledge. Whilst the embodied knowledge remains, companies here are externally safe but a key member of the enterprise or a group leaving to join the competition could rapidly reverse the situation.

Position C

Companies in this quadrant are in real trouble. They have captured a low portion of explicit knowledge and hold very little embodied knowledge of advantage. The survival of these enterprises is probably in doubt, unless something can be done fairly quickly to endow them with an area of expertise.

Position D

Most companies considering knowledge management fall into this area. They are presently successful and that success is rooted in a high proportion of embodied knowledge only some of which has been made represented. The embodied knowledge provides a temporary competitive advantage but it needs to be converted into a longer-term sustainable position. There is a great deal to be gained here from an investment in knowledge management systems technology and infrastructure.

Many medium to small companies fall into this area, particularly consulting companies, but more or less any small business in which a high proportion of knowledge and expertise is held by a small number of people. Capturing and levering this knowledge is essential if the business is to grow since obviously the knowledge resource base is very limited and very vulnerable.

The first stage of strategy determination is therefore to conduct a knowledge management audit using one of the several tools available such as that described in the Appendix. It is often said that those who do not learn from history are doomed to repeat it. In the knowledge management arena the same idea is captured by the expression, hindsight + insight = foresight. The key points on which your company concentrates its knowledge management efforts must be chosen very carefully. The initial aim is to locate niches that can provide added value very quickly. Not only does this produce a fast revenue payback but it increases confidence in the process across the enterprise. In turn this encourages acceptance and dissemination of ideas.

STRATEGY ROLLOUT

Rolls-Royce

Yes, we have strategy framework that describes what we call the dimensions of knowledge management, on both the corporate level and the divisional level. There is a human dimension, a technology dimension, a metrics dimension, content management and so on. For example, we decided first to focus on the potential of sharing knowledge. Now we have moved on to looking at the knowledge creation process, ie from the idea to the product. The strategy framework for ICN was built up in 1997 by the previous CKO and the knowledge community within ICN. It has evolved over time and we are now reviewing it in the light of e-business.

Based on an international benchmarking exercise that examined the practices of 11 international organizations, the American Productivity and Quality Centre (APQC) has identified six broad knowledge management strategies. These are not necessarily meant to be mutually exclusive.

Enterprise-wide
This is the most comprehensive approach used by companies that recognize knowledge management as vital to their long-term growth and fundamental to their ability to compete. These companies are usually well down the road of being knowledge enabled and usually have a formal knowledge champion at a very high level. A good example of such a company is Buckman Laboratories. In such organizations there is rarely a need to make a business case for the

concept. Significant resources are dedicated in all areas of the business to ensure continual enhancement and dissemination of the knowledge base through people, processes and products. These organizations frequently see knowledge as a product and it is embedded heavily in what they do. There is generally a firm conviction that it will have a substantial and direct, positive impact on the profitability and viability of the enterprise.

Transfer of knowledge and best practice

This supporting strategy is intended to improve operations and embed knowledge in products and services. The idea is to enable the company to reduce cycle times, increase customer responsiveness, increase sales and where necessary cut costs. The intention is to bring the knowledge base of the company to bear on customer needs. Such enterprises underline the importance of teams, relationships and networks as a basis for effective transfer. They have usually taken a variety of approaches to encourage collaborative knowledge transfer, such as best practice centres and communities of practice. At the same time they have usually deployed systems to organize and restructure data warehouses and distribute the knowledge.

Customer-focused knowledge strategy

Here the emphasis is on customer relationship management and is directed towards capturing, developing and transferring knowledge about customer motivations and behaviours. The distinction between this and a pure customer relationship marketing approach is that knowledge contributed by customers forms an important part of the knowledge base and directly influences how the organization responds.

Personal responsibility for knowledge

This strategy recognizes the personal properties of knowledge as belonging to individuals and groups. The strategy is therefore designed to encourage awareness and to recognize that individuals and teams must be supported if they are to identify, maintain and expand their own knowledge. The objective here is to ensure that all members of the enterprise constantly renew and share their knowledge assets, so that they are capable of performing their highly competent work. The responsibility for knowledge management thus lies with the individual employee. In this respect it is a pull strategy rather than a push strategy. The use of incentives in this situation must be handled very carefully. Performance against metrics that examine knowledge transfer can be built into regular personal reviews of performance and some rewards may be attached to coaching, mentoring and personal development. The intention is to create a knowledge intensive culture.

Intellectual asset management

This strategy revolves around leveraging assets such as patents, operational practices, customer relations and other structural knowledge assets. The relevant focus tends to centre on reviewing, organizing, valuing, safe keeping and increasing the availability of and marketability of these assets. A good example here would be Skandia, that has developed a measurement system to highlight the particular indicators of intellectual capital development and value creation.

Innovation and knowledge creation

The aim here is to emphasize the creation of new knowledge by leveraging existing knowledge. These enterprises are trying to ascend the knowledge spiral to which we referred in a previous chapter. This is a difficult strategy because it hinges on innovation and creativity. Whilst the management of knowledge is a necessary condition for creativity, it is not a sufficient condition and something else is needed in terms of culture and relationships.

Buckman Labs

I have never known us to have a knowledge strategy. My perception is that our knowledge strategy is simple, flexible and progressive. It is to implement any cultural, content or technology improvements that will improve our ability to leverage our shared knowledge in meeting the needs of our customers on a global basis. That's all that I could come up with because we don't have a great strategy… The reason I am so strongly against knowledge strategy [definitions] is that I couldn't find an adequate definition that described it. So we come up with these definitions to impress others. That's why in Buckman I don't think we've formalized our knowledge strategy.

The APQC study observed that knowledge management tends to be a decentralized management responsibility for the companies in their study but that there tends to be a systems infrastructure to support it. That infrastructure might include a knowledge leader who helps to develop a shared vision and coordinate activities. It also includes common IT platforms and corporate repositories such as databases and libraries. None of the companies in the study confined their organizational structure or infrastructure to a central corporate office or function. PriceWaterhouseCooper, for example, has nearly 200 employees dedicated to knowledge management in its consulting division with around 50,000 consultants engaged across the world in the knowledge management process.

Funding tends to mirror the pattern of responsibility. While some resources are often centrally dedicated to support knowledge management efforts for specific projects, approaches for budgets usually come from the business units themselves. Chevron, for example, allows all its funding for its knowledge management initiatives to take place on an *ad hoc* basis. The cost will be shared as required across the business units involved. The main cultural issues and enablers affecting these programmes revolve chiefly around support and collaboration. In this, senior management support is critical and an open sharing culture with a high degree of trust clearly makes a significant difference to the potential success of the programme. Sharing behaviours are therefore at a high level because people are willing and inclined to share. In only a minority of cases are formal financial rewards used to encourage behaviour conducive to knowledge management. Most companies in the APQC study were building incentives for knowledge development and transfer in their professional and career development systems. Progress, advancement and therefore salary progression are associated in some companies with contribution that has been made to the firms' structural knowledge capital.

Part of the huge problem that so many organizations have is that whilst they embrace high level concepts of knowledge management in theory, in practice they are still wedded to traditional economic ideas based on ownership and exploitation of land, labour and capital. Since it is difficult at the beginning of the 21st century to pick up a magazine or watch TV without some recognition of the change to a networked economy, many of these more traditionally rooted organizations embrace knowledge management only to the extent that they feel obliged to start at least one initiative. In these situations there is a pervasive tendency for knowledge management initiatives to bounce off some aspect of the IT operation, as that seems to offer some quantifiable output. At the very least it will produce a database or a logistic process that can be reported to shareholders. Unfortunately, they often produce little else. Expectations are formed of great transformations through a more efficient utilization of knowledge. As these expectations are ill founded they are rarely met. In turn, this leads to a belief that knowledge management does not 'work'.

The reason that knowledge management appears to fail if approached in this way is that there is no fundamental strategic underpinning. It is based on a 'Don't just stand there, do something' approach. One of the main weaknesses here is that the solution is assumed before the problem is properly structured. In other words, assumptions are made about where expertise lies and is held without analysing whether this is likely to be true. Driving a car gives an easy analogy for this situation. The instruction manual for the vehicle will tell a driver, perfectly accurately, exactly how the car works and what has to be done to make it go. In organizational terms, that might be viewed as a knowledge repository. As every driver knows, other than locating the instruments and controls (and perhaps some of the basic maintenance requirements for the enthusiast) no one uses the manual as a basis for driving. They might well read a book by an expert driver or take an actual driving course with an instructor but the essential knowledge about speeds, braking distances, whether extra care is needed because a child might run into the road, is just not in the manual for the car.

The categories of knowledge are illustrated in Figure 7.2. This describes a sort of continuum from tacit or embodied knowledge through to explicit (represented or embedded) knowledge. Within this spectrum, knowledge can be held in a variety of forms, all of which might be present in the organization. The accessibility or the potential to leverage knowledge might change according to our ability to codify or mentor it. A good example here is music. Before the invention of the bass and the treble clef, there was no way to learn music other than by copying a tune from a master musician. Musicians would have to play their composition to an audience that would seek to reproduce it. After the Middle Ages, it was possible to represent the knowledge formally by the use of a system of notation and this could, a few centuries later, be embedded in products such as CDs. Thus, initially, tacit knowledge (the tune in the composer's head) was made explicit (on paper), learnt and played by an orchestra, recorded on a CD and perhaps moved into someone else's head as he or she hummed the tune. Thus the music became tacit again with the benefit that many people could use it.

The concept of the knowledge management matrix helps to overcome the problems of understanding the form in which knowledge is held, and the extent to which it may be represented and embedded, by helping managers think about the types of knowledge that exist and where they exist. Using the research-based definitions that we have employed so far, three broad categories of knowledge are useful, as shown in Figure 7.3.

Embodied knowledge is equivalent to tacit knowledge and tends to be stored in people's heads. Represented knowledge is codified knowledge that may be either tacit in origin or explicit. A traveller's guide is a good example here. It contains explicit knowledge about hotels, restaurants and airlines along with handy tips on which restaurants provide 'good' food and service. Embedded knowledge is in processes (what people actually do in their jobs) and products.

Of course, much knowledge exists across all three categories. To create this document required knowledge of the word processor (if nothing else), background knowledge about changes in organizations and what to do to create a book and have it published. It is most important to realize that there is no broad-brush approach that can be taken across an organization to describe in total its knowledge or what it understands. Each and every department, each

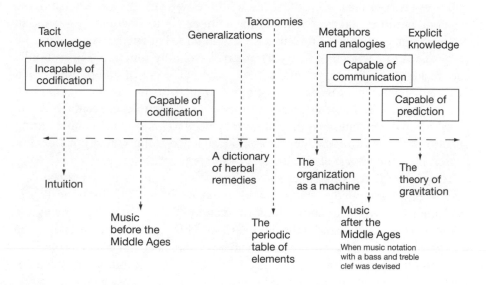

Figure 7.2 *Categories of knowledge*

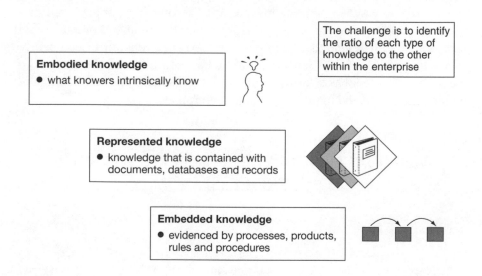

Figure 7.3 *The types of knowledge that exist in and around every organization*

and every part of the organization has all three types of this knowledge in the wisdom, intuition and experience of its members, in its documentation and in other written exchanges. Of course, whilst all three knowledge types exist, the proportions of each vary greatly by enterprise and by function. For example, the research department might have a great deal of deep, embodied knowledge, held in a form that we might call intuition and wisdom. They can use this to explore knowledge bases or they can design experiments to create new knowledge about what they think they need to know. The manufacturing function has a lot of embedded process knowledge along with a great deal of represented knowledge about the rules of the organization.

The challenge for a manager above all is how to identify the proportions of each type of knowledge and, second, what to do with it. Imagine it was possible to somehow quantify the level of intuition within a department and compare it with that held by the competition. This could be the basis of a gap analysis between where we are today and where we need to go. The problem is of course that precise measurements of something like 'intuition' or 'wisdom' are not possible in any meaningful sense. Fortunately, in practice, there is no need to measure in detail. Since we are after some sort of gap analysis what is needed is the relative proportions of all three and what tends to emerge from across different business functions is vastly different proportions of each category of knowledge. So it is not a question of measuring 31 per cent or 32 per cent of a particular category but simply of understanding how these proportions vary. When these are mapped against some ideal or preferred state, the differences against the ideal also vary by huge amounts. For example, if factors like staff retention, training, salary levels in relation to competitive salary levels and rates of innovation are taken into account, the two sets of measures provide a basis for triangulating an organization's position against both its ideal state and in relation to other enterprises.

APPROACHES TO MANAGING KNOWLEDGE PROCESSES

Reckitt & Colman

If you look at what Wal-Mart and Sainsbury's are trying to do – it's not called knowledge management but because of their VMI, ie their vendor managed inventory, they give us access to their own supply chain information in order to make sure we respond to their product needs.

Once the nature of the problem has been identified in terms of the types of knowledge in use and the relative size of the gaps, the second step is to figure out a way of managing knowledge processes better and closing the gaps. Four possible approaches are shown in Figure 7.4.

A common belief in everyday life is that plenty of choice is better than limited choice. To test the validity of that notion in practice, all you have to do is to go back to our example of children choosing ice cream. If a (wise) parent offers them a particular flavour, they will get a quick yes/no decision. If they take the children to an ice cream parlour with dozens of flavours, toppings, cones, wafers and so on they are in a problem environment characterized by combinatorial explosion or, to put it another way, chaos. More scientifically, in relation to knowledge management what is needed is a way of reducing the size of the problem space. We therefore need a working model and a method of procedure.

Most enterprises have huge amounts of knowledge in different guises. Lots of documents, lots of intuition and expertise, numerous databases and piles of paper are building up around the organization. There are some very smart people running around the business and many processes that contain embedded knowledge in them. What can managers do with it?

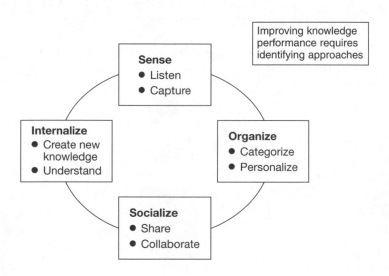

Figure 7.4 *Approaches for managing knowledge processes*

> ## KPMG
>
> There is the idea of a benefit/cost ratio. A lot of people only want to know about something if it is going to make a difference to their bottom line. People should be doing this for themselves but it's not that straightforward. Things that are not prioritized are often left until last.

The following method is not necessarily the only approach but it aims to build systematically, from the ground up, towards an overall prioritization of knowledge issues. It starts by considering the processes by which knowledge might be captured from different sources.

SENSING

Sensing is the technique to use when you have a group of people who are just working with embedded knowledge. To take an extreme example, we might imagine a group of people who never document anything. They can find ways of coping without doing so. The equivalent might be a sort of 'Memory Man' performing on a TV show who tells you how they memorized a telephone book or every last combination of a pack of cards. Basically here you have to depend heavily on mentoring. Listen carefully to what they say about their work and their route to solutions and capture it carefully. It is also important to observe what they do.

There are many documented examples where experts have had difficulty in articulating their own expertise. A well-known example was related to an attempt to automate production in a cheese factory. The systems analysts had to develop a specification for the programmers so they asked the cheese makers how they judged the point at which the cheese was ready to set. They were told it was based on the texture of the cheese. That was quite useful since texture can be determined kinetically. However, one keen observer noticed that every time the cheese makers rolled the cheese between their fingers to feel it, they subsequently smelt the result. It turned out in practice that the smell of the cheese was actually telling the cheese maker more than the feel. In another example, a manager was presented each day with a report containing many tables about the performance of a large hotel on the previous day. When an example of the report was obtained, it was found that it contained around 1,000 numbers. The question was, how did the manager make sense of that quickly? In practice it was discovered that the manager was actually using only 14 of the figures on the page. These compared actual to planned performance for key market segments. Indeed, the problem reduction was even greater since the manager actually ticked or crossed each of these two sets of seven numbers to show over and below plan. Then the manager made operational decisions based on whether there were more ticks or more crosses. In these examples the expert method can be captured and decisions made as to how to manage the knowledge better. In the case of cheese making, careful mentoring would be needed to pass a skill from master to apprentice. Mentoring in this way is used effectively by some leading management consultancies. In the case of the hotel, a different way of capturing and reducing the information presented would probably have been helpful.

ORGANIZING

The hotel manager example illustrates how better report formats and database organization can make a significant difference to the accessibility of knowledge. Many organizations complain of information overload today and of the profligate use of e-mails – why not copy the boss on *everything* I write? Coupled with Internet and Intranet access the sheer volume of information is not doing anything to make the problem of knowledge organization easier. Regulatory issues of all sorts and an increasingly litigious customer group are not helping either. To take one example, a European telephone company was faced with two statutory requirements to retain their year 2000 documentation. First, they had to have an audit trail for every document, along with a record of who provided it, for the last 9 years. Second, they had to keep audit trails of the documents themselves, and how they related to each other, for 20 years. Across a huge telecomms company employing over 60,000 people that was a fairly sizeable requirement. The challenge they faced in organizing and categorizing the knowledge they had was huge. The example underlines the importance of developing an effective content management strategy from the outset and we shall return to this point later.

SOCIALIZING

Socializing is concerned with the sharing of knowledge and collaboration. It is concerned with the culture of the enterprise and how well people work together. There are a number of things you can do to improve sharing. Mentoring and apprenticeships are of course very important to this activity. In a formal sense, management interventions to build teams and a shared set of values are also needed.

INTERNALIZING

Internalizing means examining how you understand what you know already. Internalizing also touches on learning. This is central to a knowledge-based organization, especially if a key differentiator between two enterprises is nothing more than the sum total of what they each know. If that is critical then to stay competitive there is also the issue of how quickly the organization can learn something new. Two stages are involved.

The first stage involves creativity and is concerned with how the enterprise develops new knowledge or discovers new insights. The second involves internalization. The two stages are quite distinct and may not be integrated. The detergent tablet example given earlier illustrates the point. In one organization, the creative stage was there but the internalization stage was not. In the second, new knowledge was internalized and used. This area is particularly important to relationship or transparent marketing. Here, insights are to do with understanding actual consumer behaviour in terms of what people actually do when using a product or service. A responsive organization is then needed to reshape what is offered to provide the value that customers actually seek. Internalizing is therefore to do with putting knowledge into action – leveraging knowledge.

Hewlett-Packard

Yet if you use some kind of lens from knowledge management to look at HP you will actually find many of the practices that would get listed there but they don't appear with those particular labels on them. It's not done very explicitly. There are people in the company who talk about knowledge management and there are people who will run workshops on how we manage knowledge in that part of the business. If you look at where companies talk about where they are making investments in knowledge management these days, they talk about managing their intellectual capital, managing their intellectual property portfolio, using their Intranets to improve their communications across the business. HP does all of these things yet it doesn't label them as knowledge management. These are just normal management practices that happen within the company.

STRATEGY AND INFRASTRUCTURE

KPMG

To that end, we have spent a lot of time, money and energy putting together K-World, which is our fifth generation knowledge management system. Actually, we've always had a knowledge management system. We just didn't call it that in the old days. It is global and will, in the next six months, give any one of our 100,000 employees access to our corporate databases relating to our skills databases, previous client engagements, new approaches, methodologies, client contacts and Internet access.

The strategy that is adopted affects the knowledge management infrastructure that may be put in place. The infrastructure includes the transfer specific mechanisms to ensure that best practice flows throughout the enterprise. These can be placed on a spectrum as shown in Figure 7.5. There are three general design approaches, each of which share some common processes

The self-directed approach seeks to make the technology available and encourage members of the enterprise to use it. The technology may be very simple and for companies starting on a long journey to effective knowledge management this approach may well be recommended, provided it is part of a well-thought-out strategy. For example, a knowledge map or directory can be produced quickly and cheaply on paper. Other tools such as navigation pointers round an Intranet, knowledge databases or even the creation of URL connections on a restricted portion of the corporate Web site are a little more

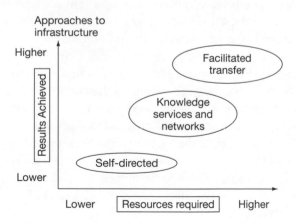

Source: after O'Dell and Grayson, 1998

Figure 7.5 *Knowledge management infrastructure – three approaches*

sophisticated. The key component is eventually the database, the knowledge repository, that is the basic building-block of knowledge management. A series of processes can then be built to surround the database in order to get knowledge in and out. A further important element therefore is locator systems such as pointers or maps that tell people where to find things. At this level of activity the approach is essentially passive and depends on people's willingness to use the system.

The knowledge services and networks approach builds on the first stage by providing a variety of knowledge management services and organized networks to assist in the knowledge transfer process. Thus managers add value by scanning information and organizing it into more digestible and applicable formats. It may also involve networks of people in communities of practice. At this level, services and networks are being incorporated to leverage collective experience and intelligence. The power that may be put behind some of these services should not be overestimated. It may include software tools on PCs, mobile telephones or PDAs. It may also include cataloguing services for gathering knowledge from internal and external sources such as the Internet. It may also involve knowledge services groups comprising of research, analysis and response teams who seek to put members of the enterprise in touch with the relevant knowledge.

The facilitated transfer approach – what the APQC call the first service level – builds on the previous two approaches. It attaches specific responsibilities for knowledge management and dissemination to individuals across the enterprise. These people have an important role not only in holding, capturing and transmitting knowledge but also as change agents. Their job is to help other members of the enterprise improve their problem-solving skills by taking better advantage of the knowledge resources available. In some cases they might act as internal consultants to facilitate implementation. The focus here is in implementation. For example, Amoco have networks of 'excellence' made up of individuals who share common business-related interests. They meet regularly to discuss how they are facing challenges. A knowledge facilitator has an important role to play in these meetings. They must have the leadership and interpersonal skills in order to inspire and to work with people. They must also be knowledgeable about the technical processes involved and should be comfortable with the technology. They will need some training and consulting skills with a considerable tolerance for ambiguity and uncertainty. They may well have their own networks for finding critical knowledge, sharing success stories and for advanced training.

It will be observed that each movement from level to level requires a greater commitment of resources but carries with it the likelihood of a bigger pay back.

MAPPING APPROACHES TO TYPES OF KNOWLEDGE

Ernst & Young

It's not all of the same importance, there are several grades of information. We have something called 'Power Packs' which are the best of the best. They are size-limited collections of information about specific themes or business areas, which have been carefully put together from a range of different sources and repositories, by experts in that field. They offer the most up-to-the-minute, cutting-edge feedback on a topic and would be referred to by consultants when perhaps needing to bring themselves up to speed on a particular area. On top of all the information though, whatever the grade, sits the K-Web search engine, which is very powerful.

In order to develop a matrix, it is now useful to apply the four processes for recording knowledge against knowledge types. This is illustrated in Figure 7.6. For each process it is possible to see which technique might be most appropriate for capturing the knowledge. For example, under sensing it is suggested that embodied knowledge might best be captured through observation, represented knowledge by gathering and collating it together and embedded knowledge by hypothesizing how and where the knowledge is held. When knowledge is organized, embodied knowledge needs to be put into context (where it is used, for whom is it appropriate), represented knowledge should be categorized, and embedded knowledge mapped to processes and products. In the case of socialization, the relevant activities are sharing, disseminating and simulating. The internalization activity for all three types of knowledge is to determine how it might be applied, to understand when and where to use it and then to put it to actual use.

From this matrix, it is now possible to build a decision-making model for managing knowledge processes. Here we have to operationalize or give effect to some of the activities described. For example, what is actually needed to contextualize knowledge? How do we improve what we are observing? Which is the more important of these two areas?

TOOLS AND DECISION MODELS

Ernst & Young

The system currently stores over 800,000 documents, although some information is filtered and is access controlled. No information held on the systems is ever thrown away. It is reviewed and rewritten where necessary. For this purpose, there are special repository managers for each business area.

Approach \ Type	Embodied	Represented	Embedded
Sense	Observe	Gather	Hypothesize
Organize	Contextualize	Categorize	Map
Socialize	Share	Disseminate	Simulate
Internalize	Apply — Decide – Act		

A Strategy for Knowledge

Figure 7.6 *Mapping approaches to types of knowledge – a systematic method for improving business performance*

Once again managers are somewhat spoilt for choice and it is a question of reducing the problem space. It has been estimated that there are between 200 and 300 knowledge-management-related technologies available. These include quantitative techniques like Monte Carlo simulations, qualitative techniques like focus groups and logistical techniques like network analysis or workflow measurement. The aim is to select tools that will support two basic processes, the use of existing knowledge and the creation of new knowledge. When applied optimally, knowledge management should allow better exploitation of existing knowledge (in support of existing operations and supply chain management) as well as faster and better creation of new knowledge in support of innovation. Examples might include:

● Processes and tools for connecting knowledgeable people dispersed over several units, locations and different time regions. The Shell oil corporation funded 150 communities of practice in which instrumentation engineers helped each other to solve problems. They were supported by Web sites, editorial help and facilitation. Processes and tools for corporate-wide accessibility of information about best practices, guidelines, experiences, good ideas, results of teams and projects were deployed. Consultants Arthur Andersen created 'the Knowledge Space', an intranet environment incorporating an enormous wealth of tools and captured experiences of past projects, which can be accessed not only by its employees but also by its customers.

- Learning tools for teams and individuals in order to improve the performance of projects and team activities. These are useful to bring a learning perspective into ways of working. BP's knowledge management team created several tools for team learning, including peer assists, after-action reviews and retrospects.
- Inventories of knowledge areas to answer questions such as 'What are the relationships between processes and key knowledge areas?' 'Which parties/individuals own this knowledge?' These tools focus on knowing what you know and what you don't know, which is a prerequisite for proper strategy formation. Unilever's knowledge development department therefore investigates where knowledge resides in relation to the value chain.

It is quite helpful to populate the matrix shown in Figure 7.6 with examples of the tools that could be employed for each cell. This provides the beginning for some kind of evaluation or measurement which can be used to develop progress milestones. This range of tools is shown in Figure 7.7. Each of the boxes in this matrix represents the start towards building a strategy of what is needed to move the organization forward. If the method of improvement is known, it is possible to apply metrics against its performance.

PowerGen

We want to be sure that if a new graduate enters the organization they can find the relevant papers and ideas easily. So the first thing we've attempted to do is produce both electronic and paper versions of new reports. Then going back in time, we've started to either scan or re-type a lot of documents. From the electronic format, we've then started a system of categorization and cross-referencing, so that you can start to pull out whatever it is you need to help you with a project.

Now that is still, I think, data manipulation rather than knowledge management.

The simplest metric, if not always the most useful, could be return on investment. Each method could be attached to a cost, however imprecise. The lack of precision is associated with the diffuse nature of some of these tools and the time taken to achieve a result. Similarly, each activity can be associated with an outcome, possibly a value such as a higher revenue or a lower cost. However, it is likely that some change in another important measure will be

Type / Approach	Embodied	Represented	Embedded
Sense	**Observe** • Knowledge surveys • Workshops/interviews • Network analysis	**Gather** • Business intelligence • Text and data mining • Intelligent agents	**Hypothesize** • Market/customer/ competitor analysis • Modelling/reasoning tools • Reverse engineering
Organize	**Contextualize** • Focus groups • Expertise guides • Knowledge coordinators	**Categorize** • Knowledge taxonomies • Libraries • Data marts	**Map** • Job/workplace design • Workflow analysis • Performance measures

Socialize	**Share**
	• Mentoring/coaching
	• Communities of practice
	• Conferencing tools/
	  groupware
		Disseminate
		• Broadcast tools/Internet/
		  Intranet/e-mail
		• Distance learning
		• Application systems
			Simulate
			• Scenario planning
			• After-action reviews
			• Training/competency
			  management

Internalize	Apply — Decide – Act		

The KM Matrix

Figure 7.7 *Range of tools used in approaches to knowledge management*

more useful. Famous examples include major oil companies that have saved millions of dollars in investment by avoiding the capital costs of new plants through more effective utilization of internal knowledge. Indeed, one oil company claims to have saved the investment in an entire oil refinery through better utilization of its existing knowledge. Essentially, however, it is a question of considering the standard risk/reward approach. A high risk, in terms of financial or other resource investments, should be matched against a potentially commensurate reward. Higher resource commitments in the expectation of greater returns are associated with higher risks. This is the basis of the final element in the process, the prioritization model. In effect a straightforward table is produced that associates the priority of each knowledge initiative against a return on investment model.

AstraZeneca

I think that the thing that's made some form of knowledge management possible is the development of groupware technologies, like Lotus Notes and the Internet.

Ericsson

You have to recognize that knowledge management support has to be different for the different roles in the organization. One thing I found to be good when I started the knowledge management programme was that we had professional journalists working in our Web group. These people went around interviewing the people involved in the project, writing a weekly newsletter, publishing on the Web site, producing a unit magazine, writing articles. This enabled us to work quickly without having to worry about documenting anything.

PRIORITIZING KNOWLEDGE STRATEGIES

Perhaps the most well-known company for valuing its knowledge assets is Skandia, the Swedish financial services group. Thanks to some pioneering work by Leif Edvinsson, Skandia began the ground-breaking approach of putting its intellectual capital on the books. There are however some difficulties with this method. It is only really possible to put a value on assets for which there is a traded market. Imagine being the first person to ever sell a house. There would not be a market value for it. Indeed, if nobody else understands the word 'house' because in that part of the world everyone calls them igloos or yats then no one will see the need for houses at all. If so, there is no point in putting a value for them on the balance sheet because no one else will be able to recognize it. A scorecard method could be used in an attempt to get around this problem. Nevertheless, what should go on today's corporate balance sheet is the value of managing and exploiting knowledge.

Based on the risk/reward approach described above, Figure 7.8 plots a sample of activities associated with an example of a knowledge management programme. Note that the high priority areas do not necessarily mean that this is where the initiatives will begin. Sometimes it is necessary to put some groundwork in place first. However, with this diagram, managers can see the things they need to do and map those against things which generate value. They can then make a considered decision where to start. These choices should necessarily be aligned with business objectives and future strategic directions.

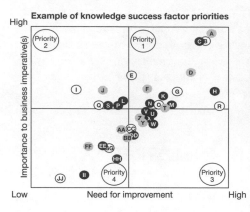

Grey – Business Intelligence Success Factors
Some possible examples include:
- Just-in-time information access
- Reliable organization-wide accessible intellectual capital
- Professionally designed intellectual capital templates
- Defined information management roles
- Professionally designed intranet and extranet page design

White – Organization Success Factors
Some possible examples include:
- Trusting and sharing culture
- Balanced work and learning objectives
- Supportive learning environment
- Results focused teaming process
- Networking encouragement and incentives

Black – Business Innovation Success Factors
Some possible examples include:
- Comprehensive, well-organized Intellectual Capital database
- Environment that facilitates and motivates work
- Technology enabled work flow management
- Priority and time given to capture, codify and manage Intellectual Capital
- Performance measures facilitate strategy goals and objectives

Figure 7.8 *Prioritized success factors associated with differing business imperatives*

SUMMARY

Hewlett-Packard

What we would really like to be able to put on everybody's PC is an icon that is the 'forgettory'. So, if you think that something might be useful you, drag it to the 'forgettory' where it becomes part of a document management system.

The main objective of knowledge management is to arrange, orchestrate and organize an environment in which people are invited and facilitated to apply, develop, share, combine and consolidate knowledge. Primarily it should focus on creating a vision of knowledge and related processes in the business by fostering an environment that supports the creation of smart businesses and ways of working.

Knowledge management needs to focus on the business challenges of the organization, otherwise it becomes the domain of professional hobbyists. The focus should be determined by both the objectives of the organization and the personal objectives of people inside. It needs to be directly related and contribute to such desired results as cost reduction, customer or employee satisfaction and quality.

There is no right or wrong answer to the question of what knowledge is. What is most important is to choose one definition and be consistent in using it. We have chosen to consider knowledge as something that is in people's heads and leads to action. What is made explicit we call information or data but knowledge management is about nurturing embodied or tacit knowledge and making smart use of represented and embedded knowledge at the same time.

Knowledge management is an aspect of the total focus of management in organizations. Knowledge management is not a goal in itself, but mainly a way of looking at reality in organizations to come up with (different) challenges, threats and solutions. Objectives for knowledge management are derived from and rooted in the strategic intentions and ambitions of the whole organization and are formulated in terms of the knowledge processes necessary to support these ambitions.

The discipline of knowledge management has not produced any new instruments by itself. The value of the discipline is in bringing together and creating synergy between knowledge-management-related disciplines and their methods and tools. Primarily, methods and tools are derived from disciplines such as business administration, communication science, organizational psychology, sociology and IT.

The deployment of knowledge management involves a considerable internal process of change in an organization. Roughly 80 per cent of the implementation and realization of knowledge management consists of the familiar problems, pitfalls, risks and conditions known in 'regular' processes of change. Organic growth and new ways of working inspired by knowledge management principles allows change to happen at a realistic speed.

The objectives of knowledge management can differ considerably, both between organizations and between departments. A vision of knowledge management should always take into account the nature of the (relevant part of the) organization and its strategic intentions and ambitions. Therefore there are no blueprints for knowledge management, and corporate-wide knowledge management plans should allow localization as much as possible.

8

Learning and knowledge

BP Amoco

These days we prefer to look at what we call shared learning, which is a term we took on board during our merger with Amoco.

We tend to have some key processes in place which we would call 'capital value processes' which amount really to a series of prompts for use by people when conducting a project, to make sure that they address the vital stages of shared learning where it could bring them advantage.

As it coincided with the merger of BP and Amoco it was decided that learning should be embedded as a personal competency rather than as something which was driven centrally.

LEARNER RESPONSIBILITIES

Earlier we referred to the changing world of knowledge. In Galileo's day, it was possible for a scientist to be the master of all that could be known in a particular scientific discipline. Today it is difficult for universities to teach even a coherent subset of knowledge in some fields during the period of a first degree. This knowledge explosion is one of the driving forces behind the move to lifelong learning and the shift from just-in-case to just-in-time education.

Just-in-time education recognizes that knowledge is expanding faster than it is possible to teach it and underpins the move to continuing professional development and lifelong learning. It is based on the assumption that people will update their knowledge and skills, as required, throughout their working lives. Simultaneously, there has been a marked shift from teaching to learning at all levels of the educational spectrum. A great deal of effort has been made in all areas of learning and training to engage learners in their own knowledge development and to encourage them to participate in the learning process actively. There is a greater recognition of cultural differences, the way in which this affects learning styles and of the differences between individual learners.

In a prescriptive approach to learning, an externally set curriculum is taught and examined by those who decide what needs to be known, imposing it on those who may wish to know. This is certainly efficient but it runs a number of dangers. If the teacher (the prescriber of knowledge) has misunderstood the problem environment, an inappropriate skill set may be shared. It also creates dependence by the learner and may discourage an active search for knowledge.

LIFELONG LEARNING AND KNOWLEDGE MANAGEMENT

Radical departures from the prescriptive approach are certainly worth considering. With due regard to the fact that while classroom-based learning has served humankind well for the last thousand years or so, it evolved in a different technological and social environment. For our purposes there are four main characteristics of knowledge, that may influence the design of a knowledge management programme.

Knowledge as a human capability

We have already noted that the storage medium for knowledge is often people or groups. Information is mediated through the person or the group and the extent to which it is translated into competence, capability, or action depends on that mediation. We recognize this in ordinary speech when we offer to share or transmit information (rather than knowledge). Thus we talk about designing management information systems. We do not usually talk about management knowledge systems or advise people that we are able to provide them with the knowledge they are after, merely with the information.

Andersen

One of the things that we're finding out very strongly as we move into this new e-commerce, Internet-driven type world is that some of the best ideas are coming from the people we just hired, not the people who are at the top of our organization. Those are the people who've been at college for five years, inventing Web sites and figuring out how to sell stuff on the Internet and they often have a great insight into it. Whereas, you know, the 40 and 50 year olds at the top of our organization are people who have to play catch-up with all this technology. So its not surprising they don't try to choose it. They certainly will have all the experience and business knowledge that might be applied in big grown up companies but don't have the sort of innovative ideas that often come from younger people.

Knowledge acquisition is dynamic

This distinction between information and knowledge is important because it means that knowledge management tools do not really manage knowledge but simply help to manipulate it. Whether knowledge is acquired following an information transfer depends on two dynamic factors

The first is a similarity between the current personal context and the context in which the information was acquired. That there are lies, damn lies and statistics is due to the fact that the original context in which data were transformed into information in order to produce statistics may not match the context in which the statistics are to be used or the purpose for which they are needed.

The second is the degree of congruence between the way in which the material is structured and how that may appear to the reader. The receiver of the information may not be able to mediate it in the form of knowledge. Thus, context and structure are highly critical to the acquisition and use of knowledge but of course they are both very subjective constructs.

Knowledge is generative

The possession of knowledge is additive. Given a set of information, the receiver creates knowledge through mediation. Someone looking at a map is able to determine direction and speed required to arrive at a certain place in a certain time. By using other information, he or she may also be able to develop new knowledge, such as whether the sight line from a particular hill will give a view of a famous landmark. This can lead to a decision as to whether to make a journey or not. Knowledge is also elaborate, knowledge is really a plural noun. We talk about a body of knowledge as opposed to a piece of information. It is set in context and related to other knowledge. Whilst it is transferred through artefacts such as books and computers, it is internalized through experience. The expectation is that knowledge, like wine, matures and improves over time. Attempts to accelerate knowledge transfer are generally unsuccessful. If this were possible, the education of young people could be accelerated and compressed into a few years.

Andersen

Now, knowledge sharing can go across different groups. We've got all these organizations springing up out there. There's one called Bright Future.com that is all about trading knowledge between different groups. You can produce a kind of on-line auction of ideas and get people to transact bits of knowledge. It's as if you write your report and stick it in there and say 'This can be mailed for ten dollars a copy or something' and see how many takers you get. If you get none, put it down to seven dollars, whatever. So there's a whole kind of auction. That's only one of the things they do and it has all happened because of the Internet.

Knowledge about work is best acquired through work

A whole field of learning called ethnomethodology has grown up around the practice of learning in work. Knowledge acquired through work comes without the abstraction and restructuring required if the information is presented through a lecture, book, or film. One less translation process means one less layer to deconstruct in order to map the knowledge to individual perspectives.

BP Amoco

The technologists in the organization are really the people who are pushing back the frontiers of shared learning, as they are the ones who have the desire for innovation and operational success.

The technologists are also very quick to catch on to this way of working, possibly because they are familiar with taking risks in their everyday jobs and therefore appreciate the value of shared learning in their decision making processes. They are definitely considered early adopters.

LEARNING AND TRAINING AS A PRODUCT

One of the most critical factors that organizations are facing at the moment is the ability to take their technology and map it against the performance required of the collective organizational competence, from the individuals, teams and communities of practice. For example, if the strategy of the business is to enter a new market or become more innovative, then organizations should be able to map that business strategy to the known competence within the organization, so as to ensure that business objectives are going to be met. In other words, organizational knowledge assets within the workforce must have sufficient capability to meet the business objectives.

The roles of each of the traditional functions in businesses are clearly changing. For example, the education and learning part of the organization, an area traditionally taken on by the training department, is increasingly being considered as part of the delivery mechanism. Enterprises are being asked to deliver capabilities in the form of training and education to make supplier workforces more competent. The former role of the personnel department is now more geared to looking at the competence of individuals. It is now their collective responsibility to recruit, retain and educate the right people. Therefore, the linkage between the human resource department and the training department is basically a lot closer. Learning and training are seen as a product, not as a support function.

What drives all this is the availability of various human resource management systems, like HR SAP and PeopleSoft. These systems are able to map the resources and competences of the organization to the delivery capability of the people within it. So, some departmental roles are changing. Whereas the training department used to have a responsibility to deliver a certain amount of training on a reactive basis, it now has to become a lot more involved with the overall business objectives. The drive for this change has to come very much from the top of the organization. Organizational performance and competency are today discussed in the board room, rather than in conversations between operational managers, although of course both types of executives are deeply interested in the issues. The main point is that the nature of the problem and the challenges presented are being understood at a much higher level.

One of the main issues that must be considered when looking at knowledge and learning is the ability to deliver a set of tools to the knowledge network which will allow individuals, groups and communities of practice to develop their competency levels. They will do this by the acquisition of knowledge and by undergoing distributed learning and training. They must then be able to map that learning back to the original business objectives. So, instead of just going on a course or extracting a piece of knowledge for personal use, everything should now be mapped directly back to the reason why that particular piece of knowledge or understanding was required.

N✱Star

Over the years, we've had very low turnover in our people, so you always had somebody you could tap on the shoulder and get the required answer. Well, more recently, we've lost a lot of those people. So it has become more and more important that we have their documentation captured, as well as their other knowledge. These are things like, 'How do you fix a problem like this?' or, 'Who do you go to if you have a question on that?' This is a form of expert knowledge that wouldn't necessarily be captured in a flowchart. We're certainly realizing that it's going to become important for us to generate this kind of knowledge and also to capture, organize and share it. Whilst I don't think we necessarily want to turn knowledge management into a training programme, we certainly want to get good leverage.

Another aspect to consider is the fact that there have been changes not only in the relationship between different departments within an organization but fundamental changes between individuals within the organization. On the one hand, there are the traditional teams within a department and, on the other, there is the growing concept of communities of practice. Communities of practice effectively cross the organization or cross the various departmental boundaries with common interests and aims. Research is an example of one such trans-enterprise activity.

SHORT-TERM VIRTUAL COMMUNITIES OF PRACTICE

N✱Star

We've had quite a few people leave recently, so we've made some attempt to capture some of the knowledge that those people had before they've walked out the door. L can probably tell you more about that as we've had discussions to try to form an idea of what we're looking for and what our expectations are from knowledge management. One of the things that I've come to realize is that there is quite a diversity, or a number of areas of specialization, within knowledge management and that some people have very different ideas of what it's all about.

147

There is also a growing interest in being able to build up short term virtual communities of practice to solve specific issues and business problems. This seems to be a very powerful concept that is being employed by a number of organizations. These companies have the ability to bring together, very quickly, a diverse but specialist group of individuals to solve a precise business problem. Each of the individuals brings with him or her a complete set of knowledge, learning, skills and competence that collectively enables the group to solve a specific problem. One of the characteristics observed generally is that a community of practice tends to exist in more of a long-term environment. Short-term virtual teams may not have a reason to exist for very long. It might only be a question of days, weeks or a month or two until a solution is achieved. One of the challenges of bringing these short-term virtual teams together to solve business problems is the difficulty of establishing common terms of reference as regards common access to knowledge, training and skills. Companies that have used this approach stress that the virtual team is all about bringing together finance people, project managers, researchers, marketers and so on, into one common arena, such as a groupware discussion forum, to do something like getting a product to market more quickly. The problem is to bring these diverse types of people together and yet get them to establish a common level of under-standing, a common perspective of the problem. This might be achieved by giving them access to a common knowledge database, perhaps sending them on some very short modularized training courses for a few hours or delivering distributed learning (see for example Cothrel and Williams, 1999). The aim is to enable them to understand each other's areas whilst collectively bringing their own knowledge to bear in terms of solving the problem more quickly.

Barclays Bank

I formed a committee two years ago which meets on a monthly basis. The people that sit on that committee are the people that are the real doers, the influencers, the people who can make decisions within the organization. We send the minutes of all the meetings to the heads of the four business divisions and other senior executives that are obviously interested. The knowledge management working party has undoubtedly built on a lot of these strengths.

DIALOGUE AS KNOWLEDGE

Cap Gemini

I guess the most exciting thing that we're doing at the moment is this process of what we called 'controlled experiments'. This involves basically putting together new ideas for knowledge management with central funding and then implementing these in controlled experimental environments, measuring the benefit and then looking at the case for wider implementation and what effect that can have across the organization. I think we currently have six of these running. They are spreading into the rest of the organization through stealth. We are purposely not publicizing them in internal magazines or internal newsletters though we're letting people whisper about them in corridors, spreading enthusiasm that way.

Dialogue knowledge is entailed in person-to-person communication. This is the social glue of most enterprises and refers to any communication, formal or informal, that takes place in the context of work. Dialogue as knowledge takes account of group dynamics that is important in any enterprise that engages more than one person. Any enterprise depends on people working together to achieve its results. If these dynamic attributes of knowledge are taken into account, the problems of knowledge capture and acquisition require the usual careful balance. If the knowledge is related too strongly to a particular context then it may not be perceived as relevant to other contexts. If however the entire context is captured then it becomes harder to distil the essence of learning and to relate it to practical situations.

Dialogue is certainly a better way of capturing the tacit knowledge in a process but whilst most knowledge management programmes are good at capturing the 'what' and 'how,' for obvious reasons they have more difficulty in capturing the 'why'. Indeed, quite often, unless the 'why' is captured close to the point of generation, it may often be lost. This is true even at the personal level. Having got themselves into hot water, individuals frequently have difficulty understanding how they got there when they retrace their steps to try to discover what went wrong and why.

THE NEW CULTURE OF DIALOGUE

Table 8.1 illustrates the co-evolutionary restructures that are needed to underpin learning in a knowledge management programme. The shift is effectively from direction to facilitation where the outcome of the learning process is essentially unknown. For the creation of wealth, the knowledge

Table 8.1 *Restructures needed to underpin a knowledge management programme*

Then	Now	Action
Hierarchy	Who are the leaders?	Redefine leadership
Push–pull	Co-evolution with clients	Understand evolution
Process	Purpose	Create transparency
Failure = bad (negative accountability)	Failure as an asset/ opportunity	Change process through purposeful action
Client focus	Content focus	Share stories of failure
Proactive	Quick reactions	Manage content to extract value
Corporate = good	Different is encouraged	Stop leading and start watching Encourage unauthorized behaviour
Controlling	Directing (as in directing the cast of a play)	State stage, create a vision, choose a cast
Value driven	Value driven	Let value emerge from clear behaviour
Business first	Business knowledge/ balance	Understand parallel knowledge universe
Teams	Communities of practice	Map communities, build new ones
Team leaders	Organizational entrepreneurs	Give entrepreneurs space to operate in
Managing for efficiency	Managing for knowledge formation/growth	Use breakthrough performance to extract productivity not cost-cutting programmes
Executive dining	Café society	Design spaces for knowledge sharing and serendipitous discovery

Source: CBI (1999: 90)

management programme may take off in a number of different directions, since it is a moving process. This is not to say that it is completely out of the control of the enterprise. Direction, values and ideas that shape strategic intent still provide a framework. The knowledge community provides implementation, infrastructure and feedback. They catalyze and use existing knowledge to populate other business areas with expertise and experience. The notion is one of emergence rather than of centralized control.

Hewlett-Packard

It's pretty clear that people working in IT across the company have become involved. They understand the various ideas of intellectual assets and are involved in providing networks and infrastructures that will help support that. You see people working in HR recognizing their role in the knowledge management game, in terms of their ability to foster good knowledge management practices. You also see it being well developed in some other areas such as customer support. I guess to summarize, take-up is variable across the business and it occurs in different ways and via different processes. It tends to happen because of basic cultural traits that run through the company rather than by any clear management direction.

CHANGING EXPECTATIONS

One of the tenets of customer relationship marketing is that customers may form expectations based on one product or service and carry these over to another, entirely different area. If your financial services provider can map your profile against different financial products, why can't your airline reservation service do the same for your travel requirements? From a customer perspective, it does not matter that the problems involved are different. The important thing is that they *seem* the same. A similar effect can be observed in the learning and training area.

The difficulty of trying to map organizational performance to organizational competences tends to rest on the lack of maturity of the various systems and tools that try to link these areas together. To make this work effectively, in terms of acquiring competence and measuring the performance of people, there has to be an easily accessible range of tools that individuals and teams can use to share that particular learning. This extends well beyond the acquisition of skills and knowledge in a classroom, to the much wider issue of knowledge sharing communities. For example, there is a range of electronic performance report systems emerging in the marketplace that promise to deliver context-sensitive knowledge and learning according to the user's job requirements. Traditionally people would have gone into training rooms and used knowledge databases to undertake a very prescriptive curriculum or set of knowledge objectives. This would have provided them with a fairly standardized form of training delivery. It would have been broadly based, designed to meet a range of possible needs and delivered with relatively little customization or personalization. The electronic performance report systems will actually give access to a much broader range of knowledge that is mapped contextually to the problem or the job in hand. So it effectively supports the individual, moving towards an individual's personal information portal in a way that is very relevant to that person. Not only do the electronic performance systems deliver knowledge and learning objects to the individual in the context of the job but they also enable the individual to feed back his or her knowledge, understanding and experiences very easily into the system. This then closes the loop. This whole process means that the knowledge base becomes much more closely correlated to the performance expectations of the business.

THE NEED FOR GREATER SENSITIVITY TO LEARNER NEEDS AND CONTEXTS

In this context, one of the most critical issues in terms of organizational competence is the ability to deliver to the workforce education which is much more learner-sensitive. It has been understood for a long time that there are different learning styles and there are various tools and models to assess people's learning. Several studies have shown that it is quite complex to actually assess an individual's learning style perfectly and then to map out the optimum learning style for that individual. Typically, something like 90–95 per cent of all learning that occurs within an organization is delivered through a classroom. The learner traditionally has not had very much of an option. If the students do not like classroom delivery or if they do not learn well in the classroom, then it is possible for them to emerge from their classes not that much better educated than when they went in. They will certainly be a lot more frustrated however!

One of the most important trends at the moment is the transfer of responsibility for learning and knowledge access from the classroom to the individual. This, in a way, means that the those individuals who prefer self-paced learning are benefiting as much as their colleagues who might prefer tutor-directed learning in the classroom. Indeed, something of a pendulum swing can be observed. For example, since 1999, IBM has delivered 30 per cent of its traditional classroom education in an online environment. It seems that in future this will be the predominant form in terms of learning styles both for commercial reasons and for the effectiveness of learning transfer. This does not mean that training delivery has to go to one extreme or the other. There is still the option to mix and match the three different learning modes, so that people are offered self-paced, one-to-one, or one-to-a-few methods. All of them are workplace-centred, although the classroom itself is progressively becoming less of an influential factor in distributing understanding. Networking and knowledge sharing is now taking place more in network environments than in the classroom, especially where continuing professional development, lifelong learning or mid-career redevelopment are concerned.

Wenger (2000) defined learning as an interplay of experience and competence. The knowledge economy rests on the inclination of individuals to volunteer information. Any system must make it attractive for individuals to put their careers and existing cultures at risk for an unknown reward. The enterprise is the business sponsor of the knowledge project and acts as an entrepreneur with backing from the knowledge team. The social and intellectual capital generated by members of the enterprise feeds into and draws from the knowledge base, evolving into a substantial and sustainable process. The reason people might choose to do this consciously is to grow their own intellectual capital through the taking of measured risks. In doing so they make a political decision as to whether it might produce benefits both personally and for the enterprise. If there is mutual benefit then both parties are inclined to continue the exchange.

Management of the learning environment becomes a question of defining how boundaries are to be set and managed. Whilst this might seem to be a problem, it has actually been going on for centuries. All individuals are already members of a number of communities; these may be social communities, work groups or professional groups. As the member of an enterprise that provides health care services, the surgeon may well exchange knowledge with other surgeons in other health care practices and may not subscribe to the values of his or her own enterprise if they conflict with more deeply held values shared with the professional community. Whilst most knowledge workers are not involved in such critical life and death situations as surgeons on a regular basis, they are making similar sorts of decisions in terms of whether to continue their participation in the enterprise by subscribing to its values. If they withhold knowledge or effort individually or cumulatively, then at the least the enterprise will operate less effectively and at worst it cannot survive.

CULTURAL DIFFERENCES IN LEARNING STYLES

Buckman Labs

The other concern I have is this… Having lived around the world, I see that all cultures have different value systems and these cause a lot of problems. So what I try to do is forget about values and focus on virtues. There are only four:
prudence, ie the ability to make the right decision or the best decision at the time;
temperance, ie shying away from arrogance, egotism, excess;
fortitude, as we all admire someone who has struggled and overcome difficulties, whatever our culture, and, finally;
justice.

From a cultural point of view, there are some fairly obvious national differences, even within Europe. For example, in Germany the culture tends to produce a preference generally for classroom-based delivery. However, in countries like the United States, where people are much more used to learning in a self-directed, self-motivated manner, online delivery is more acceptable. Not only are there country cultural issues, there is potentially a range of other professional issues. Depending on the background or discipline of the individual, he or she may be more or less used to being given a book to read and told to get on with the job of learning. Whilst certain individuals are happy to just get on and read a book or document, others may prefer the communicative 'touchy feely' type approach, and prefer to learn from a tutor or mentor. There are therefore many issues in moving knowledge transfer from the classroom to a knowledge network. In many respects, however, companies are under such a lot of pressure to retrain their workforce or to distribute knowledge rapidly, that the traditional delivery mechanisms can no longer meet their requirements.

CORPORATE MEMORY AND LEARNING

BP Amoco

It really consists of an intranet site which will have the detail, ie the lessons learnt. It will have the verbatim quotes of people talking passionately about the benefits. It will have a dynamic link to people who have the knowledge today via the Connect directory and at the highest level it will link to what you might call the distillation of key learning points. So you'll have all the experience, the war stories, the post-project appraisals and the tools in there. And you'll have the top ten points that we've learnt as an organization about that particular theme.

A further aspect of knowledge and learning is related to the feedback of experience and knowledge into what may be referred to as 'corporate memory'. There is a useful analogy with a thermostat here. A thermostat set at 20°C will always keep a room at 20°C because if the temperature drops it will fire up the heating and bring the room back to the required setting. This is what is known as single loop learning. The interesting challenge for learning is to go into what Senge (1994) called double-loop learning. Taking the thermostat analogy again, this would require a system in place to question whether 20°C was actually the right temperature for the current conditions.

From an organizational point of view, the main issues are the challenge to established ideas about access to knowledge databases. Double-loop learning means that members of the enterprise should question whether what they are currently doing is right. They should not be encouraged to follow a procedure simply because that is company policy or it has always been done in that way. The knowledge management challenge is actually corporate rather than individual learning. There are many documented case studies that relate how organizations have repeated mistakes and errors (sometimes more than once) because they have not learnt from their own mistakes. This is because they have not fed their experiences back into the corporate memory so that, in the future, individuals faced with similar problems can learn to avoid those errors. The whole idea of knowledge management applied through a double-loop learning process is to question all the time whether something is right, wrong, or effective. This is now becoming a good definition of a learning organization, one which questions its processes and practices all the time, in terms of sharing knowledge and sharing experiences.

Learning and knowledge are inextricably linked. This means that any effective knowledge management system must take into account differences between learners and the factors that may affect learning. Most social groups are ethnocentric which is to say that they favour their own culture over others. Everyone is raised in a particular cultural context and it is perfectly natural for us to use our culture as the standard for perceiving, judging and evaluating experience. As the world becomes more globalized and cosmopolitan, it seems likely that ethnocentrism will diminish but whether they recognize it or not, it remains a trait of most people's learning styles. The bad news here is that as a result people tend to devalue other cultures. This can be seen from the fact that in some languages the very word for a foreigner carries some derogatory meaning. For example: the Chinese word for foreigner also means ghost – someone you do not see. The French word also means stranger – someone who is unusual or different.

People in different cultures also have different values. People in some Western cultures such as the United States, Britain, Germany and Holland tend to be quite task-focused at work, whereas in some other cultures, human relationships are considered more important. So in a country like Spain or Mexico, the substance of personal relationships overrides task orientation. It is considered important to know the people with whom you are going to do business or with whom you are going to work. From a knowledge management point of view, this brings us back to the issue of mutual trust. In a relationship-based, trust culture, trust plays a much larger role in either doing business or in learning. This presents some interesting challenges for the design of a knowledge management system that is to be used in a multicultural environment. The basic question at its most extreme therefore, is how should the system deliver knowledge. If it is delivered in the 'wrong way', users of the system may be unable to learn from it. The 'sage on the stage' directive learning style would be very uncomfortable for students who were more accustomed to the 'guide on the side'. The former approach is sometimes referred to as the banking model, where the knowledge base deposits learning in a person's head. The latter is referred to as the midwife model where the system should be designed to help the managers absorb and conceptualize the information themselves. It is therefore useful to take into account some of the design elements that need to be considered.

Prejudice

There is not a great deal to be said about prejudice that is not self-evident. A knowledge system, however well designed, can hardly be expected to overcome prejudices that might have been acquired over years or even centuries. Prejudice is a problem for any enterprise because it is likely to affect the way in which members work together, or the way in which they relate to customers. As a result, if for purely commercial reasons alone, most management groups are concerned to minimize and reduce the effects of prejudice whether it be for reasons of race, gender, ethnic origin, or religion. Basically, this is a question of improving inter-group relationships and reducing the feeling of 'them and us'. When the 'them', whoever they may be, are seen as being more similar to 'us', then dissimilarities are de-emphasized and cooperative working can take place. Ideally, these differences may be seen as a source of advantage through recognizing the benefits of diversity. The best outcome in any inter-group situation is win–win, whether this involves supplier and customer, or manager and manager. Codified forms of knowledge storage tend to neutralize the effects of prejudice somewhat and the problem is more acute in areas to do with coaching and mentoring.

Cross-cultural training

Andersen

When we've got conscious competency then we've arrived. If you imagine a model in which the bottom left hand square is for those who are unconscious incompetence (where you're not good at something and don't even know it) the square above it is conscious incompetence. The square opposite would be conscious competence where you know that you are good at it and the final square in the bottom right is unconscious competence where you know things without really noticing that you are doing them. So it becomes almost a corporate instinct and that's where we're aiming with shared learning.

One approach to reducing prejudice is the use of cross-cultural training. There are four areas of interest:

- unconscious incompetence – when a person offends others but is not aware of having done so;
- conscious incompetence – when the person knows they have made a mistake but does not know what it is;
- conscious competence – when a person learns what to do and how to interpret what the other person is doing but they have to stay on guard all the time to be sure to think and behave correctly;
- unconscious competence – where a person has internalized the thoughts and behaviours that would be appropriate in another culture.

Clearly it is the two areas of incompetence that may require attention by raising awareness and by trying to soften prejudice.

Cultures have many levels and dimensions. It may therefore be useful to give some cultural guidelines in the knowledge base to help users to contextualize it more rapidly. To take a simple example, attitudes to time vary significantly across different cultures. In some cultures, the more important a transaction, the longer it should take. Someone from a Western culture seeking to close a deal quickly in the belief that this will appear efficient and customer responsive may well be sending an entirely opposite message to that which they intended in say, the Middle East, Africa or parts of Asia. In effect they are saying this is not very important, that is why I am dealing with it quickly. It is apparent that communities of practice are invaluable here, since cultural overtones can be discussed informally in a relaxed environment.

Work-related cultural differences

The most famous theorist in this field is Hofstede (1997). He identified four dichotomies that tend to distinguish people from different countries, relevant to the way in which they work and learn.

Power–distance

This refers to the degree of inequality amongst people which the population of a country considers as normal. If the people of a country expect that everyone is relatively equal, there will be a small power distance. This dimension is also relevant to the way in which authority is viewed. People in low power distance cultures such as the United States assume that managers and subordinates should be relatively friendly and informal and should share power and authority. That might encourage openness in the development of the corporate knowledge base. On the other hand, people from such cultures will tend to be more questioning about what is being contributed and by whom. People from high power distance cultures, such as China or Thailand, will presume that authority and expertise are more likely to be invested in more senior members of the enterprise. This means that they are more likely to accept what the knowledge base tells them but are likely to be more inhibited from making contributions if they believe that their views may conflict with those of a superior. They are also less likely to question the knowledge base, even if what it tells them turns out to be misleading.

Individualism–collectivism

This describes the inclination to consider either the individual or group membership as being more important. It broadly contrasts traditional East Asian cultures with current Western cultures. People from collectivist cultures prefer to work in groups and are more effective in groups. This is very good for the team. People from individualist cultures, such as the United States, tend to operate on the unstated assumption that the world is a competitive place and it is up to the individual to get ahead. As a broad generalization, men tend to be more orientated to individualism and women to collectivism. The implications of this distinction are explicit. In an individualist culture there is an emphasis on competition, personal reward and getting ahead by your own efforts. In collectivist cultures, people give more consideration to the effect of their actions on other members of the group and the success of the group is more important than individual success. This makes sense because in a collectivist culture the self only exists in relation to the group, so that family friends and close work colleagues are very important. In these cultures individual rewards are of lesser worth. This can be observed in Asian and Hispanic cultures.

Masculinity–femininity

This refers to beliefs in which social gender roles are expected to be clearly distinct. Men are supposed to be assertive and tough and women are supposed to be modest and tender. This is unrelated to economic development or actual gender. The most masculine culture is Japanese, the most feminine, Swedish. The United States, Japan, Italy, Mexico, Ireland, the UK, Germany and China are masculine cultures and Africa, Central America and North Western Europe tend to be more feminine cultures. In general, people from more feminine cultures are likely to adapt to knowledge-based approaches much more readily and to cooperate in the design and development of systems.

Uncertainty avoidance

This is the extent to which members of a culture may feel threatened by uncertain or unknown situations. People from countries in Latin America, Latin Europe, Germany, Japan and Korea are high on the uncertainty avoidance scale. They are therefore more likely to be uncomfortable with ambiguity and uncertainty. They will tend to prefer specific identified objectives and deadlines. On the other hand, they will also be more comfortable with emotional overtones in learning exchanges. Uncertainty avoidance is also associated with the concept of tightness or looseness. In a very tight culture there are fierce punishments for breaking rules. In a loose culture, deviation from rules is easily tolerated. A culture may be tight or loose in different areas. In general, the tighter the overall culture the more areas in which it is expected to be tight. In a culture which is very tight, the punishments for deviations can be harsh. For example, in Afghanistan, failure to observe the rules can led to death, even for what a Westerner might regard as a minor misdemeanour such as failing to wear a headscarf. In terms of storing knowledge, a tight culture may be more inclined to interpret guidelines as instructions.

Demographic differences

Whilst cross-cultural differences may be relatively easy to grasp, it is sometimes forgotten that important intra-cultural differences can also exist. Cultures can vary quite significantly between one part of the United States and another. Whilst Americans are inclined to regard Europe as a homogeneous cultural region, a European would consider this to be quite an alarming stereotype. Even a small European country such as England would profess to having substantial cultural differences between North and South, East and West.

Taking all these factors into account presents quite a headache for the designer of a knowledge-based system. People from collectivist cultures, or those where power distance is high, may be reluctant to speak up in groups. Those from other cultures could misinterpret this reticence by thinking that such people have nothing to contribute. Questioning, challenging or dissecting knowledge which is held on a database or by a person, may be considered rude and aggressive and therefore unacceptable in some cultures.

In ideographic cultures, such as in China, people have to devote a lot of effort to memorizing characters in order to learn how to read and write. Rote learning and memorization tend to come more easily to members of these cultures than some others. Problem solving approaches may also differ. Some Asian cultures will prefer to work in groups to tackle a problem and may very well find it necessary to appoint someone as a leader and to deal with very specific instructions. A visiting professor at an Irish University found that the students tended to prefer to answer the questions that they wanted to address, rather than those that had been set. They then argued for better grades because the answer to their own preferred question was a good one, even though it did not deal with the problem at hand. The design of the learning and support system may well need to clarify an understanding of the problem, before being able to offer solutions or links in these situations.

Cognitive and learning style differences

At the simplest level, cognitive and learning style differences can be divided between the intuitive and the analytical. Put another way, this refers to the 'splitters' who tend to analyse information logically and break it down into smaller parts and the 'lumpers' who tend to watch for patterns and relationships between parts.

Women are generally more field dependent than men. Field dependence includes an emphasis on relationships, wanting more emotional support, more guidance, more modelling and more constructive feedback. They expect to minimize professional distance and have a preference for a learning delivery which identifies the needs of the learner. Field independent learners tend to accept more easily messages that include instructions and tend to emphasize goals and objective tasks.

Western society is heavily influenced by the Victorian scientific tradition. This 19th century approach emphasizes objectivism, a form of scientific enquiry which seeks to distance the knower from the unknown and to avoid subjectivity. Westerners talk of scientific facts and value them in terms of their objectivity. They tend to distrust magic (intuition) and spirituality in knowledge. Thus in general, Westerners prefer allopathic medicine to homeopathic medicine and although there is a growing recognition that there is more in the world than the Victorian scientific tradition may have revealed, some differences still exist. In particular, Europeans and Americans are more likely to address problems in a linear fashion, whilst Asians and Africans are more inclined to think dialectically.

Of course these are very broad generalizations and are overlaid by other aspects of socialization, value systems and culture. Individuals in any society or culture may not conform to the norm. The key point to be made is that these differences exist and should be taken into account in the design of knowledge management support systems.

SUMMARY

If an effective knowledge management system is to be introduced it must overtly recognize individual differences and preferred learning styles. These individual differences may be influenced by a wide variety of factors. It is difficult to generalize, especially for an enterprise that may be global in scope. It is therefore essential to take these differences into account in the design of the system. It may well be that a learning style or cultural inventory may be used to establish the personal profile of members interacting with the system. This profile can then be employed to determine how the information within the system is organized and presented. In some cases this means that the information should be presented as unambiguously as possible in a strictly linear fashion. The example of a series of bullet points springs to mind (the infamous 'death by PowerPoint' approach). In other instances it may be more appropriate to present a series of discussion points which touch on different aspects of the problem at hand. The aim here would be to help managers to develop their own mind maps, so that they can organize for themselves the way they think various pieces of the problem fit into place. In the final analysis, pushing when you should be pulling can neutralize the benefits of an otherwise well-designed knowledge management system!

9

Technology and knowledge management

THE ROLE OF TECHNOLOGY

Andersen

Certainly, when we started doing it seriously, six or seven years ago, we couldn't use the Internet. So we built our own global technology infrastructure which is extremely stable, extremely well maintained and pretty expensive… I know from talking to clients and also talking to people in other management companies that we are better equipped on this side than most other companies are. I mean, we have reliable global technology infrastructure just in terms of pipes and wires and networks. Also we have a common application platform, which is rolled out to the whole organization so that everybody is using the same tools. Yes, releases are well organized, technical updates and things. We invest a lot of money and our people in that area do a great job in keeping it all running day by day. So as a whole, we don't lose time because the lines go down or because he has Word and she has WordPerfect. We work using common tools and on the same technology platform. I keep emphasizing at every available point that knowledge management is not about technology but at the same time technology is a sort of prerequisite. If you're a big global company and if you don't have technology, it's all going to be pretty difficult.

Sveiby (1997) described IT systems as the hygiene factors of knowledge management. He suggests that the technology can be likened to the bathroom of a house. People will probably be very disinclined to buy a house that does not have a bathroom. On the other hand, the bathroom is generally not the vital differentiating factor in choosing a house. Trying to implement a knowledge management system of any scale without technology is extremely difficult but the technology of itself does not make the knowledge management system work; it can facilitate and enable connections and communications but it will not make them happen. The fact that you may have Lotus Notes on your system, allowing you to share ideas and data with other people, does not mean that you are actually willing to share. Indeed, conversely, the more valuable the knowledge, the less sophisticated the technology that supports it. Take, for example, data warehouses. Data warehouses can be mined using very sophisticated statistical methods but the knowledge they contain is quite low grade. Indeed the best that can be done is to change the data that they hold into information.

PowerGen

We've got the full spectrum. We've got archives which we don't know whether we will use but we're frightened to throw away. We've spent a lot of money in the last three or four years taking things that we saw as useful and working backwards, converting them electronically. I think electronic is the only, ultimate sensible way you can do this because of the interrelationships that exist and the need to sort data. I think the key is to get the data in that electronic data format. However, having a Web site isn't sufficient as you can pass knowledge on verbally; you can pass it via paper-based methods too. I think that all too often people concentrate on the IT solution, when in fact it is a vehicle. Often it becomes the *raison d'être* when in fact is simply an enabler.

On the other hand, helpdesks are primarily driven by people using telephones, very low tech perhaps but they offer a high knowledge value. This is because they are more likely to share tacit knowledge. An intranet, however, can empower sharing efforts by integrating databases and information sources to provide a kind of one-stop shop for information. The intranet will lower communication costs, related to the printing, mailing and processing of documents. It can improve productivity by making information more widely and quickly accessible. It can facilitate higher team productivity by creating a collaborative working environment, allow for rapid implementation of solutions as a result of open protocol standards and, with the right kind of support, make transparent the use of the knowledge base in terms of business objectives. In order to achieve any of these benefits it is very important to ensure that the support requirements for the maintenance of the system are properly resourced and that a strategy for managing content has been implemented.

The ideal characteristics of such an electronic network have been set out by Bob Buckman (O'Dell and Grayson, 1998: 93):

- Keep the number of transfer steps in the transmission of information between individuals to one (or as few as possible) in order to alleviate the potential distortion of knowledge.
- Allow all employees access to the system.
- Allow all employees to make contributions.
- Make the system available from any location, 24 hours a day.
- Have a user-friendly system, able to search key words.
- Allow the users to contribute in their native language and provide the appropriate translation facility.
- Provide a system that updates automatically as information is provided.

The technology support can be divided into two broad classes:

Transfer and exchange systems which refers to databases, document depositories, pointers to expertise, document exchanges and video infrastructure.

Data analysis and performance support which includes data to knowledge conversion systems, data mining decision support and real time intelligent data analysis.

Reckitt & Colman

I would think it would have to be a partly technological and partly cultural advance. Whilst I keep saying that knowledge management is nothing to do with computers, I have to admit that we have the kind of technology around us, eg intranets, which we didn't have 15 years ago. So the availability of this new technology has undoubtedly made life easier by making information more readily and widely available. Technology is by nature an evolving medium and it can only give us better access to whatever it is we want to know in future. However, most people also appreciate that knowledge management is not just a question of technology but of people. So they are beginning to also take notice of the softer issues.

Let's look at the information offered by sales and performance support systems for example. A performance support system allows for real time customer interaction and uses expert systems to support online training and just-in-time learning. Embedded knowledge in these systems is shared through the use of scripts which guide interactions with customers.

The key to sustainability is to establish systems and choose a standardized platform. The importance of a common or shared perspective is a theme which recurs repeatedly in the knowledge management field. Even where information is being exchanged through discussion groups either on a face-to-face or a video basis, it is important to establish shared terms of reference. That means making explicit a defined vocabulary, establishing norms for the conversation in the chat room or discussion area and providing for some form of summarizing or play back to ensure that what has been agreed or discussed is commonly understood by all participants.

Standardization also ensures that there are no islands of expertise that are isolated within the user community. A variety of technologies can be used to achieve this goal, with the overwhelming guideline 'Keep it simple'. If the system is difficult to use, it will not get used. The easiest example to cite here is that of a cheque book. A cheque book contains a lot of information about expenditure patterns. Very rarely do people make use of this information to investigate their own spending habits. In general, the attitude seems to be that the game is not worth the candle, the effort involved is simply too great in terms of the reward. Software which will analyse and balance your cheque book has been available for two or three decades but very few people use it, since a separate, distinct action is required to transfer the data from the cheque book to the software. Perhaps the advent of e-cash will change all this and smart agents, linked to financial services systems, will give helpful advice about how to manage family finances better. Until then, the information sits idle in the cheque book.

Barclays Bank

Years ago, you had experts that just sat inside an organization and nobody knew they were even there. Today, this knowledge is really important to us and we are determined to use all of that expertise within the organization. One of the things we have on our information gateway, is a 'Yellow Pages' database of expertise around the organization. So if people want to do a project or write a paper on benchmarking or some development or training, something like that, they can type in the key word and... pick everybody that has that knowledge. And one of the really good things about that is everybody does their own entry into that database.

The overriding point to make is that above and beyond everything else there is not a piece of technology available that makes you smarter. Indeed, for the foreseeable future, there is no way of plugging a human brain into a nice processor or a smart bit of software. So, from the outset it is clear that technology does not do knowledge management. Technology may make it more fun, it may make it scaleable so that we can collaborate on a global basis but it does not achieve intelligence. From the technology alone there is no performance benefit, other than enabling performance.

Another important point to recognize is that if technology is going to be used, not only is the enterprise going to spend money, perhaps lots of it, but it is also probably going to reduce performance in the short term before a medium- or longer-term improvement is realized. That said, it may be worth considering for a moment whether there is a role for technology anywhere in knowledge management. The answer to that is clearly yes. That role is as an enabler, a tool that allows for scalability and global scope. The technology needs to be positioned in that perspective.

Since first and foremost knowledge management involves working with people and their ideas, what needs to be thought about is what kind of technology will fit with each small community, small grouping or small department as appropriate. It is not sensible to take a broad-brush approach that spans the entire business. This is not a case where one size fits all. It may not be possible to find one intelligent piece of software that is good for database management, sharing, collaboration or communication across an enterprise where different groups and departments may have very different needs.

We have already mentioned White's description in *The Organisation Man* (1957) of being acculturized by a large organization (in his case IBM). White decided to rethink his life when he woke up one morning to find he owned 16 white shirts and 16 pairs of charcoal grey socks, the IBM dress code of the day. IBM as an organization has changed enormously over the 50 years since White wrote his book, but amusingly there was even a comment in the 1998 annual report which shows that the pin-striped suit and starched shirt is still the stereotypical image of the company even today. Yet IBM has been taking its own medicine in knowledge management since about 1993. The company is now the largest software and consultancy company in the world, a startling difference from its earlier role as dependent on sales of hardware for its profitability. Through a better understanding and application of knowledge management across IBM, the company has reduced its internal IT spending by one third. At the same time, the technology that is being used is now a great deal more effective and is making a significant difference to the business. In this case, the technology in question is both material technology (IT, hardware) and social technology (systems and people).

It is apparent therefore that getting the right perspective on the use and deployment of material technology is important as a first step to releasing the potential for knowledge management within an organization. By reference to the knowledge management matrix shown in Figure 7.6, the technology choices can be related to the nature of the knowledge management roles to be supported, and in relation to the priorities assigned. This will vary according to whether you are dealing with a research, accounting, marketing or manufacturing department. In each case, the character of the embodied and the embedded knowledge will be different and so will the aims. There may be a need to share embodied knowledge through mentoring, in which case the role of technology could be focused on learning support. There might be a need to share represented knowledge in the form of procedures so the problem will revolve around getting 'stuff' into databases more effectively.

Therefore the technology choices, going back to the illustration in Figure 7.6, depend on what it is that the enterprise is trying to achieve, *differentially* in different departments. Having determined a direction, this needs to be broken down into its component parts as would be done in any requirements specification. At its lowest level this might translate into a need, for example, to extract elements of explicit knowledge in the form of data from a database, pass it to an e-mail system and connect that with the originators. At the other end of the exercise there would need to be people with the intuitive knowledge to create, say, a document around that. The question then is, who are the people at the other end who are going to perform that task?

PEOPLE-FINDER SYSTEMS

BP Amoco

For example, now we have a kind of corporate 'Yellow Pages' called Connect which lists over 15,000 employees details, specialisms and strengths in a series of home pages, etc.

The sometimes disastrous attractions of starting with a 'Yellow Pages' directory for a knowledge management system have been described earlier. Whilst a 'Yellow Pages exercise' is very valuable if it is correctly positioned and updated, an electronic version of the company telephone directory or organization chart alone does not usually advance enterprise capability very much. Since job titles are relatively cheap in any organization, most bosses and most subordinates happily cooperate in the creation of the most glorious job titles they can contrive. The executive vice-president for environment and ecology could actually be the head cleaner under some circumstances. It must be remembered that if someone is searching for a source of expertise and support, the very act of formal searching means that you do not know who you are looking for. It is therefore necessary to depend on external points of reference.

A people-finder system can help overcome this kind of problem. It is based on two premises. The first is collaboration – people have to want to work together in groups – and the second is disclosure. Disclosure in turn depends on a climate of trust and therefore on the culture of the organization. The basic premise is exchange – if I help you today maybe you will help me tomorrow. Some people worry that giving away personal expertise means giving away power and influence. Some resist asking questions of those outside their own organization. Yet others refuse to put information on a database because they are worried that they will be overwhelmed with requests for help from strangers. Pressure of work is a factor that affects many people's lives and taking on additional roles in the form of a sort of help desk might appear to hinder the achievement of personal goals. At the same time, however, the time invested in the system may well pay off if the effort is reciprocated. The generally accepted approach is to allow members to control the distribution of information about themselves. This tends to overcome a number of anxieties (and some legal issues) so that people can release some data generally or other data, such as, say, a home phone number, to a select group.

To be successful, it is crucial that organizations create and nurture environments where sharing knowledge and helping colleagues across the organization is not only rewarded but assumed. Technology can support those behaviours – but it cannot substitute for them.

We have referred earlier to the problems of corporate churn and a moment's thought will quickly bring to mind the impacts of the mergers such as Exxon and Mobil, Daimler-Benz and Chrysler, or Chase Manhattan and Chemical Bank. There are, of course, many other such partnerships that do not make the headlines. One effect of these partnerships is that social networks are often disrupted through transfers, redundancies and early retirements. There are simply more 'strangers' around. In larger companies, the problem is magnified by both scale and geographic scope. It is sometimes harder to make connections with others in a different state or even country.

People-finder systems serve a number of purposes:

- They help individuals to develop awareness of the background of others in the company.

- They increase awareness of what is going on by revealing which groups people belong to and which activities they are associated with. Some people-finder systems include photographs, which helps put a face (and an association) to a name.
- Other users find that the system helps them tailor their responses to people they have not met, by understanding their position in the company. For example, a new employee might need more information than a long time member of staff.
- They may play a role in creating an efficient internal labour market. Companies undertaking project work, such as those in the construction business, can use the system to assemble project teams more efficiently.
- They act as an important communications tool, not only by keeping people in touch with each other but also by providing the sort of social network that takes place in face-to-face environments. New employees can 'meet' their colleagues in remote locations.

People-finder systems do not necessarily imply the need for new technology. A personnel directory associated with other software applications can do the job. Finding people is part of everyday activities in companies of any size and very important to the effective leveraging of knowledge. This is not only an issue for very large, geographically dispersed organizations. Many companies have reported success with modest systems of a few hundred users and systems have been deployed by companies with as few as 50 employees.

Hewlett-Packard

We have established a contact database on the intranets, something we have called Connex. Anybody can nominate themselves for that, in fact everybody is encouraged. So if you want to find out if a person knows something about a particular topic, you can go to Connex and do a people or skills search.

THE PEOPLE PROFILE

A people-finder system depends on good design. We are therefore back once again into the area of content management. Creating profiles of each member of the enterprise requires careful definition.

An organization's 'Yellow Pages' is a useful starting point. Essentially this is just a basic online employee directory which can then be enhanced by mapping the directory to expertise. This might therefore include:

- Other companies that a person has worked for.
- Professional memberships (maybe with links to the home pages of those professional associations).
- Defined sets of expertise categories such as familiarity with different industry sectors, technologies, or business planning processes. This may require developing or importing a taxonomy – an organized set of concepts or ideas – to represent areas of knowledge. The easiest way to define expertise is to map ratings to those already used, such as job title, seniority, hours of formal training or level on the organizational chart.
- Details of a person's skills. Some companies rate specific skills on a numerical scale. Such systems invariably run up against the problem of determining who has the right to assess a person's skill level.

A number of policy decisions have to be made in the design of such systems. Access to personal information is regulated by data protection legislation in many countries. There is also a certain amount of confidentiality involved. Most of what is openly available is in effect broadcast and does track career movements and other aspects of each individual's work. It is also necessary to decide how the expertise categories should be reported. In some cases these are 'vetted' or approved by more senior managers. Prusak and Davenport (1998) noted a tendency for experts to underrate their abilities and beginners to overrate theirs. Profiles also need to be adaptable to changing conditions and attitudes. As the company's posture and skill base changes, there can be a substantial amount of work to update the people-finder system so that it usefully reflects the new skill-set priorities.

Once the system is implemented, a number of challenges remain. Ratings or descriptions may not adequately reflect a person's competence or willingness to give advice. After all, Dr Smith could be a PhD, a physician, a dentist or a hermit. It is also important to link the system to calendar or appointment systems. There is little point in asking for help from someone who is on vacation. Assessing and representing latent expertise is no simple matter either. For these sort of reasons, people generally prefer to consult local expertise. This also appears to overcome the fear of a potential loss of face that might be involved by seeking advice outside of the immediate work group which introduces some deeper issues. One of the most successful cultural transformation programmes was achieved by the US financial services group Bank One. Bank One grew rapidly in the 1990s, largely by acquisition. It acquired quite a large number of small regional banks, all with their own cultures. It therefore needed to leverage its own expertise and fold in these new acquisitions as effectively as possible. It did this by creating a climate which encouraged managers to seek help and advice from others. Seeking help was portrayed very positively as a strength, recognized in terms of a desire for improvement.

Too rigorous a pruning of the data in the system can be counter productive. Since wisdom in particular is based on (long) experience, it is useful to keep a reasonably long historical track of who has done what and when. Some sort of internal referencing is also helpful. Most companies have a procedure for cross referring enquiries when the key expert is busy or away. Indeed, this is essential as sometimes the relevant expert can change by the hour with shift changes. There is also a need to be able to route things 'up the line' to more senior managers in order to reach the right authority level or to create a broader awareness of a situation.

DIRECT EXPERTISE LOCATORS

AstraZeneca

We've done a number of pieces of work to try and figure it out. In terms of the quality of the stuff itself, I'm sure you can find good stuff. The difficulty is, that there is a lot locked away in different sorts of systems and repositories. We aren't instinctively knowledge management people, so a lot of it doesn't even have a title or an author on it. Anyway, our search engines try to go and find things but quite often they can't even find a title for a lot of the stuff, or a date! Having said that, there are pockets of excellence. For example, we have a document system that works in our regulatory and quality assurance area where, by law, you have to have a complete log of what's happened to that document.

Figure 1.2 illustrates the sort of hits that could be achieved by typing the word 'Bond' into an Internet search engine. Perhaps the volume of hits would not be so large in your people finder, but certainly a quite reasonable request to find someone called Bond could yield a large number of redundant hits. If this were to happen often, people would soon stop using the system. In a face-to-face situation, the communication is much richer than anything that takes place electronically. Even by just looking at the other person, it is possible to tell if they are paying attention, if they are interested in what you are saying, if they understand. The listener can communicate all that without even speaking. If clarification is needed, they can ask or they can repeat their understanding of what your question actually is. In a conversation, given good will on both sides, it is possible to develop a common language of sorts. If the listener does not know the answer to the question, they might usefully suggest where additional help can be found. So starts a chain of connections until an answer is found. Whilst an electronic exchange, even with video support, lacks something of the face-to-face contact, nevertheless, it is possible to see that chain of connections being set up, even for straightforward e-mails. Quite often, an e-mail will contain connections to other e-mail addresses or Web sites. It may contain attachments such as documents or graphic presentations. It might even just tell you who else you should contact in the message. The communication, the network, is growing organically in front of your eyes. This leads to the idea of direct expertise locators.

A direct expertise locator uses search engines where they are relevant. However, results can be improved if the information presented is organized coherently and structured around the interests of your organization. This leads to the concept of using a portal approach. A portal, as the name implies, is a gateway to other information and knowledge sources on an intranet or on the Internet, as indicated in Figure 9.1. It facilitates collaboration and provides a basis for workflow integration.

The lessons to be learnt here are taken from the Internet where there are some excellent examples of generic portals. For knowledge management, the portal must provide information based around what the individual user, or perhaps more usefully, the individual user within the context of an enterprise,

Using community portals in the enterprise can solve distributed knowledge issues – the portal becomes an organizing principle

- A portal is a framework that enables differing levels of Intranet functionality (eg content, applications) and interactivity (eg community) to members based on preferences and business rules

- The benefits of community knowledge portals are a simple Web interface that helps users rapidly sift through Intranet information managed by a large distributed computer network

- Portals provide better 'context' around work activities and add value to existing sites through customized Intranet connections

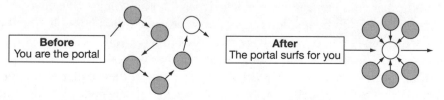

Figure 9.1 *The role of portals in accessing community knowledge*

is interested in. Thus we have seen the emergence of the enterprise information portal. The enterprise information portal has evolved quite rapidly into enterprise knowledge and enterprise community portals as illustrated in Figure 9.2.

The growth in the volume of Web pages is now so enormous that, without a portal, people using the Internet are just being turned loose into the equivalent of a library with a very primitive cataloguing system. Indeed, their situation may even be slightly worse than this because Internet search engines create the illusion of thoroughness. A portal is really that vehicle which first and foremost looks at how information can be organized to suit a user, working in a specific context. This implies that conditions of relevance and timeliness are met. It is possible that without a portal a search engine may yield the right kind of answer, though most Internet users recognize that as a lucky happenstance.

If you were the corporate equivalent of an airline pilot wanting some urgent information about instrument readings just before landing you would need something quickly which is context relevant. The portal uses subscription technology, built around enterprise-selected key words which then filters out the otherwise large volumes of data that a generic search might produce. The portal also takes account of the communities that each subscriber belongs to. It

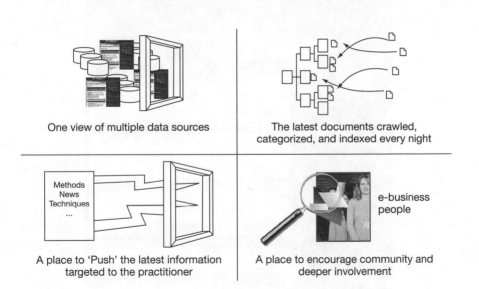

Figure 9.2 *Information provided by knowledge portals*

then provides a place for the communities to focus and it stimulates a deeper involvement in the communities because they become visible. The communities to which any person belongs will change, organically, in terms of their relevance to that person's job at that time, within a given problem space. The portal will also use crawler technology to push as well as pull information and links into the portal. Unlike a standard search engine, it will therefore crawl through intranets and Internets, examining databases and other objects, using natural language key word searches, to find terminology, expressions or people that are working in that area. The filters that it uses can be refined to make these searches more focused and when results are combined with those of other persons in a community, perhaps linked up through the people-finder function, the system turns from a fire hose into a sort of three dimensional map of knowledge sources that is starting to work for the user. Portal technology has advanced into a very significant technological step and, when coupled with advances in the graphical presentation of information, makes a substantial contribution to leveraging knowledge and ideas. An example of a knowledge portal based on the IBM product Raven is shown in Figure 9.3.

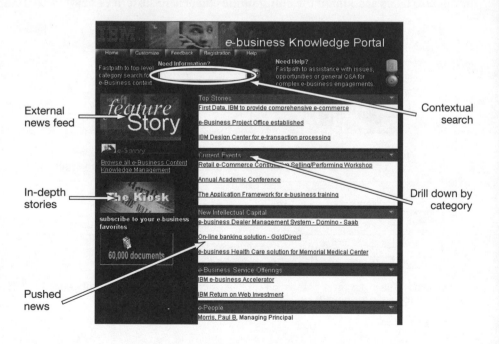

Figure 9.3 *Knowledge portal for the IBM Global Services community*

Andersen

So you look at those two people [analysts and partners] and their needs are clearly completely different. For the analyst, what's important is that the package of knowledge that he has to address a particular task is clear and relevant. That he's got access to someone who can explain things if he has questions and enough context knowledge in order to apply the particular piece of knowledge in the context that he's working. That'll be his needs. Partners would have, perhaps, much more proprietary needs and would need to be able to commission the packaging or customisation of particular knowledge in a different way.

For example, if I'm going to meet with client X, I need all the latest breaking news on that client, so that in the discussion I'm well up with what's happening at their company and the public perception of it. Also I want any intelligence, or internal stuff that we may have access to, that will help to put me in the know. Maybe it will useful to have a career profile of the executives that I'm going to meet. I'd also like to know the history of our own relationship with this client and the work we've done for them. All the knowledge that exists within the company would have to be prepared in a quite a specific way.

So the knowledge that different grades are interested in is different topics and completely different types of knowledge at different levels and it tends to be prepared by different people in the organization with different types of skills. So again it's important to look at the breadth of knowledge management and say, 'Yeah sure, everybody touches knowledge management in the organization, everybody has a need for something but their needs are all very different'.

CONTENT MANAGEMENT

Procter & Gamble

It's not all there at the moment and there's an awful lot of out-of-date stuff. We train people to share but people aren't very good at deleting their knowledge once it's out of date and not useful anymore. It's hard enough getting them to share but getting them to clean up afterwards is almost impossible. That's why we're going for this very structured approach with expert knowledge because it really will be current and up to date.

Content management is a major factor in the more efficient management of knowledge. In some ways it is the key that unlocks the door to the sharing of knowledge. It is a behind-the-scenes enabler. Done well, nobody knows it is happening. Done badly, nothing works and people turn away from the knowledge systems because they are too muddled, out of date, irrelevant or simply inaccurate.

Lawrence and Giles(1999) of the NEC Research Institute state that:

Redefined by e-business, content management involves the collection, management and electronic distribution of all forms of business information – including documents, e-mails, audio, video and images – and linking it to core business processes.

With corporate data doubling every 6–8 months and Intranets deployed in more than 90 per cent of major companies, it is increasingly important for companies to leverage the complete spectrum of data assets within their enterprise and share it electronically among suppliers, customers, partners and employees.

Content management identifies and defines the types of content, how the content is stored, maintained, published and distributed.

Content management organizes content in terms of owners/creators, content life cycle and implements security measures.

The content to be managed might be held in a wide variety of forms ranging from ordinary documents through to images, video and audio clips. As anyone who works in an organization will know, despite the ubiquitous use of PCs and other computers, the amount of paper generated in a week even by an individual quickly mounts up. Electronic communications have actually only added to that as people copy their e-mails to others. It might almost be imagined that there is a kind of corporate game here. Since electronic copies are so easy, you might as well copy an e-mail to everyone you can think of. This both overwhelms the recipients' in-box (so they start to disregard some messages) and allows the originator to state correctly that everyone was informed when a decision was taken.

Nokia

Basically, because of the 'page owner' system then we have practically no old documentation on the Intranet. To my understanding that's not a problem.

THE PURPOSE OF CONTENT MANAGEMENT

The problem of organizing content has to be looked at in two dimensions. The first concerns the person who is hoping to access the knowledge, the second organizational flow and the form in which information and data are held. In turn, these require a consideration of both the technology being used to store and circulate information and the skills and behaviours needed to use it. This mix of purposes, technologies and attributes is illustrated in Table 9.1.

A knowledge management initiative that only addresses one or two of the quadrants in Table 9.1 is unlikely to be successful because it will overlook the balance needed in the other sections. For example, if individual uses of information are not considered, the question of how people will add value to information would be missed. Providing e-mail or videoconferencing systems raises questions of access and training. The skills of note-taking and synthesizing are not as universal as might be imagined and this is an area where training will help. Over and above all these is the question of organization culture, sending the right kind of signals from the top of the organization.

The primary objective of content management is to help improve the quality of decision making based on managing the content behind the portal interface. Content management labels and defines types of content which then determines how it is stored and accessed. The labelling identifies the source and the context of the information being stored. However it is useful to go back briefly

Table 9.1 *Individual uses of information and organizational flow*

	Individual Uses of Information and Knowledge by People	**Flow of information and Knowledge within the Organization**
Technology	● Search engines ● e-mail filters ● Intelligent agents ● Information visualization ● Push technology from the portal	● e-mail ● Intranets and groupware ● Electronic bulletin boards ● e-yellow pages ● Videoconferencing
Skills and behaviours	● Filtering out overload ● Reading and note-taking ● Analysis and synthesis ● Making effective decisions ● Communication skills	● Organizational culture ● Propensity to share ● Teamwork and team objectives ● Group processes ● Facilitation skills

Source: Dawson (2000: 75)

and revisit one of the ideas that is central to the success or failure of the knowledge management system. Quite simply, however well knowledge is stored, if it is not used, for whatever reason, the system will fail. An example was given earlier of ineffective practice but the point is easily illustrated by a common corporate practice. Essentially this involves putting policy manuals and procedures on the Intranet in electronic form. There seems to be a belief that, say, the HR manual, that nobody ever reads when it is circulated on paper will somehow become attractive when its contents are presented as electrons. However, unread on paper it will be unread electronically unless the content of the communication is changed. An electronic document is not the same as a paper document. To begin with, electronic documents are presented in the form of Sumerian scrolls, a technology that was superseded by books in about the 4th century. It is hard to read from a scroll. On the other hand, an electronic document can do a lot more than its paper alternate. It can be self-indexing, it can be searched more quickly, it can cross-reference to other sources more quickly, it can suggest other, relevant topics to the one being examined, it can present itself in a variety of languages and forms at the choice of the user. The job of content management is therefore to ensure that 'slow dull' does not just become 'fast dull'. The materials must be organized so that users are attracted to them and encouraged, by good results, to use them. In other words, content management is about marketing. The objectives of content management are to:

- Improve the quality of decision making based on common understanding of information.
- Improve office productivity/efficiency through electronic facilities.
- Extend the reach, quality and value of information.
- Improve customer service/responsiveness.
- Capture and share corporate knowledge.
- Reduce cycle times and times to market.
- Improve regulatory compliance.
- Use 'best practice' processes.

THE IMPORTANCE OF CONTENT MANAGEMENT

PowerGen

OK, I would say that our electronic systems are the most useful and are certainly now the most used. I believe them to be accurate but I'm not sure I can prove that everything that we know is on there… But we're working towards full coverage. The trouble is, it is such a labour intensive task to convert and it's not exactly a stimulating task. Those are your two problems. People become bored. Somebody needs to be either very dedicated or have a particular mindset to actually do the job well. But whenever I sample the databases, I'm reasonably happy with what turns up.

Swiss Re

One of the main problems we have is that we often have the right information or knowledge but we don't know where it is always. It could be on any one of 2,000 Lotus Notes databases. But we not just interested in accessing data. We also want to be able to identify people who are interested in the same topics and to make connections with them. So, we're certainly trying to do something around putting a tool over the top of all these 2,000 databases.

Figure 9.4 illustrates the rapidly growing importance of content management as a discipline within knowledge management. The problem has to be considered in relation to the different characteristics of the communication channels by which knowledge may be transferred. Some of these have been around for a while, others are quite new.

Digital convergence is encouraging organizations to hold increasing amounts of data electronically but however fast the technology might change, people still tend to hold and transfer quite large amounts of information in traditional ways. The content management exercise is analogous to the contact management problem in relationship marketing. A customer might touch an organization in a variety of ways, in person, by letter, by fax, by e-mail, through a friend, on the phone and so on. Yet, despite perhaps the enormous size of the organization with which they are working, they will expect everyone with whom they deal to have knowledge of their problems and concerns. So it is with content management. Despite the fact that knowledge may be generated in a variety of forms, the requirement – perhaps even the ideal – is to draw all these different sources together so as to leverage the expertise they contain.

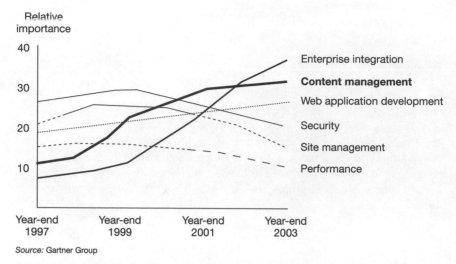

Source: Gartner Group

'. . . research indicates that the content management market is expected to exceed US $10 billion by 2004. Companies are beginning to demand greater management capabilities for a wide variety of digital formats.'

META Group

Figure 9.4 *The importance of content management*

Table 9.2 illustrates some of the knowledge transfer capabilities of different communications. In this table, the term bandwidth refers to the amount of information that can be communicated in a given period by the channel. It is one of the most important issues in knowledge transfer and is an essential element of media richness, certainly in terms of its ability to achieve changed understanding. The more communication channels used, the broader the total bandwidth.

Knowledge sharing and transfer depends on communication, so the channels by which transfer takes place must be managed. Content management aims to ensure that features such as interactivity, bandwidth, structure and reusability are considered so as to facilitate the transfer of knowledge. Whilst content management is also concerned with the important task of indexing knowledge, so as to ensure relevance, reliability and currency, it must also take account of the portfolio of communications by which information should be harvested and shared. Digital channels are of course becoming more important because these technologies lend themselves to easier management, but it is important not to disregard other important forms of transfer such as say, coaching and mentoring when designing the content management system. Figure 9.5 illustrates the architectural approach required.

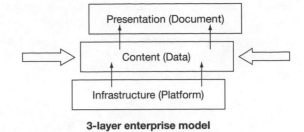

The architecture requires processes to be in place, which ensure integration between business objectives and the supporting technology

3-layer enterprise model

Figure 9.5 *Architectural approach to content management.*

Swiss Re

We have put in place a number of knowledge managers whose role it is to review documents and we hope this will help improve the accuracy and relevance of everything on the system. In terms of recency, when we're talking about our knowledge community database, we have an automatic review every six months. We felt that this was particularly important for the knowledge community because it was our first try at a global depository, where contributions are made by people who have not yet met one another. So, every six months, the author of a document has to go back and say whether or not it's still appropriate, before resubmitting it for review to a knowledge manager. We also encourage users of the database to post feedback on documents. Interestingly, we've been thinking about the fact that you might find that some documents on the system from the UK are very old because the market has moved on and the documentation has been replaced by more up to date findings.

Table 9.2 Knowledge transfer capabilities of different media

	Interactivity	**Bandwidth**	**Structure**	**Reusability**
Documents	Nil	Low	High	High
e-mail	Medium	Low-Medium	High	High
Phone	High	Medium	Low	Low
Meetings	Very High	Very High	Low-Medium	Low
Presentations	Medium	High	High	Low-Medium
Workshops	Very High	Very High	Medium	Low
Computer-based Training	Medium	Low-Medium	High	High
Coaching	Very High	Very High	Low	Very Low

Source: based on Dawson (2000)

The task is clearly substantial for organizations of any size and to assist with it there are a number of tools and technologies on the market, such as Professional Content Manager. These tools are designed to organize a variety of media ranging from simple text documents, through to images, e-mails, Web pages, audio files and video clips.

Ericsson

We do get too much information. Often you have an idea of where to get information but not a detailed view. You do not get 100 per cent accuracy in the system but it can give you enough to move into the right direction. We do have a local updating process but it is difficult to keep date recording up to date. People have many tasks to do in each day and something like knowledge management can be easily forgotten about. Often, you only update what is on top of your thoughts.

SUMMARY

Knowledge management systems do not necessarily imply the need for new technology. For example, people finder systems do not have to be designed around a technology or even for that specific purpose. At a pinch, personnel directories associated with other software applications can help people make the connections they need. However, to be successful, it is crucial that organizations create and nurture environments where sharing knowledge and helping colleagues across the organization is not only rewarded but assumed. Technology can support those behaviours but it cannot substitute for them. The hard work is the process of cultural engineering that needs to take place alongside the technical development. If the organization has the right kind of culture and systemic processes then adding automated tools is easy. However, people within the organization have to be prepared to engage in collaboration and sharing

BP Amoco

There's nothing maliciously wrong with the information, it's just that in terms of accuracy, some of the information is three or four years old and it is still there because nobody knows who owns it anymore. A lot of our stuff doesn't have owners or expiry dates or even creation dates. We have some material which is graphically quite clever but its content is actually quite boring and it doesn't really develop your thinking greatly. There are also some issues around gate-keeping because the tools which place your content on the Web aren't easy to use and therefore you often get a personal perspective rather than a team view.

People-finder systems can help individuals develop awareness of the background of others in the company and can link people who might never have an opportunity to meet face to face especially when employees are far away from home base. Such social networks are powerful mechanisms for transferring and translating latent knowledge through the organization. They have been called the 'central nervous system' that kicks in when unexpected problems arise. They can however be very brittle, especially in fast-moving business environments. They are very difficult to scale up for large organizations since, as informal structures, they are often *ad hoc*.

Organizations can and should be structured to foster the transfer and sharing of knowledge and this requires a consideration of both the technologies and the social networks. Disregarding part of the interaction between these two elements can substantially reduce the effectiveness of knowledge sharing.

Barclays Bank

So, it's about the integrity of the data. It's also important that we value the information we keep and continually review it to keep it valuable. The way we have organized the system means that when you go on to a particular Intranet site, everything is pulled together and you are aware that there is an owner for each particular page or document. This person is responsible for ensuring that all information on that page or whatever is maintained as current and relevant.

Organizations need somehow to make the knowledge exchanges between social networks more systematic. It is the function of content management to organize different information and knowledge sources so that they can be inventoried and accessed. If content is well organized and accessible, technology in the form of people finder systems can strengthen social networks and increase the probability of making valuable connections between members of an organization. However, the technology must be combined with sensitivity to both personal and organizational issues if innovation, responsiveness, productivity and competence are to be improved.

Reckitt & Colman

It fits into an overall management strategy. People have to be incentivized to share and, in the same way, they have to be disincentivized not to share. The strongest direction would be for the CEO to say in a document that he wants everyone to share information and then sack somebody when he realized that they had concealed it! It's not nice but it would be effective. Lots of initiatives fail because people on the ground say, 'That looks like a very good idea' but people in the middle just want to stay the same and do nothing about it. In that instance, it should be for senior management to ask the middle men to pull their fingers out and adopt these new methods or move on. So if we do start to adopt knowledge management in a more formal way at Reckitt, then we need to make sure that we reward people whose ideas go on to make money for the company, in the most tangible ways possible; through performance appraisal and ending up with promotion and financial incentive.

10

Measurement and evaluation

In theory, there's no difference between theory and practice but in practice, there is.

Carter Brooks

Any business manager can relate to the need for measurement. It is almost axiomatic in management that what you cannot measure you cannot manage. So perhaps we should start looking at measurement by creating a measure. It is possible to create a metric which will determine, albeit crudely, the degree to which your organization might respond to a knowledge management initiative. Award a score out of 10 for your company on each of the following parameters, weighted as follows:

- Technology – weighted as 1.
- Culture – weighted as 2.
- Economics – weighted as 3.
- Politics – weighted as 4.

So, for example, if the enterprise is fully networked, has all the latest groupware and provides access to its knowledge base around the world for all enterprise members, customers and many alliances, it might score 10 for technology. If the technology is largely used for e-mails and the chief executive uses a secretary to print them before they are read, it might score 2 for culture. The score of 2 with a weight of 2 would give a subtotal of 4. Similarly, an evaluation would be given against economics in terms of market share and market dominance. Finally, an assessment could be made of trust, openness and commitment to sharing, under politics. As a rule of thumb, scores below 60 would be poor, between 61 and 80 fair and scores of 80 and above indicate a greater likelihood of success for knowledge management initiatives.

Of course, the actual score does not mean anything 53 per cent is not especially different from, say, 55 per cent but the valuation does at least give an overall assessment of position and, in a broad sense, is probably quite fair. This exercise does demonstrate three aspects of the measurement and evaluation of knowledge management programmes. First, it is possible to develop metrics. Second, they are not very precise, they are highly contextual and depend very much on their value to the individual. Third, they are to some extent necessary. It is actually useful to have some way of assessing whether such a programme would have worth or, in this case, get some kind of idea of the stage your company is at in terms of its knowledge management.

Cap Gemini

We have reward mechanisms for excellence and best practice called OTACE (On Time Above Customer Expectation). [OTACE] is a customer measure of our reuse or re-application of best practice. It's a very valuable way of measuring that we are delivering the right solutions to clients.

The basis for the measurement and evaluation of knowledge owes its origins to the work of Leif Edvinsson at Skandia. Putting knowledge as an addendum to the company's balance sheet was always a troubled issue because a balance sheet is an auditable, accounting record designed to measure visible assets. In the public domain, it also purports to affirm that the calculations behind the accounts have been measured and audited by independent accountants. The assets are transferable from one set of accounts to another. By seeking to put knowledge on the balance sheet there seems to be a suggestion that two people, taking independent views, would value something as intangible as wisdom or intuition in the same way. That is very hard to achieve. For example, take any newspaper headline and offer it to six different people, asking each one what they make of it. Quite possibly there will be six different interpretations and six different answers. That sort of evaluation cannot be part of a balance sheet. The Skandia experiment really could not progress much beyond the level of an experiment because the approach used was not really transferable. It worked in the context of one, individual company.

BP Amoco

Similarly, financial considerations don't block our way.

Yes, we do undertake some financial measures but I personally don't think that this is the most important or accurate way to reflect the success or otherwise of the activity.

ASSESSING INTELLECTUAL CAPITAL

The approach pioneered by financial services group Skandia can be summarized in six major phases.

- Missionary. The first step is to articulate a deeper understanding of the hidden capabilities within the enterprise and the contribution that they make to greater future value for shareholders and other stakeholders. This is achieved by establishing a systematic taxonomy that helps to make visible the intangibles. It is also achieved by metaphors, such as a knowledge tree, where nourishment of the roots is considered more important for the future than harvesting of the fruits for today. This then requires the development of a series of metrics to describe the position, evolution, velocity and direction of the hidden capabilities. In Skandia this is done by report format called a Skandia Navigator.
- Financial focus. This looks at conventional areas such as return on investment and operating outturns but also calculates a financial outcome for value added per employee.
- Customer focus. Again, this starts with some straightforward measures of things like number of contracts sold and proportion of insurance policies surrendered (a measure of retention) but also looks at items such as telephone accessibility, number of points of sale and customer satisfaction.
- Human focus. Following a count of number of employees, managers and women as a proportion of the management team, this considers employee profile in terms of age and numbers and also training expenditure and number of training days per year.
- Process focus. This is concerned with number of contracts per employee, administrative costs per employee, number of IT employees as a proportion of total employees and IT expenditure as a proportion of administrative costs.
- Renewal and development focus. This looks at trends in performance, the values in the claims assessment system and the number of new ideas filed with the central group, the share of staff under 40 years of age.

Every six months the company publishes on the Internet an intellectual capital index. Skandia uses a system called Dolphin which allows senior managers to navigate the organization electronically through PCs, in order to nurture future earning capabilities based on the following intellectual capital themes:

- Technology – to develop the structural capital of human capabilities. Technology is regarded as one of the most essential multipliers for productivity, helping to package, recycle, distribute and trade on human skill. Technology is seen as the tool for participating in the global digital economy.
- Capital – the creation of value from intellectual property can be achieved by trading on patents, trademarks, copyrights and new ideas. The aim is to discover how to package the human capabilities into structural capital as well as to look for alliances with others to leverage this structure.
- Future – to amplify and embody the leadership and management efforts towards future capabilities, Skandia have established a number of future centres with the theme of turning the future into an asset. The first future centre was inaugurated in Sweden in May 1996 and it has attracted more than 5,000 visitors.

THE VALUE OF INTELLECTUAL CAPITAL

Intellectual capital has always existed but an explicit recognition of its importance to business is a relatively new phenomenon. This is because other, more traditional sources of competitive advantage are increasingly open to substitution and copying. Capital markets have recognized this trend by placing substantial premia on companies with demonstrable intellectual assets.

Nokia

Out there in the market there is really only one market price but here there are many available functions, which customers might pay for. In order to be able to develop this functionality you need superior knowledge.

Further impetus will come from regulators who are placing a responsibility on directors to establish a system of controls for all the assets of their business, not just the financial ones.

Rolls-Royce

I would argue that whilst sharing knowledge may cost us time and money initially, it will pay back handsomely in the long run. We can see this manifesting itself in the various quality issues that we have had in our design processes.

The gap between the market value of a company and its tangible net assets is now often so wide that investors have become more concerned about each company's intangible assets and its relative strengths. When the gap was small, investors could see that assets, or at least a reasonable expectation of future income streams, basically backed their investment. If the company were to fold, the assets could be realized and value could be returned. Assets in the form of brands or knowledge are much more difficult to realize and much more vulnerable. At the same time, it is harder for investors to take comfort from press releases by brokers about the value of patents or the future revenue stream from new knowledge initiatives, in the absence of consistent and reliable measures to value them. It has been suggested (Powell, 1999), that real value is a function of two factors, raw value multiplied by robustness. It is useful to consider these two elements.

MEASURES OF RAW VALUE

Originally, the difference between the value of assets and the value of the company was described as goodwill. Subsequently, this has expanded to take account of, for example, undervalued tangible assets or purchased intangibles such as brands. There were also methods used to help estimate the greater earning power following a merger or acquisition. As intellectual capital came to the fore, measures were developed to monitor three underlying assets:

- Human capital – the documented skills and experience of the staff.
- Structural capital – patents owned or pending, the infrastructure, 'everything that remains in the company after the office is closed'.
- Customer capital – the history of customer relationships in place, the value of the customer base in relationship marketing terms.

> ## Andersen
>
> However, I think that you've got to do it as best you can. You've got to link what you do with knowledge management, to whether the organization can sell more work or generate more business, whether it can be more productive or lower costs. Whether it can innovate or get into new markets faster. All these kind of hard business measures have to be used and you have to try to make some deductions between the effort you put into knowledge management and your performance across key indicators.

The methods employed can be divided between those with an accounting basis, such as Tobins Q or EVA, and those with an indicator basis, such as the balanced score card, and various tools such as navigators or monitors. These approaches have tended to focus on the visible or content components of assets, ie those aspects that can be counted or valued. This is essentially a static and historical view of intellectual capital. It is not very useful if the assets are very vulnerable – for example if the expertise of a group of employees can quickly be lost.

ROBUSTNESS IN INTELLECTUAL ASSETS

It is therefore useful to attach a value that cannot be affected by factors beyond the company's control, for example, the risk that a competitor might develop a better patent or that a rival might poach a key employee. The resilience of intellectual assets is therefore dependent on the relationship they have with the company:

- Human capital. The biggest question here is how well is this asset managed. Measures associated with job satisfaction or morale might be employed. Some account might be taken of the care and effort that is put into maintaining staff relationships or even attempts to lock in staff by means of loyalty bonuses.
- Structural capital. The enterprise derives value from the basic quality of its structural elements in the way that they work together. This is based on how the elements fit together in a process or a technology and how those operating the process or the technology cooperate – for example when an outsourcing contract that is taken back in-house because of poor cooperation between the parent and the outsourcer. Again, therefore, there is a key relational aspect to realizing the maximum potential value from structural elements.

- Customer capital. The importance of customer relationships is now recognized as a primary marketing focus. Measures here could be those used to evaluate the progress of any relationship marketing programme in terms of customer satisfaction, customer loyalty, lifetime value, cross-selling and up-selling.

Swiss Re

There are also some discussions going on at group level around measurement and evaluation. It seems to focus on two elements. Measuring intellectual capital and measuring the success rate of knowledge management projects. But they both seem to be coming up with the same difficulty regarding accurate and valid measurement. We haven't got that one cracked yet!

The Relationships Foundation was one of the pioneers of metrics which looked at relationships within the organization. Having first published a book, *The R-Factor*, to test their applicability to public and private organizations, they then designed a series of tools, along with consultants KPMG, to look at the robustness of relationships and to identify ways in which they can be improved. Accounting bodies and governments are increasingly exploring ways to report intellectual capital. The Danish Government has already moved to define national standards for intellectual capital account statements and the Canadian Institute of Chartered Accountants has produced a Canadian performance reporting initiative. It is clear that there is some way to go in establishing relationship measures of robustness but there is wide support for these initiatives in the business, investment and regulatory communities.

TARGETING KNOWLEDGE MANAGEMENT APPLICATIONS

KPMG

I think there will be two things, recognition that knowledge management is here with us to stay and recognition that it needs to become embedded in organizational processes in the same way that quality assurance has been accepted and incorporated as a common sense course of action. I also believe that IP value will be recognized . That is, that intangibles such as an organization's tacit knowledge and expertise will have an impact on its market valuation.

CRITICAL FACTORS IN TARGETING AND MEASUREMENT

Buckman Labs

You could have 10 Nobel prize winners within your organization but if they're not sharing their knowledge, they're worth nothing. The thing about intellectual capital is that it's different to normal capital. Intellectual capital actually appreciates through use.

Teltech Resource Corporation of Minneapolis studied 93 knowledge management applications in 83 different companies (Hildebrand, 1999). Based on factors such as the demonstration of realized benefits, comparative usage levels, trends and levels of advocacy and enthusiasm, they divided these projects into high, medium and low impact, according to the effect on business performance. Of the projects studied 45 per cent were intended to generate revenue; 35 per cent contained expenditure; 10 per cent were to enhance customer service; 6 per cent to improve quality; and 4 per cent were to refine internal processes. Teltech identified five key criteria which will help to increase the impact of the knowledge management project on enterprise performance:

- Target business critical areas. Nearly half the projects that fell into the high impact category were not labelled by the term knowledge management. Essentially they were focused on business issues and were solving business problems by managing knowledge. The common theme was a measurable business outcome.
- Research the problem to be addressed. This requires that you develop a strategic framework for solving the problem before you begin the search for a solution. Three-quarters of the high impact applications in the study were based on advanced planning. In each case there was a well-defined business goal and a clear strategy.
- Organize content. Teltech identified two primary methods for organizing and transferring content. The first was the storehouse model, using a database. The second was the pointer model, by which users are directed to a source of knowledge. As we have observed, this does not always require technology, it is essentially more efficient networking. The enterprises found to be most effective at organizing and transferring knowledge used both methods. The storehouse method employed alone had much lower levels of success. Similarly, even pointer models had less success if they were not used in association with knowledge repositories. It was the inter-action between the two that proved critical. Once a person has retrieved

information from the storehouse, knowing what step to take next, or who next to ask for advice, transforms performance.

Ericsson

We have been driving the measurement of intellectual capital for at least 10 years. We are running a knowledge management programme and looking at the measurement of intangible assets, ie paying attention to the intangible value created within our businesses.

- Invest in content maintenance. 84 per cent of high impact applications were associated with a continuing investment in content creation and maintenance. This requires two types of people – subject matter experts to decide what goes into the content and librarians to extract, organize and manage the content. Unless the information is properly farmed and harvested, it cannot support growth.
- Recognize that knowledge means change.

Hewlett-Packard

HP is operating in a very advanced market, in a very competitive industry. So there is a real orientation towards the new, towards discovery, toward sharing around here. There is probably more emphasis on this innovative kind of activity than there is on capturing intellectual property. In fact, I think there is less emphasis on capturing intellectual property because there is recognition that things degrade very, very quickly.

Nearly three-quarters of the high impact projects were supported by explicit change management efforts, such as user training, usage promotion and programmes to recognize and reward the use of the application. None of the low impact applications had incorporated any kind of change management measures. The important thing to remember is that in terms of a process, what is being sought is a shifting of culture. A knowledge management programme depends for its success on people and it is therefore vital to ensure that new roles and responsibilities are made apparent.

Siemens

I think you can make a judgement as to whether knowledge management was a major contributor to the success of an activity or in the achievement of a target. The way we have devised our business plan, all knowledge management targets are optional and incentivized but next year they are obligatory and I will only be paid my full salary if I can show that we have made the required savings and additional revenue streams.

THE VALUE OF KNOWLEDGE

One of the main attributes of knowledge is context. Knowing the names of all the kings and queens of England is probably not much use until, one day, you happen to be on a quiz show where that is the US $64,000 question. At that moment, this particular piece of knowledge has great value. In fact, you can attach an exact value to it at that point – failure to remember the names will cost you US $64,000. Outside the context of the quiz show, to all intents and purposes, the list of names is not worth very much. It just clutters your memory. The same principal can be applied to the valuation of knowledge generally. Thus one way of valuing knowledge is to fragment it or break it down into its constituent parts. The elements of knowledge can be fragmented. Thus instead of trying to value all the knowledge held by the enterprise onto a balance sheet, it becomes more possible to identify components. Then, each component can be associated with a transactional value inside the business.

Andersen

We try to build it into the culture. Some groups have tried incentive schemes of one type or another. I think there's some good stuff being written which explains why that doesn't work. If you artificially incentivize people to do things in a rather shallow way, you can get temporary compliance. It's like loyalty bonuses or whatever from retailers. You think 'Oh yeah, I'll do that' and then, when you realize that you can't do anything with the points they give you that's of any value, you kind of lose interest. The other thing is that the points tend to devalue something which is quite serious, because you're saying, 'Well, we'll reward you for doing this'. In a way it kind of implies it isn't really important. Do you see what I mean? It's as if it's not really that valuable so we have to give you a special incentive to do it.

So I think you've got to be really very careful. I think a lot of the rewards are internal for people in that it's actually part of job satisfaction and self-esteem in a way. It's feeling valued that you're part of a community and that you have something to contribute with shared knowledge. I think the way to reward people is to make sure that those communities of interest and of practice are supportive of each other and that people feel that that's something that they should be doing that has value for them. I think that's the way to evaluate it.

Let us take an example. Imagine that a researcher is working on a new product, in a medium-sized company with four or five competitors. Every supplier in the business has its eye on this product and each has an idea of the value of getting it to market first. It is now possible to attach a series of values to that particular piece of knowledge. The value (benefit) of first mover advantage, the value of a certain market share or niche where the product will fit, the value of a premium price, and so on, all offer ways of attaching a value to the knowledge.

THE VALUE OF TRUST

A similar approach can be made to the valuation of trust but using a reverse principle. In other words, it is possible to determine the cost of *not* having trust. The cost of not having trust is based on the failure to have confidence in communications. In an effective group, where trust is high, recognition of peers, of other members of the community, provides a background of trust which enables communications to be internalized and used more rapidly. Indeed, if it is internalized, committed to memory in part or in full, it can be recalled at a relevant time and used without further concern. The archetypal example of this is a joke. If someone sends a joke to a friend, they may commit it to memory. When retold, the joke may well be funny but there will certainly be many times when it will not. Telling it to the wrong audience or at the wrong time may make the teller look foolish. That humour of the joke has a value in terms of a person's position in a community. In the same way, the value of trust is associated with what is being done and how the knowledge is positioned. It has to be placed in the context of a role. Another illustration can be given by the use of formal qualifications. When someone is ill and they visit the doctor, the sight of the certificate on the wall, 'proving' that the physician has studied long and hard to pass certain exams, 'proving' that they are accepted as a physician by their peers as members of a medical association, is a basis for trust. The advice given can then be used with more confidence and put into effect straight away. In a business situation, people do not wear the equivalent of formal qualifications on their sleeves but it is equally valuable to establish the same confidence.

Cap Gemini

The biggest concern is that people are unwilling to share valuable knowledge. I'd say that this was totally untrue because if you don't share knowledge, nobody knows you've got it. It's only in the application of knowledge that people become aware of your holding it and therefore of your value and worth. I've never found any organization where people are unwilling to share knowledge. What I found was organizations where people were unwilling to listen to knowledge. The problem is far more with the receiver. The other barrier to knowledge exchange is to get the organization to realize that knowledge has to be a core component of their business. They need to put in mechanisms to enable knowledge to flow and if they don't put those mechanisms in place it will flow inappropriately.

There is a kind of fool's gold to be had from the belief that an enterprise can put huge amounts of knowledge into an intellectual capital management database and then simply manage that asset. Whilst the notion of capturing all the expertise in the organization is attractive, even were it to be done, it is doubtful if it would be used very much. Take this example. The new British Library, opened in London in 1999, contains a vast amount of manuscripts, literary works of art and scientific documentation. Yet there is hardly a great queue of people outside, desperately waiting to access it. When people are going about their day-to-day jobs they have the option of going into the British Library, or the corporate knowledge base to search for that nugget of information that will help them in their work, but knowledge management does not happen like that. The British Library analogy is perhaps less than exact since its electronic search and retrieval facilities undertake powerful generic searches across vast amounts of information. People tend to use corporate knowledge bases where retrieval is also supported by local (internal) expertise and frames of reference. Thus the creation of a knowledge base is really about creating an internal market place where people recognize what knowledge they need, the value of that knowledge and its relevance to their current problem environment. The greatest value of the exercise is in capturing and harnessing intellectual capital across the business and then ensuring that it is used.

Of course it is the usage that is the most important aspect. Trust, belief in the value of the knowledge, is fundamental to that. The use of a common language is also a key factor. This means introducing a framework by which people can identify the 'right' knowledge. Having a common language across the business soon starts to accelerate the value of the knowledge base. A conversation with someone speaking absolutely fluent Cantonese holds little meaning unless both people speak that language. Until there is a common frame of reference and language across members of the enterprise which helps to filter and put in context each piece of information there will be very little market value in the knowledge base.

The conversation with our Cantonese speaker might turn into a dialogue if some form of machine translation were used and here again we can pursue an analogy. Machine translation of language has been an important research area for decades. Early research showed that purely algorithmic approaches to language translation did not work well. It is certainly not possible to get sensible translations by looking up the meaning of words in a giant database. Nor even is much improvement possible by adding phrases to that database. Reasonable translations are only possible when the social context of words is taken into account. Thus, in English, the word 'interview' sounds very like 'into view' but in a conversation in the social context of, say, a job application, the meaning of the sounds is perfectly clear. Similarly, there are words that have two opposite meanings such as 'cleave'. This can mean 'to cling to' or 'to split'. Again, it is social context which allows for interpretation. By programming some aspects of 'social context' into the translation software, the machine can do a more reasonable job.

The fragmentation of knowledge into elements for valuation and developing algorithms to establish a contextual basis for trust is an area that needs a lot more research.

VALUING THE KNOWLEDGE OF THE INDIVIDUAL

A further dimension of the problem is that particular nuggets of knowledge have different values at the individual level. The problem here is one of setting a value on the processes for capturing knowledge, analysing it, mentally positioning it, breaking it apart and then replacing selected elements with another person's anecdotes and experience. The value of that nugget, in both directions (being added to or extracted from the knowledge base) depends on the direct relevance to the individual.

Cable & Wireless

The only thing that is common is that permission is granted for an amount of money for human development of each employee in Cable & Wireless. That figure is set on an annual basis and it's normally something like £500 per annum per person which equates to about £20,000,000 per annum across Cable & Wireless. There is also a meeting twice a year, of the top 100 people within Cable & Wireless to reflect the current thinking on strategy, on development, on the way the company is going. The learning from that is then cascaded down to the other levels of management.

If members of the enterprise are going to be measured and rewarded in terms of their contribution, team work, willingness to share, trust and commitment to community development then the reward system is likely to be very subjective. At the individual level therefore, an approach which values contributions in terms of outcomes (whether the individual is able to change his or her behaviour so as to achieve a more effective performance or whether he or she is able to impact bottom line results more effectively) would suggest itself.

XYZ of San Francisco illustrates this type of scenario. XYZ was set up by 'Bob' as a new software development company in 1996. The company went from strength to strength. It grew rapidly to the point where it employed 250 people and Bob was just starting to panic because he recognized that to continue this growth he probably needed another 80 or 90 people in the next 9–12 months and might possibly need to double the numbers after that. When the company had 250 people, Bob had employed everyone, interviewed everyone and seen everyone, from the warehouse people who were doing packaging through to the research and software development people. The values and beliefs were shared capital across the business. He knew as he had touched and felt it that everyone else had that same inspiration. Doubling the business meant that he would have to trust other people in terms of sharing the core values and beliefs. The problem was, could growth be sustained in these terms? Bob observed 'We have grown this quickly and successfully because of the way that people share knowledge. How we have worked together at the moment is crucially important. The fluency, the negligible internal transaction costs and low internal friction of developing a new idea was because people communicated freely. They spoke about what they knew, what they wanted, what their drives were, what their challenges were and shared ideas on how to get them resolved'. The company responded at maximum efficiency. It might not be possible to maintain this in a much larger organization.

This is a classic business growth scenario. Bob then called for help from a knowledge management consultant. The two worked together intensively over a 5-week period trying out a huge number of different frameworks and models for valuing and sharing knowledge. The net result of all of this came after one weekend when Bob and the consultant had been up to the Napa Valley to visit someone who owned a vineyard. Good wine and good company on Saturday evening were followed by a pleasant lunch on Sunday and Bob and the consultant spent the time talking through different ideas, churning the problem around. At 4.30 am on Monday morning, Bob rang the consultant, hugely excited, 'I've fixed it!' he said, 'I've finally cracked all of the ideas and I've put it all together in terms of what we want to do for the company. We've got to get to the office!' The consultant walked into XYZ offices at around 6 o'clock that morning to find that Bob was already there. He and his secretary were running around the office feverishly, going to every one of the notice boards. On each one he was pinning up a document, alongside an envelope with some forms. The consultant looked at the first document with some surprise. On it were some 250 names, those of every employee of the company. Against every single name it had exactly what that employee earned, from Bob downwards. The first reaction of the consultant was to say to himself 'Gosh, look at how much Bob gets.' He then looked at the little plastic envelope that came with the forms. Each of these forms said 'There is no authorization, there is no sign-off, you take this form, you fill it in yourself and you can pay yourself whatever you want next month and every month after. You decide your own salary.' His second reaction was to assume that, obviously, after they had left each other on Sunday, Bob had been drinking something stronger than wine because this proposal seemed so extreme.

But Bob was stone cold sober. He said that he had taken all of the principles and concepts about value management and the role of knowledge. He had extrapolated them and put to himself the questions 'If you want to value and put a price on knowledge, or if you want to pay and reward people for their knowledge, who is the best arbiter of that value?' 'How can you establish the worth of your knowledge and your perceived contribution to the business?' He felt that the best arbiters of these issues are an individual's peers, the colleagues that he or she works with. If an individual wants to pay himself or herself US $10,000, US $15,000 or US $20,000 next month, colleagues will get to see it. Peer pressure will then raise the question are you worth that? Have you contributed enough intellectual stimuli? Have you helped others enough? Have you shared enough of your knowledge?

Bob had identified all of the conundrums of knowledge hoarding and knowledge blockers. He had picked up on all of the issues around the measurement of knowledge and how to reward people. The salary choices were made not by going to your boss and asking for a million dollars a month. The salary level was sustained based on assessments by members of your community. Bob actually ran the company on that basis for

18 months. The only reason that it stopped was that he made an acquisition of another company. The system then got to the point where there was a degree of discomfort. In that first 18 months, there was only one change in salary. One of the client directors actually had three weeks off in one month – a week because of domestic problems followed by a two-week holiday. He actually signed a form that went to the finance group to pay himself less on the grounds that his perceived contribution to the business was lower. He thought he had better get in quick before his colleagues said that he was a lightweight and had not contributed so much that month.

KEY PERFORMANCE INDICATORS AND CRITICAL SUCCESS FACTORS

It is obvious that the method used by XYZ would not be easily transferable. What the case illustrates is that there is a natural market for knowledge in society and in organizations. However, the approach is interesting because it very much underlines the view that the value of a person lies not only in what they know but how quickly they can let others around them have access to that knowledge. The knowledge hoarders are much less useful.

PowerGen

I'll pick one topic – advanced coal. The world has been concerned for a while that energies such as nuclear, gas, etc will run out and yet coal was seen to be a very long-lasting resource. Unfortunately, most of the ways of burning coal result in a high level of pollution although there are now various systems which will burn coal in a very clean manner. Most of these are experimental, rather than commercial. So, we started to put together groupings of information about that area, where we can pull together the facts and convert them into a knowledge base which is accessible to everybody. However, it isn't just a collection of facts, it is really an entire overview of the field, comments on performance, who has worked already in that area, etc – proper knowledge.

The key idea from the San Francisco example is the importance of not so much the team, which is a sort of corporate artefact, but of the community of practice. This is related to the organic structure of the enterprise and how its members communicate. It is concerned with who communicates to whom and what the value might be of that communication. Gradually it becomes clear that social capital exists inherently in communities. Communities of practice, as a peer group, will very quickly agree, refine and re-refine amongst themselves where value lies. They will determine what the critical performance indicators might be for the current task assignments. They will be able to suggest what key factors are going to make for success. The members of the community will then recognize each other's roles and pose the three 'What' questions to individual team members: 'What do you know? What do you need to know? What is the best way of getting it?' Two or three iterations of this process will distil the most important issues and enable the community to recognize more fluently what they need to know. A community is based on mutual agreement, a version of what was put in place explicitly by Bob of XYZ.

CUSTOMER VALUE MANAGEMENT

Customer value management takes an outside perspective on the value of customer knowledge. The reason that a technology such as the Palm Pilot is so successful is that it is a connectivity tool. It is not the people you connect to that defines value in your business but how you can connect through those people to their social networks. That is how you drive value. The power of the connection is the power of their social network. In other words, each person is considered as if they are a node or a gateway to eventual solutions. Customer value management is about trying to get through your customers, or your customer's customer to their social networks. Then the aim is to open up your business sufficiently so that you can respond to identified customer needs in terms of the solutions that they are seeking to their customer or business problems. In other words, a customer need is seen in terms of a problem-solving exercise and the objective is for your business to solve it better on the customer's behalf. This requires a responsive form of enterprise that changes with the market. In other words, it is about openness, listening and responding.

During 1992–93, IBM had access to possibly more business analysts than any other company. No matter how many times those business analysts pointed out that the market was changing, the company found itself unable to absorb and respond to the advice. There was so much other clutter around it was swamping any marketing decision. Eventually, a poor end-of-year outcome gave force to the analysis. In turning itself around, IBM had to make clear decisions about how to use filters to eliminate noise and clutter from a huge number of messages. It had to find a way of prioritizing. It had to listen, sense and respond in a better way. The signals being sent internally were weak in organizational terms. It therefore had to find a way to amplify those weak signals. The best way of doing this is to correctly position the customer value managcmcnt proposition. Communitics can bc uscd for this. Thcy will filtcr out redundant signals and amplify weak signals very quickly. They will add context and value to them from inside the business. They will then provide a structure for acting on those signals within the business.

MERGERS AND ACQUISITIONS

The problem is even greater when mergers, acquisitions (or divestments) occur. Sometimes, an acquisition can alter the basic core values of a company, as it did in XYZ. If a business is nothing more than the sum total of what it knows, how quickly it learns something new when it makes an acquisition is critical to success. At one level, the millions of dollars paid to acquire a new business may change the strategic position, alter the overall capability or take the enterprise into new business areas. At another level, what is happening is that the acquiring firm is buying business knowledge or even just acquiring a business's ability to learn. It is another, more acute form of the problems associated with corporate churn. For success, the new business must assimilate a whole new set of contacts, networks, customer links and, of course, knowledge. The value proposition revolves around the knowledge being acquired. Therefore it is very important to start a new knowledge management initiative with each major change of structure.

KNOWLEDGE PUSH

Mergers or acquisitions act as a form on knowledge push. When two organizations come together, like the confluence of two rivers, the flow of potential is increased. The new river is bigger, faster, more powerful and can be used to generate more energy. Software downloads from the Internet or the Intranet produce a similar effect. With the increasing use of knowledge portals more software will be available to acquire and filter information. For example, if someone likes theatre he or she might run two or three automatic Internet searches (Web bots) to push information about new plays and performances onto a PDA. In a corporate context, this sort of tool has enormous potential value. This is largely because the conceptualization and personalization of the information are inherent within the software. In other words, this moves away from the overwhelming generic search tools to something very specific and relevant. It is personalized and customized to the individual. Knowledge is as personal as what we eat, how we dress, where we live, what we drive, what we like to drink and what we do. How companies manage knowledge and how we move forward with it will reflect the sum total of those personal decisions.

Web bots linked to individualized portals will trigger a chain of thought and actions that will connect with other similar sources of knowledge and information. They will be connecting to embodied knowledge and eventually to communities of practice. Bringing them together will be the basis for greater activities. This can drive innovation, which in turn will spur the vision for what is next in the field of knowledge management. This will be to achieve a better understanding of how people work severally and alone: how people work as individuals and how working with others leverages their performance. Much of this will be based on fresh developments in the way people collaborate, fresh developments in organizational design and fresh development tools to enable higher performance inside the business. To some, the notion of knowledge management appears like an attempt to create a hive of worker bees. Everyone shares in the corporate honeycomb. In reality, knowledge management is about the power of the individual. It is about a future driven by individuals who are working within a community and who use the power of the community to make their own performance more effective.

SUMMARY

Buckman Labs

The rewards, how do we get rewards? I don't know about universities – how do they reward you? Do they reward you for publishing? Or do you find the fact that your peers recognize your contribution and they actually quote your papers? That makes you feel good – it is recognition. It's the same way within Buckman really. If I share my knowledge and somebody writes and says to me 'Thanks, that was really helpful', then that is my incentive to do it again.

The problem of designing measurements and evaluation of knowledge management programmes has not been fully resolved. It is certainly possible to identify metrics, based on a sort of balanced scorecard approach, which set out to report on secondary effects and benefits resulting from knowledge activities. The best known of these was developed by financial services group Skandia, but there are some doubts as to whether it provides a generally portable model.

The essence of knowledge is that it lies in communities and that it has a value that varies enormously according to context, both at the individual and the organizational level. One approach might therefore be to leave the problem of developing metrics to the relevant communities themselves. As long as some sort of agreed measures are developed and used consistently, the organization will be able to assess whether its store of knowledge is being nurtured and exploited effectively.

Appendix

The questionnaire in this appendix is intended to allow you to assess your organization's predisposition to implement what might be called a knowledge management philosophy. There is no one best way to interpret the results. If you score 5 out of 5 for every question, you will achieve 1,750 points but it is not likely that anyone will do that. Nor is it important. Different aspects of knowledge management are differentially important to individuals and to companies. Perhaps a more useful way of interpreting the results is to calculate a percentage outcome for each page and use the comparison between each of the 10 areas as a way of understanding where your company is strong or weak. Another possibility is to take the two scales – importance and effectiveness – separately, and to produce a single graph plotting the coordinates of each topic. This will allow a comparison of what you consider to be important against how effective your company is at that aspect of knowledge management.

Answer the questions quickly – without too much reflection – be honest.

Awareness and Commitment	IMPORTANCE				EFFECTIVENESS				SCORE
	Critical (5)	Important (3)	Beneficial (1)	Not Important (0)	Complete (5)	Improving (3)	Inefficient (1)	Not Approved (0)	
Do the staff in your company understand the concept of knowledge management (KM) and are senior management committed to its use?									
If I use the term knowledge management anywhere in my company, most people will understand what it means for us and how it is applied to the business									
There is board-level representation for knowledge management with a CKO position or something similar									
Senior management 'walk the talk'. They demonstrate their commitment to KM with resources, action, guidelines and activities									
Senior managers support knowledge sharing, learning and other KM desired behaviours. This is often talked about in meetings.									
KM is seen as a vital element of business strategy and knowledge is widely recognized as the basis of our competitive position									
There is a senior level ongoing review of the effectiveness of KM in the whole company									
Intellectual assets are inventoried or recognized and some measure of value (hard or soft) is attached to each									
TOTAL SCORE									

Strategy	IMPORTANCE				EFFECTIVENESS				SCORE
	Critical (5)	Important (3)	Beneficial (1)	Not Important (0)	Complete (5)	Improving (3)	Inefficient (1)	Not Approved (0)	
Has your organization committed to a programme of KM improvement by trying to manage it so as to ensure maximum business benefit?									
There is a vision for how KM should integrate into the business									
There is a shared understanding, based on a scenario plan, on what KM should be doing for us in two years' time									
It is clear how KM initiatives support the business plan									
There are defined responsibilities and a budget set for KM initiatives									
KM principles are well established. There are definitions of key knowledge and guidelines for the creation and management of knowledge									
There is clear ownership of KM initiatives either by the business unit or the whole business									
There is a programme of initiatives within the business plan to improve KM									
TOTAL SCORE									

Culture	IMPORTANCE				EFFECTIVENESS				SCORE
Do the behaviours in the company enable effective KM?	Critical (5)	Important (3)	Beneficial (1)	Not Important (0)	Complete (5)	Improving (3)	Inefficient (1)	Not Approved (0)	
Failure is not punished, rather it is seen as an opportunity to learn. Regular reviews or debriefings are used to see what we have learnt from projects									
Recording and sharing of knowledge is routine and second nature. Next time I have a good idea, I know exactly how to share it									
We constantly seek best practice and try to re-use existing projects and knowledge whenever we can									
Time is allowed for creative thinking. For example, staff are encouraged to reflect and thinking time is allowed for									
Knowledge sharing is seen as a strength and the amount of mentoring and coaching practised is discussed in appraisals									
Everyone is willing to give advice or help on request to anyone else in the company									
Changes to day-to-day working are seen as normal and there are no rigid definitions of where people can contribute good ideas									
TOTAL SCORE									

External Focus	IMPORTANCE				EFFECTIVENESS				SCORE
	Critical (5)	Important (3)	Beneficial (1)	Not Important (0)	Complete (5)	Improving (3)	Inefficient (1)	Not Approved (0)	
To what extent does the company see itself as part of a knowledge network? Is the business looking beyond its boundaries to maximize business opportunities?									
We are actively connected to external networks and knowledge sources which cause us constantly to re-examine what we are doing									
Technology is shared with both suppliers and clients where appropriate to enhance relationships									
There is a programme of active participation in business conferences and other discussion forums to share ideas and experience									
The company is recognized for its innovative approaches									
Ideas and alliances for joint ventures increase intellectual capital and are constantly reviewed and acted upon where necessary									
There is a strategic programme in place to collect and analyse business intelligence, so as to develop the company's strategy									
We have identified a range of learning partners and develop training and learning programmes collaboratively									
TOTAL SCORE									

Incentives	IMPORTANCE				EFFECTIVENESS				SCORE
	Critical (5)	Important (3)	Beneficial (1)	Not Important (0)	Complete (5)	Improving (3)	Inefficient (1)	Not Approved (0)	
Does the company reward those who contribute to its KM efforts?									
There is a strong belief that only by sharing our ideas can we all do well. There is no special need for incentives in my company									
Hoarding of knowledge and being secretive about the best way to do something is actively discouraged									
Good KM behaviour is monitored and built into appraisal systems									
Individuals are visibly rewarded for team work and knowledge sharing									
Training and development programmes in KM behaviour and procedures are encouraged from recruitment onwards									
Good KM behaviour such as sharing knowledge and re-using it are promoted on a day-to-day basis									
Asking for help from expert co-workers is monitored, encouraged and rewarded									
TOTAL SCORE									

Information Technology	IMPORTANCE				EFFECTIVENESS				SCORE
Do you have the right kind of IT and is it used effectively enough to support KM?	Critical (5)	Important (3)	Beneficial (1)	Not Important (0)	Complete (5)	Improving (3)	Inefficient (1)	Not Approved (0)	
Technology 'fit' for knowledge sharing (not just technical compatibility) is the main item on the agenda when new IT initiatives are being discussed									
The information services team are constantly checking to ensure that our IT supports our knowledge needs									
Technology is a key enabler in ensuring the right information is available to the right people at the right time									
IT makes the search for information much easier. Our IT is leading-edge and is fully supported									
IT allows effective communication across boundaries and even time zones									
Our hardware and software are updated routinely without significant debate									
People use the IT in place effectively as a normal working practice (for example, everyone shares the same templates for word processing)									
TOTAL SCORE									

Maintenance and Protection

How well does the company protect and maintain its information and knowledge assets?	IMPORTANCE				EFFECTIVENESS				SCORE
	Critical (5)	Important (3)	Beneficial (1)	Not Important (0)	Complete (5)	Improving (3)	Inefficient (1)	Not Approved (0)	
We know who our leading experts are in all areas of activity. We take active steps to ensure that they share knowledge and do not leave without leaving their knowledge in the organization									
Effective cataloguing and archiving procedures are in place for document management whether the data are held electronically or on paper									
Key information to be protected, such as customer information, is identified. Intellectual assets are legally protected									
Measures are in place to ensure that key information is captured quickly and accurately									
There are regular reviews to delete out-of-date information and there is a procedure to ensure regular updates from designated information owners									
There are complete IT security procedures in place (back-up, recovery, etc). In fact we have a disaster drill without warning from time to time									
Regulatory and compliance requirements for our industry are published and clearly understood by key managers									
TOTAL SCORE									

Ongoing Assessment	IMPORTANCE					EFFECTIVENESS					SCORE
Does the company measure the impact of KM and particularly the management of intellectual assets on the organization?	Critical (5)	Important (3)	Beneficial (1)	Not Important (0)		Complete (5)	Improving (3)	Inefficient (1)	Not Approved (0)		
When we find that we don't know something we discover to be important, we set up a programme to ensure that systematic learning takes place											
There is a type of balanced scorecard or similar framework in place covering innovation, people, customers, finance and operations											
There is a regular measurement of the impact of KM on the way people do their jobs and on the bottom line											
The value of intellectual assets is measured regularly											
Action is taken at a senior level on the assessments to further improve the position of the business based on the KM measures											
Key performance indicators for KM are in place											
We have established a system of internal benchmarking to measure each area of performance against company best practice regularly											
TOTAL SCORE											

Organization	IMPORTANCE				EFFECTIVENESS				SCORE
Is your company organized to make the most of its knowledge resources?	Critical (5)	Important (3)	Beneficial (1)	Not Important (0)	Complete (5)	Improving (3)	Inefficient (1)	Not Approved (0)	
We categorize our products and services according to whether we think we are working in a simple, complex, uncertain or ambiguous environment									
A flexible, well-structured, up-to-date knowledge map exists to point staff in the direction of the knowledge they seek									
Informal networks across the organization are encouraged, in fact management meetings often discuss our communities of practice									
Information with use across different units is available to a number of different users in different formats, ie in formats they can use and understand									
Formal networks exist to facilitate the dissemination of knowledge									
Virtual or remote teams are supported effectively in terms of access to knowledge or networks									
Staff are rotated to spread best practice ideas or natural staff turnover is positively used to assist with the dissemination of best practice									
TOTAL SCORE									

Using and Applying Knowledge	IMPORTANCE				EFFECTIVENESS				SCORE
Does your business use and exploit the knowledge inherent in the company in an effective manner?	Critical (5)	Important (3)	Beneficial (1)	Not Important (0)	Complete (5)	Improving (3)	Inefficient (1)	Not Approved (0)	
For each new initiative, we identify a number of knowledge transfer outcomes (eg productivity, learning, quality, etc) that we later review									
We have a number of people who are designated as 'gatekeepers' from time to time to ensure that knowledge is transferred internally and externally									
We look very carefully at whether we support our major decision points in key business processes with the right kind of knowledge									
Use of knowledge and information is controlled in line with regulatory and compliance requirements									
Multi-disciplinary teams are effectively formed and managed									
There are a number of dedicated knowledge workers in place whose job is to assist in the capture, recording and dissemination of knowledge									
Ideas to exploit pools of information are reviewed and acted upon for business benefit									
TOTAL SCORE									

References

SOURCES

This book is designed for managers and MBA students seeking to understand how knowledge management might impact on the organizations and companies that they work for. As a measure of how important knowledge management has become it should be recognized that this list of references represents just a tiny portion of what has been written about the subject. In terms of pointing you in the direction of further sources, we can hardly do better than practice what we preach by connecting you to our network.

The best working reference on how to design and implement knowledge management programmes we have come across is:

Tiwana, A (2000) *The Knowledge Management Toolkit*, Prentice-Hall, New Jersey

For an extremely comprehensive set of sources including a huge bibliography, an annotated bibliography, a directory of knowledge management resources online, discussion lists, professional knowledge management organizations, periodicals and even a calendar of events, refer to:

Cortada J W and Woods J A (2001) *The Knowledge Management Yearbook 2000–2001*, Oxford, Butterworth Heinemann

Cortada and Woods also contains sets of readings though the quality is a bit variable. Your best jumping-off point is of course: www.km.org

REFERENCES

Barladi, P (1999) Knowledge and competence management: Ericsson Business Consulting, *Business Strategy Review*, **10** (4), pp 20–28

Blake, R and Mouton, J (1978) *The New Managerial Grid*, Gulf Publishing, Houston

CBI (1999) *Liberating Knowledge*, Caspian Publishing, London

Cothrel, J and Williams, R L (1999) Online communities: helping them form and grow, *Journal of Knowledge Management*, **3** (1), pp 54–60

Davenport, T H and Prusak, L (1998) *Working Knowledge: How organizations know what they know*, Harvard Business School Press, Boston

Davis, M C (1998) Knowledge management, *The Executives Journal*, **98**(1), pp 11–23

Dawson, R (2000) *Developing Knowledge Based Client Relationships*, Butterworth Heinemann, Oxford

Drucker, P (1999) Knowledge worker productivity: the biggest challenge, *California Management Review*, **41** (2), Winter, pp 79–94

Edvinsson, L and Malone, M S (1997) *Intellectual Capital – Realising your company's true value by finding its hidden brainpower*, Harper Business, New York

Gamble, P, Stone, M and Woodcock, N (1999) *Up Close and Personal?: Customer relationship marketing @ work*, Kogan Page, London

Ghoshal, S and Bartlett, C (1998) *The Individualised Corporation*, Harper Business, London

Goffee, R and Jones, G (1996) What holds the modern company together? *Harvard Business Review*, **74** (6), November–December, pp 133–48

Gummesson, E (1999) *Total Relationship Marketing*, Butterworth Heinemann, Oxford

Hall, R and Andriani, T (1998) Analysing intangible resources and managing knowledge in a supply chain context, *European Management Journal*, **16** (6), pp 685–97

Hansen, M T, Nohria, N, and Tuerney, T (1999) What's your strategy for managing knowledge? *Harvard Business Review*, **77** (2), March/April 1999, pp 106–16

217

Hildebrand, C (1999) Making knowledge management pay off, *CIO Enterprise Magazine*, February 15

Hofstede, G (1997) *Underlying Cultures and Organisations: Software of the mind*, McGraw Hill, New York

Inkpen, A (1998) Learning, knowledge acquisitions and strategic alliances, *European Management Journal*, **16** (2), pp 223–29

Nahapiet, J and Ghoshal, S (1998) Social capital, intellectual capital and organisational advantage, *The Academy of Management Review* **23** (2), p 243

Nonaka, I (1994) A dynamic theory of organisational knowledge, *Organisation Science*, **5**, pp 14–37

Nonaka, I and Takeuchi, H (1995) *A Knowledge Creating Company: How Japanese companies create the dynamics of innovation*, OUP, New York

O'Dell, C and Grayson, J R (1998) *If Only We Knew What We Know*, Free Press, New York

Pfeffer, J and Sutton, R (1999) The smart talk trap, *Harvard Business Review*, **77** (3), May/June, pp 134–42

Powell, T (1999) Valuation of intellectual capital, in *Liberating Knowledge* ed CBI, p 58, Caspian Publishing, London

Prusak, L and Davenport, T (1998) *How Organisations Manage What They Know*, Harvard Business School Press, Boston

Prusak, L and Lesser, E (1999) Communities of practice, social capital and organisational knowledge, *EFMD Forum*, **3**, pp 12–17

Quinn, J B, Anderson, P and Thinklestein S (1996) Managing professional intellect: making the most of the best, *Harvard Business Review* **74** (2), March/April, pp 71–80

Senge, P (1994) *The Fifth Discipline: The art and practice of the learning organisation*, Doubleday, New York

Stewart, T A (1997) *Intellectual Capital – The new wealth of organisations*, Doubleday/Currency, New York

Sveiby, K (1997) *The New Organisational Wealth*, Berrett-Koehler, San Francisco

Teece, D (1998) Research directions for knowledge management, *California Management Review* , **40** (3) pp 289–92

Townsend, R (1970) *Up the Organization: How to stop the corporation stifling people and strangling profits*, Alfred Knopf, New York

Wenger, E C and Snyder, W M (2000) Communities of practice: the organisational frontier, *Harvard Business Review*, **78** (1), January/February, pp 139–45

White, W H (1957) *The Organization Man*, Jonathan Cape, London

Index

Visit Kogan Page on-line

Comprehensive information on
Kogan Page titles

Features include

- complete catalogue listings,
  including book reviews and
  descriptions

- special monthly promotions

- information on NEW titles and
  BESTSELLING titles

- a secure shopping basket facility
  for on-line ordering

PLUS everything you need to know about
KOGAN PAGE

http://www.kogan-page.co.uk